Adolf Grünbaum

PHENOMENOLOGY OF DEPRESSIVE ILLNESS

PHENOMENOLOGY OF DEPRESSIVE ILLNESS

Edited by
J. John Mann, M.D.
Payne Whitney Psychiatric Clinic
New York Hospital — Cornell Medical Center,
New York City

Vol. I in the Depressive Illness Series

HUMAN SCIENCES PRESS, INC.
72 FIFTH AVENUE
NEW YORK, N.Y. 10011-8004

Printed in the United States of America
987654321

Library of Congress Cataloging-in-Publication Data

Phenomenology of depressive illness.

(The Depressive illness series; vol. 1)
Includes index.
1. Depression, Mental. 2. Symptomatology.
3. Depression, Mental—Classification.   I. Mann,
J. John (Joseph John)   II. Series. [DNLM: 1. Depression.
2. Depressive Disorder. WM 171 P541]
RC480.5.P475 1988   616.85'27   87-2593
ISBN 0-89885-369-9

CONTENTS

CONTRIBUTORS

Shelley Fox Aarons, M.D.
Clinical Instructor of Psychiatry
Department of Psychiatry
Cornell University Medical College
14 East 4th Street
New York, New York 10012

George S. Alexopoulos, M.D.
Associate Professor of Psychiatry
Department of Psychiatry
Cornell University Medical College
The New York Hospital — Westchester Division
21 Bloomingdale Road
White Plains, New York 10605

Richard P. Brown, M.D.
Assistant Professor of Psychiatry
Department of Psychiatry
Cornell University Medical College
1300 York Avenue
New York, New York 10021

7

David Cella, Ph.D.
Instructor of Psychology in Psychiatry
Department of Psychiatry
Cornell University Medical College
1300 York Avenue
New York, New York 10021

Elizabeth Charney, M.D.
Department of Pediatrics
Albert Einstein College of Medicine
Pelham Parkway South
Eastchester Road
Bronx, New York 10461

Martin R. Cohen, M.D.
Associate Professor
Department of Neuropsychiatry & Behavioral Sciences
University of South Carolina
School of Medicine
P.O. Box 202
Columbia, South Carolina 29202

Allen J. Frances, M.D.
Professor of Psychiatry
Department of Psychiatry
Cornell University Medical College
1300 York Avenue
New York, New York 10021

Jonathan H. Holt, M.D.
Instructor of Psychiatry
Department of Psychiatry
Cornell University Medical College
The New York Hospital — Westchester Division
21 Bloomingdale Road
White Plains, New York 10605

James H. Kocsis, M.D.
Associate Professor of Clinical Psychiatry
Department of Psychiatry
Cornell University Medical College
1300 York Avenue
New York, New York 10021

J. John Mann, M.D.
Associate Professor of Psychiatry
Department of Psychiatry
Cornell University Medical College
1300 York Avenue
New York, New York 10021

P. Anne McBride, M.D.
Assistant Professor of Psychiatry
Department of Psychiatry
Cornell University Medical College
1300 York Avenue
New York, New York 10021

Samuel W. Perry, M.D.
Associate Professor of Clinical Psychiatry
Department of Psychiatry
Cornell University Medical College
1300 York Avenue
New York, New York 10021

Theodore Shapiro, M.D.
Professor of Psychiatry
Department of Psychiatry
Cornell University Medical College
New York, New York 10021

Peter E. Stokes, M.D.
Professor of Psychiatry
Department of Psychiatry
Cornell University Medical College
1300 York Avenue
New York, New York 10021

Milton Viederman, M.D.
Professor of Clinical Psychiatry
Department of Psychiatry
Cornell University Medical College
1300 York Avenue
New York, New York 10021

Deborah Weisbrot, M.D.
Assistant Professor of Psychiatry
Department of Psychiatry
Albert Einstein College of Medicine
Pelham Parkway South and Eastchester Road
Bronx, New York 10461

Myrna M. Weissman, Ph.D.
Professor of Epidemiology in Psychiatry
Chief, Division of Clinical-Genetic Epidemiology
College of Physicians and Surgeons of Columbia University
722 West 168th Street, Box 14
New York, New York 10032

George Winokur, M.D.
The Paul W. Penningroth Professor and Head
Department of Psychiatry
University of Iowa College of Medicine
500 Newton Road
Iowa City, Iowa 52242

Robert C. Young, M.D.
Assistant Professor Psychiatry
Department of Psychiatry
The New York Hospital — Westchester Division
21 Bloomingdale Road
White Plains, New York 10605

ACKNOWLEDGMENTS

I wish to thank the contributing authors for their valuable suggestions, and in particular, I would like to mention that the constructive comments of Dr. Gerald Klerman greatly enhanced the quality and organization of this book. Ms. Renee Azima-Heller assisted me in the editing and preparation of the text. My secretary, Ms. Isadora Johnson, patiently and expertly typed several sections of the book. I would like to thank my wife, Margot, and my children for permitting me the time to work on this project. A research scientist award from the Irma T. Hirschl trust provided partial support for this work.

FOREWORD

There has been an explosion of research activity in depressive disorders in the last 25 years, spurred by the advances in neurobiology and the discovery of effective antidepressant drugs. At the same time, the lifetime prevalence of these disorders has been estimated at 20 percent for women and 10 percent for men and appears to be increasing. Although many books have appeared describing new theories of the cause of depression, the descriptive aspects of these syndromes have been neglected. The time has come to pause and reexamine this disease according to the dictum of Thomas Sydenham, who stated:

> In writing the history of a disease, every philosophical hypothesis whatsoever, that has previously occupied the mind of the author, should lie in abeyance. This being done, the clear and natural phenomena of the disease should be noted—these, and these only. They should be noted accurately, and in all their minuteness; in imitation of the exquisite industry of those painters who represent in their portraits the smallest moles and the faintest spots. No man can state the errors that have been occasioned by these physiological hypotheses. Writers, whose minds have taken a false colour under their influence, have saddled diseases with phenomena which existed in their own brains only; but which would have been clear and visible to the whole world had the assumed hypothesis been true. Add to this, that if by chance some symptoms really coincide accurately with their hypothesis, and occur in the disease whereof they would describe the character, they magnify it beyond all measure and moderation; they make it all and in all; the

13

molehill becomes a mountain; whilst, if it fail to tally with the said hypothesis, they pass it over either in perfect silence or with only an incidental mention, unless, by means of some philosophical subtlety, they can enlist it in their service, or else, by fair means or foul accommodate it in some way or other to their doctrines.

Some of the finest descriptions of the phenomenology of melancholia have long ago appeared in the literature and no doubt the reader has come across such works. Examples of landmark texts include *The Anatomy of Melancholia* by Robert Burton[1] first published in 1652 and *Manic-Depressive Insanity* by Emil Kraepelin, published in English in 1921.[2] Robert Burton wrote from the vantage point of a sufferer of melancholia and Emil Kraepelin wrote as a physician. Both recognized a variety of forms of the disorder, but Kraepelin's broader range of clinical experience and brilliant clinical mind led to his unification of much of the presently recognized range of syndromes under a single rubric.

Language represents a major challenge to the diagnosis of depressive disorders as well as to the effective education of the public regarding the distinction between feelings of depression and a depressive illness. This volume begins by attempting to deal with the semantic aspects of describing depression. In a juxtaposition reflecting the historical linking of Kraepelin and Burton described above, the viewpoint of the doctor and the patient are presented. The opening chapter by Drs. Shapiro and Weisbrot attempts to deal with semantic problems involved in the communication between doctor and patient about depressive symptomatology. In his poetic synopsis *The Anatomy of Melancholia*, Robert Burton wrote:

> When I lie waking all alone,
> Recounting what I have ill done,
> My thoughts on them tyrannise,
> Fear and sorrow me surprise,
> Whether I tarry still or go,
> me thinks the time moves very slow.

And then, in desperation, he goes on later to write:

> I'll change my state with any wretch,
> Thou canst from gaol or dunghill fetch,
> My pain's past cure, another hell,
> I may not in this torment dwell!
> Now desperate I hate my life,
> Lend me a halter or a knife,
> All my griefs to this are jolly,
> Naught so damn'd as melancholy.

Sadly, it was rumored by his students, that Burton eventually ended his own life by strangulation. Today we have not only developed effective treatments for depression, but we have progressively extended the range of recognizable and treatable forms of depression. Such successful recognition and treatment of depression led C. K. to comment in Chapter 3, "I have talked to people who are despairingly depressed.... I advise them, if they have not done so already, to get good professional help immediately. All the while I am smiling to myself at how indirectly and unimmediately I seem to do it." Education of the public, physicians, and other mental health professionals remains an urgent imperative since it is estimated that less than half of the population suffering from a depressive disorder are currently being treated. Part of this process involves recognition of the range of depressive syndromes, their special forms at the extremes of life as well as in the physically ill, and their distinction from normal grief.

The descriptive aspects of depressive disorders are divided along several axes. Bipolar disorders are distinguished by the presence of manic or hypomanic episodes. The unipolar disorders are considered to be divisible on the basis of: chronicity; atypicality; the presence of delusions as in delusional depression; and depression in the context of physical illness. A third axis is the developmental dimension and the two extremes of the life span are represented in describing the particular characteristics of childhood and adolescent depressions at one pole and geriatric depressions at the other pole. Finally, the important practical and theoretical problem of distinguishing normal and pathological grief from depressive illness is addressed.

An integral part of a description of depressive disorder must be at the ecological or epidemiological level. Drs. Charney and Weissman describe the current state of refinement of methods applied in this field and then provide, not only a review of the present state of knowledge, but also a report of the most recent results of the landmark epidemiological study sponsored by the National Institute of Mental Health.

Attempts at a classification of nosology of mood disorders have been made for many centuries. The introduction of specific diagnostic criteria in the past 15 years has finally permitted the development of systems of classification that could be validated: across centers; over time; by biological measures; by family and genetic studies; and on the basis of natural history and treatment outcome. Drs. Cohen and Winokur describe both the historical development and the process of validation of current systems of classification of mood disorders.

Description of specific depressive syndromes begin with the depressive episodes associated with bipolar disorders by Dr. Stokes, a pioneer of lithium research in the United States. The presence of manic or hypomanic episodes as well as mixed affective states distinguish this category from the so-called unipolar depressive syndromes. This subgroup is validated by: differences in pattern of family history where there is a clear predominance of relatives with bipolar versus unipolar disorders; biological differences; clinical differences in terms of phenomenology; and treatment effects including the triggering of manic episodes by antidepressant treatment.

Chronic depressive disorders and dysthymia have only been recently recognized in terms of prevalence and a positive response to antidepressant medication. Drs. Kocsis, Frances, and colleagues were the first to demonstrate the efficacy of imipramine for this condition and their chapter is a major scholarly review of the latest findings on this condition.

Nonendogenous and atypical depressions have long been a confusing group of disorders with multiple overlapping definitions. Dr. Aarons brings clarity into this area by a combination of tracing the historical evolution of the various definitions of atypical depression as well as by an application of current data to test the validity of these definitions. For example, initial work was based on delineating the characteristics of a depressive syndrome that responded to monoamine oxidase inhibitors. The subsequent demonstration of the efficacy of these drugs in both endogenous *and* nonendogenous depression required alternative strategies and led to an emphasis on phenomenology, particularly reactivity and anxiety, as a starting point for defining this syndrome.

Depressive episodes characterized by the presence of delusions which are usually mood congruent has defined a syndrome that may be distinguished not just phenomenologically, but also biologically and by treatment response. This syndrome responds less favorably than nondelusional depression to antidepressant drugs alone, but does respond very well to electroconvulsive treatment. Dr. Brown, who has studied delusional depression for many years, has reviewed the literature that addresses the validity of this syndrome.

Childhood depression is not common, but recent studies have shown that it does respond to antidepressant medication. Although developmental aspects may modify the symptomatology, its validity appears confirmed. There are some important differences from adult depression in terms of natural history including a longer duration of episodes. Adolescent depression is more common and its response to antidepressant treatment remains to be established. Drs. McBride and Shapiro review the presentation of depressive disorders in these age groups. The hope is that better recognition will ultimately lead to better treatment.

Just as developmental aspects color the symptom patterns of depressive disorders in childhood, effects of aging, physical illness, and drugs do the same in later life. Dr. Alexopoulos and colleagues describe this complex interaction. Appropriately this chapter is followed by that of Drs. Cella and Perry describing the interrelationship of physical illness and depressive disorders. It may be difficult to distinguish symptoms of depression from those of physical illness, but some useful guidelines exist and their application is discussed.

Freud spoke of mourning and melancholia. The similarities of the two states led to his psychodynamic formulation of the cause of depressive disorders. However, the clinician is faced with making the distinction between normal grief, pathological grief, and a depressive disorder. Dr. Viederman invokes developmental and psychodynamic models together with a detailed review of the phenomenology of these states to guide the clinician in this task.

Ultimately this volume aims to meet the challenge of Thomas Sydenham and thereby provide the reader with the detailed knowledge of the clinical characteristics of depressive disorders that will permit both judgement of the generalizability of the various theoretical models of depressive disorders as well as improved recognition and therefore treatment of these syndromes.

J. John Mann, M.D.
New York, 1986

REFERENCES

1. Burton, R.: The Anatomy of Melancholia. London, Chatto and Windus, 1881.
2. Kraepelin, E.: Manic-Depressive Insanity and Paranoia. London, E&S Livingston, Ltd. 1921.

Chapter 1

THE SEMANTICS OF DEPRESSION

Theodore Shapiro, M.D.
Deborah Weisbrot, M.D.

Give sorrow words, the grief that does not speak
Whispers the o'er-fraught heart and bids it break.

William Shakespeare

INTRODUCTION

A person identifying a feeling of depression may verbalize this state or affect by saying "I'm depressed," or he may use terms such as "down," "upset," "bad," "blue," "sad," "low," or "exhausted," "weak," "loggy," among other choices of expression. The observer might note that he appears silent, withdrawn, is pacing, speaks in monosyllables, or complains of a headache, stomachache, or backache. The inquiry, "Where do you feel the feeling?" may lead to complaints of heaviness in the head, heart, or legs, a lump in the throat, total body ache, emptiness in the pit of the stomach, or a pressing feeling on the chest, and leaden limbs. An autistic adolescent, defining affects primarily by the facial expressions and activities associated with them, responded to the above inquiry by saying, "I feel sad in my eyes." He knew sadness by the observation of and sensation of tears and contractions of the periocular muscles rather than by an assessment of his inner experience. He was unable to define his affective state except operationally.

The various complaints and signs may be construed according to prior convention as clinical depression or other similar designations: melancholy, sadness. Once named, it becomes more than its component parts and a designation that signals that interpretation has taken place. Names carry the burden of denotation and connotation that may require careful analysis of both local and universal usage. We should proceed with caution clinically if the patient tells us the name of his symptoms in a shorthand form as a diagnosis—depression. The patient's depression may not be the depression of DSM-III or any other restricted use. Moreover, medical depression is made up of signs and symptoms, exclusion criteria, and a discriminant function that may not be what the patient's complaints are about. The name may mislead as well as guide.

Knowing the context in which the feeling of depression is expressed is also crucial to the comprehension of its intended or appreciated meaning. When a person describes "a pain in my chest" to a physician, the signifiers may imply various conditions from organ pathology of the cardiopulmonary system to anxiety, depression, or psychosis whose organ is said to be the brain and its outflow paths. Although we take it as a basic assumption in medicine that the somatic disorders must be considered first and ruled out, studies suggest that 25 percent to 50 percent of patients visiting their physicians are actually signaling psychological distress rather than organic disorders by their physical complaints. In both Western and Eastern societies such as China, a somatic complaint is a frequent semantic idiom for depressed mood. It seems, however, to be a more acceptable semantic vehicle in China than in the West. The Chinese word for depression, *Men*, Arthur Kleinman[1] notes, is composed of two striking ideographs: the heart sign enclosed by the doorway sign, entrapping it. So much for the virtues of ideographic conciseness and poignancy.

The origins of the English word, *depression*, are equally intriguing. *Webster's Dictionary*[2] indicates that the term originates from the Latin, *deprimere* (*de* = down, *premere* = to press) or, to press down, to sink. An even more ancient source can be traced back to an Indogermanic root, *Angh*. This is believed by some scholars to be the original and global word for all unpleasant emotions including anxiety, the modern word which it most closely resembles in English, French, and German. From ancient times onward, then, the concept of depression has developed in popular forms along a continuum of pleasure-unpleasure. From this perspective, it is not surprising to find the diagnoses of depression and anxiety sometimes difficult to disentangle. Only during the modern era beginning with Darwin[3] and Freud,[4] have attempts been made to explicate the psychological variants of pleasure-unpleasure, and with them anxiety-depression. Indeed, the nuances of feeling that Western cultures designate by distinct names reminds us of the botanically discrete nomenclature Europeans require, while in some aboriginal cultures "edible/non-edible" is the only relevant lexical cleavage necessary.[5]

Regrettably, knowledge about the origins of the word, depression, tells us less than we wish to know about what the word means or for that matter how we use it in medicine and psychiatry. To understand that, we must analyze the referential complexity of depression and the various social, psychological, or biological constructs currently applied as well as the purpose and use to which they are put. If we admit that language is the primary organizer of one's experience of the world, then such a study is crucial to an examination of our "explanatory model"[6] of depression. Semantics or referential significance encompasses not only the external event, or inner referent (that which is signified) but the meaning of the event as well. Almost all that we know about how a person feels when he or she is depressed must pass through the filter of language as people who may become patients attempt to communicate their perceived states to others.

Language provides many alternative formats by which a personal experience of depression is relayed to others. Despite the uniqueness of each person's experience, we are able, nonetheless, to share individual states by access to a communication system which transmits messages by a number of channels—visual, auditory, and linguistic. We then invoke an intuitive and perhaps naive assumption of intersubjectivity and also assume isomorphism between the biological substrate and mental experience. These shared "basic assumptions" are certainly relevant in the case of affect designation and particularly in the denotation of depression—a central and universal human experience.

FROM SUBJECTIVE STATE TO NOMINALIZATION

From these original positions we have gone on to develop more complex and diverse semantic networks by which we communicate the idea of depression. There are many levels of subjective and objective criteria by which we reference depressed states. At the least within psychiatry they range from the categories in DSM-III-R through psychodynamic formulations and learning-theory formulations. In fact the proposed revisions include renaming the category of affective disorders as mood disorders. We are sometimes offered bewildering choices between lexical or imagistic signifiers, metaphorical or abstract statements, generalizations or self-reports, computer simulation or statistical analyses of self-report or observational checklists. Contemporarily, there is a growing trend within the medical community to reduce the concept of depression to a definition of the experience as a series of biochemical phenomena correlated to the experience. Willy-nilly, direct semantic links are being made between mind and body in the path of a tidal wave of research on the biology of depression. Thus, we now must take responsibility for the emergence of such terms as "chemical depression," a clear example of how the feeling can yield to the biological substrate within the medical frame of reference and the public's understanding.

In such a system the equivalent of the gold standard is reversed from symptom complex to biological data—the validity of one is measured against the other. Despite the new generation of codes and signifiers, what continues to seem evident is that within the person, linguistic symbols are the social link between depressive symptomatology and the undefined. It is the individual's idiosyncratic descriptive lexicon that requires unraveling when the clinician sits with the patient. An interesting example of medical renaming is apparent in the construct "alexithymia" which has been developed to categorize the inability or difficulty some people have in describing or being aware of emotions and moods. Sifneos and Nemiah[7] suggested this bastardized term while they were studying patients with so-called psychosomatic symptoms (another lexical anathema). It was hypothesized that these patients, who were found to have inadequate object relationships, developed somatic complaints rather than psychologically designated discomfort. The psychosomatic style of communication is seen as a pathological variant, implying concreteness and lack of vividness of fantasy. Whether alexithymia actually designates a disorder where people lack words for mood is unclear, but the term has taken hold in some quarters and links feelings to affective contact or lack of contact with others. Is alexithymia a linguistic failure, a cultural variant, or a global lack of appreciation of affective life? The current theories of emotion are essentially speechless and as yet cannot answer such questions until development in our field gives them words. A child's affective understanding follows a similar developmental path. Emotions are there from the beginning, but their appreciation and designation is ontogenically determined.

Despite the variations in communicative style, language does provide an essential vehicle for the recognition and sharing of all experiences including depressive experiences. It is similar to another technique of expression, music, in which the "blues" are clearly recognizable in many different styles. For jazz, the "blues" employs an indigenous medium, having its own distinctive twelve-measure progression utilizing "blue notes" the third, fifth, and seventh degrees of a key. Even if the listener or musician can't read the musical notation, the audience can appreciate the meaning and the player can improvise within this style. Basic elements of tone and quality of presentation seems to transcend the interpretation each individual brings to the same note, and a recognizable theme of musical mood emerges from different keys.

Thus, affects may have some preordering in various stimuli and their corresponding brain responses *but* the affect is not the sound of blues, nor is it the cochlear's transduction of the sounds. It is an interpretation that labels an appreciated state of feelings.

DEPRESSION AMONG DARWINIAN EMOTIONS

The idea of essential, universal affects shared by all humans is far from new. Darwin[8] was one of the first to observe and write about basic emotions and their accompanying facial expressions. "Surprise, fear, disgust, happiness, anger and sadness" were observed across the mammalian species and in infancy. Darwin viewed depressive emotions as normal, universal, and potentially adaptive—and even permitting survival. It, among other affects, became a pivotal structure in the evolution of our current theories. As Klerman points out in *The Scope of Depression*,[9] "Darwin himself first applied the evolutionary approach to behavior, especially to emotional responses." As he noted, Darwinian theories and observations of emotions have been rediscovered in contemporary research and in mother-child dyadic studies. This adaptational approach "examines neurobiological mechanisms, environmental milieu, genetic mutations, etc. which mediate the input of the environment and organize, integrate and terminate the emotionally metabolic and goal-directed activities of the organism." Darwin also pointed out the signal value of depression as an appeal for help. As such, the affect provides an adaptive survival function for mammals requiring long caretaking and auxiliary aid in parenting during which maturation can take place. The appeal function will be considered further at a later point in this chapter because of the postulated value of the affect as a vehicle of communication. Suffice it to say that the move from *expression* to *appeal* represents a developmental advance toward attachment and socialization.

Although depressive affect may be called "primary" it should not be considered simple, nor should it obscure the complexity of its study in mature persons. This is true in the semantic domain, too, where the identical word "depression" may assume multiple meanings (polysemy) and reflect various values. *Depression* is often used in daily language to imply boredom, loneliness, anger, fatigue, or anhedonia. Freud[10] and then Abraham[11] made critical distinctions between mourning and melancholia based on the presence of or absence of unconscious hostility, while other theorists distinguish grief and bereavement reactions from depression based on the temporal relation of the emotions to actual loss. These distinctions notwithstanding, the clinical presentations of people in depressed states are not always easily differentiated without history or personal report and familiarity with the social and intrapsychic context of the mood. Although the grief-stricken individual only rarely presents for psychiatric help, the diagnosis of a pathological state on the basis of signs and symptoms may not be easy. We know little about the continuity or discontinuity between these depressive experiences.[12] The psychoanalyst may argue that the distinction is best made in the clinician's sensitive listening as he explores the intensely personal and idiosyncratic meaning of words which point to structural and dynamic organizations. From another perspective, Beck[13] and his colleagues indicate the need to listen for the "cognitive triad" of depression: consisting of negative cognitions regarding oneself, the world, and one's future. These data are closer to the empirical surface. Whether one applies a cognitive or psychoanalytic model of depression (and they are not mutually exclusive) subtle shifts of meaning and interpretations are likely to occur if one model is emphasized above the other. Neither model is immune to arbitrariness of the classification system and ethnocentric bias. Theses biases are embedded in the names and categories in use within our community.

CATEGORIES AND ASSUMPTIONS

While it is currently stylish to speak of discrete categories of psychiatric disorder, "spectrums" and polarities were the rule in the recent past. This is only one of numerous examples of a shift in terminology which accompanies and even structures our parochial conceptual cubbyholes. In the recent past and now, polarities such as "primary-secondary" endogenous-exogenous (reactive), major-minor, neurotic-psychotic, unipolar-bipolar, formed and form the semantic underpinnings of our models of depression. Our current classification system can be shown to have evolved out of a melting pot of terms deriving from various conceptions, dating back to the Aristotelian idea of melancholia and then dysthymia. Melancholia, of course, was revived seriously by Galen to account for mood on the basis of excess black bile out of balance with the other humors. Even then the body was the source of the feelings and mind's work. Dysthymia, in turn, has a recognizably Greek origin referring to the thymus as the seat of emotion rather than the liver. The current shift in our nomenclature to bipolar from manic-depressive sanitizes one form of affective disorder from the conceptual dead wood of the past. On the other hand, the retention of dysthymia and melancholia firmly links us to the past.

The number of categories and subcategories our nosologies and classifications can incorporate may have a critical maximum, perhaps akin to the number of objects which normally can be remembered at any one time. It is likely that when this hypothetical maximum occurs, multiple nuances and shadings require consideration of the "spectrum" concept rather than that of discrete cuts. Interestingly enough, as we struggle to determine the truth (validation) of critical boundaries between clinical entities on empirical grounds by parceling out symptoms, we must acknowledge that the continuities among sadness of everyday life and states of clinical depression or grief tend to defy decisive demonstration. At the same time, familiar notions such as primary-secondary, endogenous-exogenous have become shadows of their former selves as studies fail to substantiate those distinctions. This may be so because their use implied attempts at an etiologically based nosologic system rather than a cross-sectional descriptive nomenclature of disorder as it is coded in DSM-III-R.

Nonetheless, from the ashes of these theoretical discards, a phoenix has arisen. This is the psychiatric positivism spoken of earlier, where one finds "chemical depressions," "DST positives and negatives," "rapid and slow cyclers," "MHPG positives and negatives," and "chemical restraints." In our language—even if not fully in our belief—we find the assumption of direct one-to-one correspondences between neurophysiological aberration and the subjective experiences of the depressed person. Current research findings may have made the gap smaller, but we have yet to solve the mind-body dilemma. Common psychiatric jargon frequently implies otherwise these days, sometimes leading us into a false tranquility that giving something a name or changing a name represents new knowledge. However, empirical caution has prevailed in the long arduous battle to link our feelings to biological measures. DST correlations with depression began with the optimism that we finally had a measure at the level of the substrate. But evidence could not be ignored that hopes were not yet fulfilled and that high correlations were not enough to designate exclusivity either of trait or state. However, the direction and model are distinctly medical and empirical.

FEELING, DIAGNOSIS, BEING

Currently, the nominalization of depressive states seems to be in greater flux than in the case of the schizophrenic disorders. There are intriguing linguistic usage differences between these two groups of disorders. For example, in everyday speech we tend to say: "He *is a* schizophrenic," rather than, "He *has* schizophrenia": whereas, for depressive disorder we are more likely to say: "He *is depressed*," (the verb form), and not as frequently, "He *is a* depressive," or "He *has* depression."

The psychiatrist's signifier, "Schizophrenia" appears to define who the person is as though it were inexorably connected to his being, whereas depression is something that a person experiences, usually for discrete periods of time. Depression is or can be a temporary modifier—a state designation. We can speculate that the semantics of psychiatry reflects degrees of societal stigmatization or discomfort that is felt with a particular psychic state or behavioral designator. All of us experience depression; a minority can conceive of experiencing schizophrenia. Indeed, in common usage, schizophrenia is more frequently used by laypeople to reference being of two minds. Thus, common usage is closer to etymologic concretism than professionally agreed-upon definition. Attributions such as, "He is a schizophrenic," "She's a borderline," may signal our unease with what we consider to be permanent and frightening states of mind that are less universal and therefore less understandable than depressive feelings. Meanwhile, the universality of feelings of sadness, disappointment, grief, and rejection are so common in the human condition that their familiarity is reflected in the appointed syntactic tendencies of using the forms as attributions rather than as copula* forms of equivalence—"He *is* a schizophrenic." In a gray classification zone between the poles of alienation and familiarity one can find persons with psychotic depressions, lifelong characterological depressions and schizoaffective disorders. Ironically, it may be the automatic and unthinking use of these contemporary depressive semantics which leads to some of our blind spots.

The subtle ways in which we have arbitrarily linked classification systems is worthy of note. Klerman[14] points out that the endogenous-reactive dichotomy has unfortunately also been used interchangeably with the psychotic-neurotic distinction. They have become semantically equivalent. Furthermore, the differential reactions of subculture to such experiences as bereavement, traumatic, or other life events are difficult to factor in when symptom pictures and profiles are detailed out of context. Our ability to clinically diagnose is dependent upon how our patient's pattern and history is construed. And how it comes to be construed is itself based upon the shifting definitions and interpretation at different levels of meaning. It is for this reason that data from epidemiological surveys must be validated against clinical examination—too many false positives in epidemiology may ensure that we are gathering in all the cases *but* there may be too many that are not *clinical cases* in the sweep. There is a rich interaction among three levels of the clinical process:

The complaint of the patient

(A)

The depth and sensitivity of inquiry of the doctor

(B)

The constellation of complaints and responses to specifically formulated inquiries which create syndromes.

With Process A in motion, the level of inquiry has been triggered by the complaint arising out of an already learned semantic network. Furthermore, among all the complaints, the physician then selects certain signals which fit into the syndromic constellation of his voice via Process B.

---

*The verb *is* renders the subject and its post-verb designation as equivalents: "He *is* schizophrenic," "A schizophrenic *is* he."

The patient who comes to this situation well-informed further influences this process, as does the patient who styles his symptoms to fit the anticipated questions. Bühler,[15] the developmental psychologist, suggested that the *expressive* function of an utterance gives way to an *appeal* function as the environment of humans begins to respond. The latter responses shape future utterances in the expectation that selective responses will be forthcoming. Only with fuller maturity can humans with well developed language propositionalize, i.e., tell in order to share experience with each other. However, throughout the life cycle, we return to our need both to express and to appeal. The latter function becomes most prominent in situations of need such as in visiting a physician or in seeking help. The attentive psychotherapist will listen for the appeal in the *words*, the *prosody*, and the *kinesics* while also placing the references into a coherent system that is brought to the clinical situation by prior training as a frame of reference. In this sense patients may wittingly or unwittingly lead the listener astray. He or she may tell a story to influence the clinician, i.e., to force a drug treatment; to force shock treatment; to direct toward hospitalization, etc.

Mirroring this process are those complaints which are not spoken, those questions not asked, and that which does not become incorporated as a symptom into a syndrome. Is this the manner by which the "not-asked" becomes potentially nonexistent? The emphasis upon particular dimensions from both the distressed individual and the therapist is patterned in accordance with our cultural belief system and past education regarding depression as well as in accord with empirical findings. It is possible that the current fluidity and emphasis upon spectrums in our classification systems reflect the increasing awareness of the difficulties with a rigid schema. What is named "atypical" may mean no more than that we cannot classify it now. The inherent causal inferences under which we function continue to lead to the exclusion of certain questions and the misinterpreting of unanticipated responses. We select from what is said, and we also lead our patients' responses, i.e., a review of systems or queries about side effects leads to suggestion and compliance in some individuals and defiant denial in others.

Thus far, the appeal function of depression and depressive language forms has only been alluded to. As noted, the semantics of depression has a powerful link to the appeals: "Do something!" "Help me!" The form adopted by a culture to articulate distress relies upon its idea of what legitimately constitutes distress. That form is also dependent upon its idea of what is an appropriate expression of distress and upon what one has to say in order to obtain the desired reaction from others. In certain situations and personality configurations those words are, "I'm going to hurt (or kill) myself" or the equivalent gesture. How the expression is labeled by the observer is crucial. On prison wards, for example, such statements are likely to be interpreted as "manipulative" by the correction officer rather than as an expression of psychological distress. In less restrictive human environments the expression of distress and its nonverbal accompaniments of tears, postural, and motor retardation are intense modes of social communication, frequently evoking sympathetic reactions from others; yet under certain circumstances we may respond with helplessness or anger to the same depressed individual. There are culturally predetermined time periods after which the depressed person is expected to "pull himself together."

In some situations, an "idiom of distress" leads a person not to a psychiatrist, but to a church or spiritual leader in the community or a friend. In all cultures the experience of grief is viewed as primary; such spiritual suffering is not described as illness, unless it exceeds a culture's expectations of (or prescriptions for) bereavement reactions. In our society, the individual who continues to hear the voice of the deceased for a prolonged period of time, i.e., greater than 12 months, may then be referred to a psychiatrist. In other societies, such as subcultures of India, mourners may be expected to grieve for a lifetime or wives to commit sati. A recent report of the Institute of Medicine[16] describes our current understanding regarding states of grief and bereavement reactions and their relation to states of clinical depression. The questions regarding continuity between these normal reactions and disorders continue to be the object of scientific inquiry.

The temporal dimension of depressive reactions has an important role in the delineation of illness and health. We apply a linear construct of acute versus chronic which then becomes a part of the criteria for psychopathology or normality. The bereavement reaction, which is pathological when prolonged past a culturally defined time period has been noted. Reactions to traumatic events are expected to be resolved within briefer time spans without any of the underlying neurophysiological indices becoming positive, as in major depression. Meanwhile, the observer of trends in hospital psychiatry may note that the use of the term "chronic" has become an anathema because it is so strongly associated with a failure of treatment. Moreover, this word has additional social impact because it is a semantic signal for insurance companies paying for psychiatric care to investigate and threaten withdrawal of payments. Such predicaments have even generated specific staff positions in many psychiatric hospitals focusing upon the auditing of medical records. The objective is to ensure that the wording of reports on severely disturbed individuals will not carry the image of chronicity. "Chronic" now carries the additional burden of "hopelessness," conjuring up, for some, the image of a homeless psychotic patient. This linkage can be seen even when the disorder itself is not of great severity. It belongs in the semantic and social cubby of stigmatization. Thus the language of depression—and psychiatry itself—functions simultaneously as a professional, clinical construct and a biased popular vehicle to express and define life experiences. Physicians must be aware of the dual tracking of significances as they go about their professional work.

In these ways, as well as many others not mentioned here, our capacity to conceptualize depression is limited by our linguistic frames and temporospatial metaphors. The patient and his depression now fuse and become inseparable. They are, in fact, defined by each other. (The very sick mental patient becomes as the schizophrenic is: his disease!) Ironically, the firmer description of depression as a diagnostic entity can become a barrier to its diagnosis.

The experience of depression in childhood may serve as an example of this as a potential problem. The young child, with his incompletely developed use of language may confound our expectations about how a depressed mood is expressed leading to problem in empirical study. The criteria for the identification of clinical depression in childhood are far from clear, although we are now certain that some prepubertal children fit the diagnostic bill for major depression. This difficulty in identification has occurred in part due to the fact that a depressed child's reactions may differ significantly from an adult's.[17] The problem may have been further confounded by the development of theories relating the psychogenesis of adult depression to the infantile and early childhood experience of loss. The term "masked depression" was in the recent past frequently applied to adolescents and children. Both these age groups were felt to be unable to fully express their depressed mood. The adolescent's inclination to enact, rather than to express distress was confusing to the clinician seeking simple diagnostic criteria. Others have since complained that the diagnostic and statistical manuals treat children like "little adults" and therefore misunderstand that the psychopathology of childhood is part of other developmental considerations. Adolescent psychiatrists claim that the "acting out" adolescent would have described clear-cut depressive symptoms if he had been asked about it in appropriate terms, hence the former popular concept "masked depression" or "depressive equivalent." We seem to require relative conformity to disease patterns in order to delineate subjective states of depression regardless of developmental stage. In our sharing the assumptive world it is easy to lose track of the variations in reactions which are possible during the flux of developmental change or across cultures. Whatever emotions we can distinguish in the face of what the child knows of his reactions is based upon the names a culture provides for its members.

CULTURAL AND ETHNOCENTRIC CONSIDERATIONS

Ontogenetic changes is one species of problem. Contrasting the names different cultures apply to similar experiences also can illuminate our perspective. The profound influence upon cognition and constructions of illness exercised by a culture are difficult to study if we remain closed in our own backyard. Kleinman's[18] work within China, previously mentioned, provides a valuable crosscultural reference point for studying the semantics of depression. He relates how somatization, accompanied by a medical professional's diagnosis of a "broken kidney" may be one of the few culturally sanctioned signifiers for psychological distress although it is cast in a metaphor of bodily distress. It is fascinating to note that, whereas the expression of mood disturbances are in the form of physical complaints, the treatment prescribed by non-Westernized physicians tends to be psychological (i.e., spiritual) requiring a visit to a shaman or a priest.

A study[19] of an Australian preliterate society, the Pinturi, similarly reveals a lexicon of terms that refer to variants of depression ranging from disappointment to serious mood, extreme loneliness, and reduced speech and appetite. These various terms have been categorized into constructs that refer to affect, behavior, cognition, and vegetative signs. Most interesting, perhaps, is the tendency to project cause and effect for overlapping words to express both anger and depression. If we contrast these styles with what Wiig,[20] an Indian psychiatrist, calls the Western propensity toward "psychologization," it is clear that we are much freer to label our emotional distress as such. Despite Western "psychologization," biomedical tests, neurophysiological and neurohumoral analyses, and pharmacological interventions are at the forefront of investigation and treatment of depressive complaints in the West. One must wonder how this reversal of the Chinese tendency for psychological treatments and somatized complaints has developed. Perhaps it is linked to the preeminence in Western society of a medical model in which the diagnosis of depression is made in the same way as a diagnosis of congestive heart failure by symptom clustering even as we search for correlations with substrate changes.

These correlations reveal concisely materialistic value systems in our thinking. The mentalist-social dimensions are looked at as temporary and even discarded as spiritual as we await the messianic hope of a *maker*. Even Freud[21] began his mentalist speculations as a neural analogue in the *Project* and wrote of his metapsychology as a mythology one day to be replaced by physicalistic propositions. It is not inconceivable that the two models are closer to one another than at first viewing. The Chinese "broken kidney" represents a much broader category than we are comfortable in applying in the West. It encompasses diagnoses of hysteria, depression, anxiety, pathophysiological reactions, and hypochondriacal personality. Kleinman relates how the Chinese have even absorbed and adopted an out-of-vogue Western explanatory diagnosis, neurasthenia. The neurasthenic model— with its allusion to an exhaustion of the nervous system giving rise to various forms of depression and organic pathology—is an attractive concept for a somatized psychiatry. Moreover, we are not so far removed from our own past to remember that Freud[22] in his earliest formulations considered neurasthenia to be an actual neurosis consequent to neurohumoral exhaustion or depletion occurring secondary to excessive sexual activity or masturbation.

The essential point in describing crosscultural studies is to permit us to see that various and conflicting interpretations are believed to be true by their respective users. On the other hand, we all may be referencing essentially identical states by diagnoses that we in Western medicine call depression.

The names we apply to our emotional and mental states not only have changed the classification system, but the very ways in which we perceive our subjective states. Since medical practice is embedded within its cultures, doctors tacitly force patients to fit their complaints into prescribed and well marketed culture-bound propositions. Words are not empty labels, but conceptually full and restrictive in their demarcation. They also carry affective valence. Cancer is a word loaded with intimations of death. AIDS is new to the public, but it spells hopeless. ARC (Aids Related Complex) is not as medically onerous, but try to tell that to a public full of apprehension.

Balancing out this weighty cultural factor is the profound significance of personal meaning upon how a person chooses signifiers or words to express a state, experience, or symptom. Classification processes may obscure the primary affects such as depression which are more meaningful to the individual than the secondary public terms with which he shares his experiences. Although somaticized metaphors for depression are not ignored, it is rare for the general practitioner or internist to both recognize and treat for depression on the basis of what may be the next layer of meaning of those physcal complaints. The reason for this is far from clear. However, when viewed in light of the vast amount of antidepressants and anxiolytics prescribed by nonpsychiatrists, it may be that there is a partial recognition of the meaning of the somatized complaint, but not enough to raise the treatment response above the level of a pharmacological intervention for a vaguely hypothesized neurophysiological derangement. On the one hand, the medical model forms the structure of such interventions. However, such actions may also have a social dimension: the physician is too busy, he judges his patient an unlikely psychiatric candidate, or an attitude prevails that symptomatic treatment is the best that can be done in the face of vague etiologic inferences. Medication seems practical, quicker, concrete, and less demanding on professional time. If it works, it is cost-efficient. Moreover, the dissatisfied patient may not return, and follow-up is lost.

Another factor worthy of consideration in the semantics of depression involves the environmental or individual stimuli which are commonly accepted as stressful precipitants to a depressed state of mind (and body). The presence or absence of stressors were previously utilized to distinguish between "neurotic-reactive" depression and "endogenous" or "biological" depressions. The significance of precipitants appears to wax and wane in importance to our theoretical and empirical constructs. The introduction of stressors may have been responsive to a type of patient who spontaneously describes environmental factors as concomitants to the onset of depression. These individuals may be "cause seekers"—they need an etiology for their ills and attach contiguous events to give meaning to their symptoms.

Hirschfeld[23] reported that a group of patients with diagnosed "situational" major depression defined by a precipitant did not differ significantly on clinical grounds from a group of depressed patients without a precipitant. No significant difference in life events, family situations or social supports was identified. In contradistinction to this, George Winokur[24] and others have revived interest in the diagnosis of "reactive-neurotic" depression. He argues that it should not be made a "diagnosis of exclusion"; that there is a specific subgroup of depressed individuals with this disorder. A family history of alcoholism is said to be a validating factor for the existence of this depressed subgroup and is correlated with long-standing personality problems. The old debate about whether depression is to be called an illness or a syndrome is rejuvenated by such studies despite many efforts to eliminate it. Meanwhile, attempts by Casper, et al.[25] to discern subsets of depression by typing somatic symptomatology were reported as unrevealing. Thus the significance of somatization may not be related to its value as a classifying marker within our culture.

The referential questions of how we classify and name can be approached more deeply if we address the issue of what can be said to be most basic and universal about depression. As physicians we want to know what goes beyond culture-bound considerations, and is there a core presentation that cannot be missed and yet is specific. Anthropologists refer to the *etic* as that which is universal while the *emic* refers to the meaningful form within a specific culture. The designations derive from a linguistic heritage of the words *phonetic* vs. *phonemic*, the latter referring to meaningful sound units, the former to the basic universal sound variants common to any speech group. As this mystery continues to be probed, one aspect looms large: the semantics of depression always seems to supersede our discoveries. This is particularly true when we work on multiple levels of investigation ranging from the biological to the phenomenological. The semantic processing of dysphoric affects is a pivotal mechanism, intimately involved with the awareness of depressed mood, of somatization and of psychologization.

When a child looks at the face of another and identifies the emotion saying, "He's sad," for the first time, a considerable amount of learning has already occurred. For that matter, the later designation of that child's inner state by learning a label is also subject to the systemized rigidity of a classification system by naming it. It is the culture that provides the child with a name. That name only approximates the experience. As the child grows to adulthood, the development of psychic and semantic defenses such as intellectualization, denial, dissociation, stigmatization will all become operative to reduce the intensity of unpleasant emotions. All of these devices are rooted in linguistic processes as they are added to the developmental flux.

DEVELOPMENT OF AFFECT AWARENESS IN VERBAL CONSCIOUSNESS

There are at least two directions of exploration. One direction is to review developmental theories and biological perspectives on bodily states. The other applies the cultural perspective previously discussed. Bowlby's[26] and Spitz's[27] work on effects of separation and attachment theory are primary examples of the developmental perspective. These investigators used separation experiences as a model for the observation of the development of depressive experiences. The basic underlying concept of loss was modified from the earlier psychoanalytic perspectives of Abraham[28] and Freud.[29] Bowlby's work, also, has led to experimental paradigms with laboratory animals over time in order to study the development of depression. Similar paradigms have been developed for the study of young children as in the Ainsworth[30] "strange situation" that is widely used.

Emotion elicited by separation is a concept which appears to have universal application to the human condition and is consonant with the Darwinian perspective of prolonged dependency for survival in higher mammals with small broods. The development of depressive affects is intricately linked to the growth of psychologically meaningful relationships which precede the display of such affects. Bowlby's notion of an "instinctive response system" in humans includes sucking, clinging, following, crying, and smiling. These functional capacities facilitate the attachment behaviors which occur when behavioral systems are activated. When the maternal figure as a mental representation becomes and remains unavailable, grief and mourning occur in successive pathological phases: numbness, protest, despair, and detachment. As Malmquist[31] delineates, Bowlby's concept of mourning referred to a psychological process of grief, the subjective state in response to the loss of the loved object. Depression is the affective state observed when mourning occurs. This is an integrative theory, in which the semantics of depression are not classified into distinct and separate categories, but rather are stated as a composite of behaviors that are responsive. Separation, anxiety, mourning, grief, and defense all operate as part of a unitary process.

Although Bowlby originally postulated identical mourning in children and adults, developmentalists now consider the differences between successive developmental stages in reacting to object loss. For the very young child, (under six months) the experience may be one of helpless withdrawal which Spitz describes as an anaclitic state rather than something comparable to the adult mourning process where the adult goes through a painful psychological process of gradual detachment from the inner representation of the deceased person. Thus, this is presemantic, perhaps a part of the conservation/withdrawal phenomenon. Bowlby's studies and those of others who followed of the relationships between early maternal deprivation and the susceptibility to depressions in adult life documented some of the earlier analytic theories in which early ambivalent relationships with parental figures were related to later states. Most of these investigations were retrospective, but they suggest the survival of meaningful unconscious complexes activating psychological and behavioral states over long time spans.

The developmental perspective on depression also demands that we examine the inner language of the self, focusing in on the evaluation of devalued self-concept and negative bodily conception in the narcissistically vulnerable child. Self-derogatory thoughts such as "I am bad" or "I hate myself" form the basis for narcissistic disorders in later life and refer also to subsequent suicidal preoccupations. This depreciated self is also the template for somatic manifestations of depression. The relationship of childhood anxiety to later vulnerability to depression is a close one in this context. In the face of real or feared object loss in adult life, these earlier intrapsychic influences may become operant. Brenner[32] refers to the developmental calamities that activate response to anticipated loss, anxiety, and response to loss itself as depression. In this sense the signals to affective arousal are coded in meaningful units that have semantic valence. Situations and contexts interpreted as threats to well-being or as generative of affects become triggers to mood states. Thus, from a developmental perspective, meaningful units of experience are scanned and interpreted and affective responses serve as self-regulating units of influence on the basis of their semantic reference. The word begins to dictate to the body just as the body responds to the meaning of the context. This schematization is consonant with cognitive and psychoanalytic dovelopmental propositions. It is also in line with our studies of biological substrate changes as a complementary science to linguistic studies.

The basic questions regarding the semantics of depression have not changed dramatically over time. We still must wonder how changing diagnostic labels may transform our concept of the feeling. At the least, the power of words to shape our theoretical positions is clearer. Not only do affective disorders need to be further studied, but the different patterns of cognitive processes and illness behavior as well. The consequences, expectations, and treatment of depression are molded in many ways by the categories and labels we apply to the phenomena or experiences. What is not yet classified in the depressive universe may still exist. It may be discovered (or rediscovered) once we decide to name it. However, as the philosophers[33] tell us, we must be silent about that for which we have no words.

References

1. Kleinman A: *Patients and Healers in the Context of Culture*. Berkeley, University of California Press, 1980.
2. *Webster's Third New International Dictionary*. Edited by Grove PB. Springfield, Massachusetts, Merrian Company, 1963.
3. Darwin C: *The Expression of the Emotions in Man and Animals*. New York, J. Appleton, 1929.
4. Freud S: *Beyond the Pleasure Principle (1920), Standard Edition, Vol XVIII*, London, Hogarth Press, 1953-1974.
5. Levi-Strauss C: *Introduction to a Science of Mythology. Vol 1, The Raw and the Cooked*. Translated by John and Doreen Weightman. New York, Harper and Row, 1969.
6. Kleinman A: *op cit.*
7. Nemiah JC, Sifneos PC: *Affect and Fantasy in Patients with Psychosomatic Medicine*. Edited by Hill O. London, Butterworth, 1970.
8. Darwin C: *op cit.*
9. Klerman G: *The Scope of Depression in the Origins of Depression: Current Concepts and Approaches*. Edited by Angst J. Berlin, Dahlem Konferenzen, 1983.
10. Freud S: *Mourning and Melancholia (1917). Standard Edition of Complete Psychological Works of Sigmund Freud, Vol 14*, London, Hogarth Press, 1957.
11. Abraham K: *Notes on the Psychoanalytical Investigation and Treatment of Manic-Depressive Insanity and Allied Conditions*. Edited by Gaylin W. New York, Science House, Inc. 1968.
12. *Sociocultural Influences in Bereavement: Reactions, Consequences, and Care*. Edited by Osterweis M, Solomon F, Green M. Washington, DC, National Academy Press, 1984.
13. Beck AT: *Affective Disorders*. Edited by Arieti S. American Handbook of Psychiatry, New York, Basic Books, 2nd Ed. 1974.
14. Klerman GL, Endicott J, Spitzer R, et al: Neurotic depression: A systematic analysis of multiple criteria and meaning. *Am J Psychiatry*; 136:57.
15. Bühler K: *The Mental Development of the Child*. New York, Harcourt, 1930.
16. Osterweis M: *op cit.*
17. Poznanski E, Mokros HB, Grossman J et al: Diagnostic criteria in childhood depression. *Am J Psychiatry 142 1985; 142:* 10, 1168-1173.
18. Klerman G: *op cit.*
19. Morice R: Language and Diagnosis in Transcultural Psychiatry. Edited by Simpson MA. *Psycholinguistics in Clinical Practice*, New York, Irvington Publishers, Inc, 1980.
20. Wiig: Personal Communication. *ADAMHA:WHO Meeting*, Copenhagen, 1982.
21. Freud S: *A Project for a Scientific Psychology, Standard Edition, Vol. I*, London, Hogarth Press, 1953-1974.
22. Freud S: *Introductory Lectures on Psychoanalysis (1916-17), Standard Editions, (Part III), Vol XVI*, London, Hogarth Press, 1953-1974.

23. Hirshfeld RMA, et al: Situational major depressive disorder. *Arch Gen Psychiatry* *1985;* 42:1109-114.
24. Winokur G: The validity of neurotic-reactive depression, new data and reappraisal. *Arch Gen Psychiatry 1985;* 42:1116-1122.
25. Casper RC, Redmond E, Katz MM, et al: Somatic symptoms in primary affective disorder. *Arch Gen Psychiatry 1985;* 42:1098-1127.
26. Bowlby J: *Attachment and Loss,* New Work, Basic Books, 1969.
27. Spitz RA: Anaclitic depression. *Psychoanal Study of the The Child,* 2:313, 1946.
28. Abraham K: *op cit.*
29. Freud S: *op cit.*
30. Ainsworth M, Bell SM, and Stayton D: Infant-Mother Attachment and Social Development: Socialization as a Product of Reciprocal Responsiveness to Signals. Edited by Richards M. The Integration of the Child to a Social World. Cambridge, Cambridge University Press, 1974.
31. Malmquist C: Depression in Childhood, in *The Nature and Treatment of Depression.* Edited by Flach F, and Draghi S. New York, J. Wiley & Sons, 1975.
32. Brenner C: *The Mind in Conflict.* New York, International Universities Press, 1982.
33. Wittgenstein L: *Tractatus Logico-philosophicus.* London, Routledge & Kegan Paul, 1951.

Chapter 2

THE SUBJECTIVE EXPERIENCE
OF DEPRESSIVE ILLNESS

C.K.

Today is quite an appropriate day to think about depression. The night before was slightly insomniac, in and out of unpleasant, self-deprecating dreams in which I played the antiheroine in every reel.

I get up this morning, vaguely disgruntled, grumbling to myself that I will have to clean the house, get flowers, buy food, and be friendly with two good old college friends who are coming to lunch. Last night I was looking forward to this; today I wish they weren't coming; I feel too busy. They don't know what I am in the midst of.

In the course of the cleanup, I break a green glass dish that belonged to my great-aunt. It has thistles cut into it; they lie on the floor in pieces. The sun shines through the green and the thistles are still beautiful. Picking up the shards, I cut my finger, bleed on my dress, and, all in all, the tone of the day is set in an intensely blue state of dislike.

Nevertheless, I somehow stagger through the rest of it, fake the housecleaning, skip the flowers, slap together an easy lunch, and let my old friends do all the talking.

I think Sylvia Townsend Warner defined the fatal law of gravity, which is that when you are down, everything falls on you. I know, by experience, that to get good and down, you start by falling on yourself.

If you have ever had a major depressive episode, you, like me, may be in the habit of taking your mental temperature. Am I just tired? Or am I slipping-sliding down down into the ineluctible depressive mud? Is this just a passing zephyr of a low mood? Is my sleep permanently off? Is my coordination ajar? Or was that just an uninteresting tennis game? Am I unaccountably touchy? Am I getting more and more unfriendly? Should I drive on with the activities that yesterday's energy and enthusiasm plotted for today? Or should I become my own nurse and plan some defenses?

Usually, the answer to these questions is merely wrong-side-of-the-beddedness; the following day is productive, bright, and interesting.

Unusually, the answers point to the inadvertent beginning of a dark journey that seems convincing proof of the existence of hell.

All you rationalists seem so fine in the sunshine. You tell me that I should be glad I am not starving, or hijacked, or bomb-blasted; remind me that this glorious country, the land of opportunity, is made for all of us to succeed in. Individualism and self-reliance, the great American ideals, urge us on. There is no reason why anyone with backbone cannot succeed. So why am I so inconsolably discouraged?

I want to be my best. I want, most of all, not to disappoint myself.

Yet, sometimes, the many roles I expect myself to play become unplayable: poet, wife, mother, daughter, housekeeper, athlete, conversationalist, correspondent, hostess, bookkeeper, dreamer, and doer of good. These demand the entirety of each.

But.

If you add depression to my regular routine, I am now talking about working two full-time jobs at once during the day and a third full-time job during the night. I am talking about trying to do what I usually do without thinking about it, but now must try to hold my exterior together tightly so that colleagues, friends, and strangers won't know that my interior is a hopeless shambles of shards more shattered than that green glass dish. Not only am I lugging a major depression, but I am also risking being found out by those lucky people who have no experience with it.

I know that they think depressed people are indulging themselves, just goofing off. They say that depressed people could, if they wanted to, get rid of it by an act of will. Undepressed people enjoy the superiority of their own present mental health; yet, they think nothing of complaining about and getting treated for their hearts, livers, allergies, teeth, and broken bones. At the same time, the majorly depressed are thought of as either tetched, or weak, or both.

Now, do not misunderstand me; depressives as well as anyone with a so-called "medical illness," must take responsibility for their illness. It is vital not to get so bogged down by depression that nothing is done to ameliorate it. Depression must be admitted to be the affective disorder it is while the decision is made to get back to life and work.

But what is a depressive most likely to do? You guessed it; a depressive is likely to be unmoved by this essential imperative. For example, I am, at my worst, rolled in a dirty storm wave, in a seascape tatally devoid of other human beings. All alone, I am tumbling over and over and no one and nothing either can or will help. No pill, no friend, no lover, no child, no doctor. I am so low, so dead low, that I truly have no hope. So, I do nothing except turn my back to the storm.

Depression, to many experts, is just one more disorder with its vegetative and cognitive symptoms, easy to tick off. But to me, depression is a deep and unrelieved grief without any feeling in it, without any object for it. Along with this grief is the sad recognition that without feeling, both the rational and the lyrical parts of the brain are useless to me.

I tend to be unaware, despite my experience in the past, of how debilitated I have become, so the call to the doctor comes late in the descent. Still, everything I try to do is a part of a complicity of dead lines scheming against me. Little threads of living come loose. My work is at a standstill; blocked. I begin to forget things, to be late, to make mistakes. I write a check, but forget to sign it. I drop my gloves. I lose my keys. I spill milk all over the kitchen. I put my letters in the incinerator and mail my garbage. I hate listening. I cut people off in mid-sentence. I can't decide, not even the smallest decision: which to do first, the dishes or the beds, which bill to pay, which message to answer first. Most decisions are resolved by doing neither. I want only to lie down, to be by myself, to do nothing. I know I am irritable, but I believe, with good reason. I wish everyone else would be more considerate. Love and appreciation seem to have flown out of my life just when I could use them the most.

Getting through the day is a pointless and unfocused effort at mere survival. My IQ has been lowered to 75. The things I used to do without thinking now take deliberation, concentration, and four times the time.

Time!

Time begins to lose its shape; mostly it stretches out while, at other times, it shrinks. The day is interminably long, although, to be honest, I do very little in it. Clock-watching reveals imperceptible advances; eons unroll from sunup to sunset, except for appointments for which I am invariably late—if I can remember them.

Any ability I may have had has disappeared. My self, which used to be optimistic, energetic, funny, sympathetic, is now dwindled down to a small flame on an uncertain pilot light. What remains of me has defensively withdrawn to wait in the minimal inner center of the flame.

Hyperbole, this is not.

Sleep perversely eludes me. I am exhausted all day; by seven in the evening, I cannot stay awake. I doze in and out of the news and the slapdash supper I have presented. I leave the dishes and crash into bed.

Heaven.

But by midnight, I am at attention, tangled in the sheets and watching my brain repeat and repeat at breakneck speed. My brain is a Rolodex of thoughts that spins through the rest of the night. Time has done its ultimate stretch. Round and round they go, refusing to hold still so I can deal with them. The night lasts and lasts and lasts, ample time to show me failures: failures in work, creativity, friendships, feeling; misses, mistakes, meanness, monotony, monogamy. There is ample time to spiral by other people looking successful, sought after, young, lovely, lovable, loving, beloved.

It is blazingly clear why I am not in that category. I am old, ugly, messy, incompetent, boring, and probably repulsive. Plainly unlovable. I can't write, can't work, can't listen, can't talk, can't remember, can't feel. I can't even cry; can't find a way to express the sadness that overwhelms me.

Can't is a recurring theme with variations.

Separated as I am from all living things, I can't even exchange comfort with my dog.

On and on they go, these tatters and snippets of thoughts that blow cyclonically round in my head.

I try to change the subject, think back on how I was before I slid down here. It is a cold view. I clearly see that all I worked for was illusory, of no importance, a piece of shit.

While this is going on inside, no one seems to be aware of it. That may be the biggest hurt of all: that my best self is so similar to my depressed self, there is no perceptible difference.

A few days ago, Linda said to me: "You are so strong and wise...so generous, so goodhearted."

How could she *not* know that I am nothing of the kind? I consist of what I can only describe as a blob of putrefying flesh around which I have thrown up an inadequate wall to hide it. The smell must be awful. The wall threatens to break; it must be inspected constantly, day and night. It has to be shored up. This takes all the physical and mental strength I have; the unremitting effort takes all my attention.

I writhe at the hypocrisy of seeming. I vacillate between hating the things people like Linda seem to think I am, and trembling at the thought that I am transparent, that the pitiful thing I really am shows through.

What I really lack is content. I am absent. I will never come back.

While my mind is doing this to me, my body keeps itself at a peak of tension, at the ready at all times, yet totally unable to act. My neck is stiff; my shoulders and back are rigid; my stomach carries an unremitting pain of fear, because of all the blame and guilt and disgust.

Be realistic, I say to myself: life is nothing more or less than losing. People spend their lives going around afraid of an inadvertent, surprising debacle. Why should you be different? We are all afraid of losing someone who loves us. Afraid of losing the ability to love, we are also afraid of losing our minds, our memories, our health, our youth, our sex appeal. The fear in my belly is the fear of losing.

I still remember that this philosophy is not the one I usually operate under. The thing is that depression can flip my philosophy in one fell swoop. This can happen while my husband is walking to work, or while my friend is drinking a glass of wine, or while a complete stranger is going to the bathroom. People can be getting married or getting elected or getting hijacked or getting stoned. They are all oblivious, while I sink in this black ooze to my chin, to my nose, to my eyes, to my all.

The pain of depression is something indescribable and no one can comprehend it who has not had it.

Still, try to imagine a crucifixion, an invisible interior crucifixion. Even if you cry out, no one will hear you, or if they do, they will not know why you cry. The pain cannot be measured in terms of blood lost or fever height or bones broken.

This being the case, what lover or friend or child can gather up, much less sustain, empathic feelings for such a silent and deeply interior suffering?

Worse, what depressive could feel such empathy even if it should miraculously be there?

Christ, the exhaustion of being utterly alone with this thing.

I might as well be dead; except the dead are not, as far as I know, enduring the omnipresent, omnipotent flagellation that depression lashes.

I think it might be better if someone would punish me. In spite of my obvious guilt, I do not get canned. The biggest part of the pain is that I deserve an F in life and nobody will give it to me.

Talking has stopped, eating is minimal, work stops, and human relations are cut.

But suddenly, there is a hiatus. I feel decisive at last. I see I will have to do it for myself.

I quit.

As a prelude to quitting, I pay my bills, give away some special books, write some checks to causes I care about, neaten my closets, throw my journals on the fire, and think about a plan.

First, I must not injure anyone else. Second, it must seem to be an accident: car...water...a fall.

The next two days I will be alone in the house. I have made a decision.

In these choices and in the basic decision, there is a lovely burst of purposes, a release from all the accumulated effort to keep going, a light feeling of important accomplishment. It feels like joy.

It is elating to think that I shall soon be rid of my miserable, barren, meagre, unsatisfactory, unlovely, dull, thin, dry, unnourishing self. That is the definition of jejune; depression is certainly jejune.

The anticipation of relief is what brings joy. In ordinary times, I am repulsed by the thought of being a corpse. I am terrified of losing myself. But, this time, I long for the silence. The peace.

Early, early in the morning, I drive to the shore. My bathing suit is under my coat. The sun is just sending the first blinding rays of morning light across the surface of the water. I start swimming slowly away from the shore. After swimming for a long time, farther than I have ever gone by myself, I roll over on my back to look at the shore where I left. It is a long way off.

I lie there, suspended between the sky and the earth on a huge bed of water.

All is calm. The sun is entirely above the horizon.

At that moment, I feel a flicker in that tiny pilot light. Why that should be, I don't know: maybe cowardice, or selfishness, or the innate imperative of all protoplasm to survive.

What am I doing???

Maybe this is not such a good day to die.

My resolve dissolves.

The immediate problem is how to get back to that shore. There is not a soul in sight, but of course I planned it that way. The joy and the calm that pleased me so much have left me to the panic of possibly not making it back.

What the hell was I thinking of?

Now I'm cold despite the rising sun. My fingers are wrinkled. My limbs feel weak.

I talk to myself, like a coach: "Take it easy. You're a good swimmer. Go slowly. Don't think about being cold and tired. Rest on your back when you need to. The main thing is to keep going." This settles me down enough to function. Eventually, I come close enough so that I dare to feel for the bottom with my foot. And it is there!

I walk out of the water shaking, cold and embarrassed, although there is no one there to see me.

I put on my coat and drive home, chastened. If nothing else, I have demonstrated conclusively that I, for one, cannot manage a depression by myself. It is time to call the doctor who treated me once before.

As soon as I walk in the door, still wet, I look up the number. I get a wrong number. Damn. I redial carefully. Finally, I get through and get an appointment.

Howling for help is the first right decision I have made in this thing. Major decision for major depressive episode.

Now that I have done this much, the horrible spectre of getting to the doctor's office arises. I will have to get dressed and then walk fourteen blocks.

So, you may reasonably say, "What's the big deal?"

The enormity of that scenario looms up to the point of insuperability. Take a bath. No, take a shower. Skip it and just warm up with a big towel. Wear the red skirt; no, it's dirty. Wear the black skirt and a black sweater. No, you look dead enough as it is. Wear the white one; no, the button is off; wear it, anyway. Run in my stocking; change it. Comb your hair without looking in the mirror. This dawdling indecision and vanity has made me late.

I'll call and say I can't come. This really is cowardice.

I run all the way, though I was certain I could not.

I do get the doctor's office. He knows me; he knows what is to be done. I share my problem equally with him. My half feels much lighter already. We begin the cleanup with antidepressants and psychotherapy. I take the pills and begin to talk.

The pushmepullyou of recovery begins. I feel noticeably better, at least at the end of the day. I still start off most mornings in the classical depressed condition. I still cannot work. So, after breakfast, if I can, I go back to bed and read until noon. It is my only means of shutting off the Rolodex. I have to read fast adventure stories: *The Bounty Trilogy,*[1] a Dick Francis mystery, *Far From The Madding Crowd,*[2] anything that moves and has an obvious story line.

Then I get up. As the afternoon progresses, I feel better, positively good. I can talk to friends; I can do some work. I am really quite good; I am greatly encouraged. I admit that I am on my way out of this mess.

But, the next morning, I am flattened again, worse by far than the morning before. I am discouraged, hopeless again. After two or three dog days like this, I am thinking suicide again. Since I feel so rotten, and since I am at least in this with the doctor, I call and treat him to my muddleheaded rationalizations, about how I will never come out of this depression.

But this doctor is on to me. We have an argument in which he takes the optimistic side: "Of course you will; you are already better, and you certainly recovered completely the time before. Isn't that so?" He, with all his faculties, and probably most of them tied behind his back, overwhelms my fuddled logic.

I come away comforted. I think he would be sorry to hear I was dead after all the time and effort he has spent on me. I find this terribly comforting.

Slowly, despite some slippage, in an incremental fashion, I choose to live. This probably sounds soapy, but, the truth is that as the gloom lifts, life comes to be a good thing in itself. And I believe I have been in such powerful control of my destiny, that I have chosen it. I am convinced that people who have been close to death and, by good luck or good people, escape from it, are truly born again. Just being alive, with no trimmings, is an exquisite experience.

As I pick up my pace and my emotional range, both my outer surface life and my private interior life are atingle with pleasurable variety. Exhilarating. Each in its own way can be dangerous, incomprehensible, uncontrollable. It comes to me that life cannot be lived preventatively. And, even if it could, prematurely, deliberately leaving it, is the best prevention.

During the depression-prone years of my life, I have tried to learn as much as I can about the disorder. These inquiries have helped me to better understand both myself and others like me.

And, during this time, I have talked to people who are despairingly depressed. Obviously, I empathize. If they want to hear, I tell them what I know. Always, I advise them, if they have not done so already, to get good professional help immediately. All the while I am smiling to myself at how indirectly and unimmediately I seem to do it.

Furthermore, I tell them that, although depression is not as chic as alcoholism, it is nothing to be ashamed of. It is perfectly OK to admit it to yourself and to get treatment for it. It is time for a little destigmatization.

Every person's little story is probably more similar to every other than it is unique. In the world of statistics, percentages, and large regional studies, individual experiences do not matter. And though these numbers are not the real world we live in, they do represent the research on which our hopes for a depression-free future for all potential depressives depend.

As one in that number, I feel particularly lucky that I am still here to benefit from the progress that has been, is being, and promises to be made in the prevention and the management of affective disorders.

REFERENCES

1. Nordhoff, Charles: *The Bounty Trilogy*, Little Publishing Co., Boston, 1936.
2. Hardy, Thomas: *Far From the Madding Crowd*. Airrmont Publishing Co., New York, 1976.

Chapter 3

EPIDEMIOLOGY OF DEPRESSIVE ILLNESS*

Elizabeth A. Charney, M.D.
Myrna M. Weissman, Ph.D.

At present, it is estimated that at least 10–14 million Americans are afflicted by some form of major affective disorder. Recent studies indicate that as many as one in ten Americans may experience, at some point in their lives, the severity of mood disturbance associated with an affective disorder. Moreover, the WHO has established a world-wide annual prevalence of depression at 3% to 5%, approximately 100 million people. Such a preponderance has led some to consider depression as "the common cold of psychiatric disorders," and its apparent increase in occurrence among the generations coming to maturity in the recent decades has prompted some researchers to characterize the present one as an "age of melancholia."[26, 37] Furthermore, the current epidemiologic findings underscore not only these rates of occurrence but also their variation and risk factors.

*This work was supported in part by Alcohol, Drug Abuse and Mental Health Administration grants NH 28274 from the Affective and Anxiety Disorders Research Branch, National Institute of Mental Health, Rockville, Maryland; by Yale Mental Health Clinical Research Center, National Institute of Mental Health grant MH 30929; and by the John D. and Catherine T. MacArthur Foundation Mental Health Research Network on Risk and Protective Factors in the Major Mental Disorders.

Sections of this chapter also appear in: Charney EA, Weissman MM: Epidemiology of depressive and manic syndromes, in Georgotas, A., Cancro, R. (Eds.): *Depression and Mania: A Comprehensive Textbook*. New York, Elsevier Science Publishing Company, Inc., 1987.

This chapter on the epidemiology of depressive illness will begin with a presentation of the key concepts, definitions and scope of investigations necessary for interpreting the current research findings. Interpretation can often be enhanced by an understanding of historical context. Accordingly, a summary discussion of psychiatric epidemiology will follow with inclusion of the historical development of the refined methodologies currently employed in state-of-the-art investigations. The core of the chapter will focus on the recent findings of the NIMH-ECA (Epidemiologic Catchment Area) Program, NIMH Collaborative Depression Study, and family-risk studies. The extent to which these findings confirm or challenge those of previous research will be analyzed. When possible, comparisons with concurrent research will be noted and areas of dispute presented. This chapter will then conclude with a brief summary of the key points of the preceding discussions and will aim to emphasize their clinical relevance for the individual physician.

EPIDEMIOLOGIC APPROACH

Conceptually, the epidemiologic approach in psychiatry extends beyond that of a quantitative description of the occurrence of psychiatric disorder within the population under study. The approach presumes that variations in these rates of occurrence are not random, but are related to factors of time, place, and person that exert influence on that population. Such factors are called risks, and it is the hope that identification of appropriate risk factors will provide clues to etiology and consequently suggest interventions designed to control and prevent psychiatric disorder. Thus, the epidemiologic approach serves to elucidate, as do the other investigative sciences, the etiologic factors associated with the origin, course, and outcome of psychiatric disorders. Additionally, it seeks to apply knowledge toward the planning and evaluation of mental health care services as provided by an informed administrative policy.

The fundamental quantitative unit in epidemiology is a *rate*, which may be defined as the number of persons affected with disease (psychiatric disorder or characteristic) per unit of population per unit of time. The numerator reflects the number of persons affected, or "cases." The denominator indicates the reference population among whom the affected persons are observed. This reference group is often defined as the *population at risk* and quantifies the number of people in a population capable of manifesting the specific disorder under study.

A *risk factor* is a specific characteristic or condition which seemingly increases the probability of the present or future occurrence of a specific disorder. This implies a statistically significant association between the presence of a disorder in one group with the risk factor when compared to a comparable group without the risk factor. The risk factor associated with the disorder may be causative; innocuous but correlated with another, perhaps unrecognized, risk factor; or a sequelae of the disorder. Risk factors can be defined by time, place, or person (e.g., sociodemographic, biological or genetic factors).

Epidemiological analysis utilizes a variety of rates in measuring the frequency of disorders. It must be emphasized that in the rates defined below, the numerator and denominator must be similarly restricted as to sex, age, race, etc.

Incidence is defined as the number of new cases of a disorder with onset during a defined period of time among individuals referred to in population at risk. Most incidence rates reflect onset of disorder over a one-year period. In the recurrent affective disorders, these rates may reflect onset of previously remitted cases.

Prevalence is the number of both old and new cases in a population for a defined period of time. *Point prevalence* is defined as the proportion of the population manifesting the disorder being studied at a given point in time. *Period prevalence* is defined as that proportion of the population with the disorder for a given period of time (one year, six months). The *lifetime prevalence* is a calculation of that proportion of a population, alive on a given day of ascertainment, who have ever had the disorder under study. In essence, it reflects the proportions of survivors affected with the disorder at some point during their lifetimes.

Lifetime risk differs from lifetime prevalence in that it attempts to include the entire lifetime of a birth cohort, past and future, and includes those deceased at the time of survey. It is the proportion of a birth cohort that would be expected to have the disorder develop before a specified age, if all unaffected persons survived to that age. Morbid risk is another term used to indicate an individual's lifetime risk of having a first episode of illness.

Two commonly used measures of the degree of association between hypothesized risk factors and disorders are relative risk and attributable risk. *Relative risk* is the ratio of the incidence of disorder among the exposed and nonexposed groups. It is also termed the "risk ratio." *Attributable risk* is the incidence of the disorder in exposed individuals that can be attributed to their exposure to a hypothesized risk factor and thus provides an assessment of the causal association between risk factor and disorder.

Psychiatric epidemiology may be conducted descriptively by ascertaining the extent and type of psychiatric disorder in a defined population as well as analytically, by attempting to determine why rates differ among particular groups in identifying the risk factors that influence origin and clinical course.

Cross-sectional studies as exemplified by the NIMH-ECA are descriptive studies that comprise observations made at one point in time. The cross-sectional approach has limitations in assigning causality to disorders. Because one is making observations at a single given point in time, it is impossible to assess temporal sequence between the putative factor(s) and the disorder in this approach.

Thus, longitudinal studies which follow a population at risk of manifesting the disorder over a given time period are perhaps most suitable for identifying antecedent risk factors. Also called *cohort*, prospective, or follow-up studies, these generate incidence rates and information on the clinical course and natural history of specific disorders. A cohort is defined as a group of people sharing a common experience. Studies begin with identification of a group exposed to suspected risk factors. The Lundby[26] and Zurich[34] studies exemplify this approach in their prospective assessments of depressive disorder in two Swedish communities. A cohort study can also be retrospective and reflect a "case-history" design.

A *case control* study is an example of a more analytic functional design. In these studies, a selected sample of those people with the disorder under study (the cases) are compared to a comparable group of people, selected from the population at risk, without the disorder (the controls). These two groups are compared with respect to differential exposures to certain factors of characteristics deemed relevant to the disorder investigated. A relative risk is derived. The Yale-NIMH Family Study project represents this approach.[61] The study sought to determine the differential risk of psychiatric illness in families of psychiatrically ill patients compared to families of normal controls. The findings concerning affective disorders will be presented later in the chapter.

HISTORICAL OVERVIEW

Epidemiologic studies conducted during the century prior to World War II were characterized by indirect methods of assessment which relied primarily on the reports of key informants, hospital and other records. During World War II, however, studies were pursued by the military with a more vigorous precision reflected in advanced sampling and survey techniques yielding data exposed to statistical analysis. Furthermore, the employment of screening questionnaires and scales of impairment disclosed an apparent correlation between environmental stress and symptomatology. After the war, subsequent community surveys of the 1950s and 1960s adopted not only the direct methodology developed during the military experience but also the unifying concept of "stress," proposing analogous factors such as poverty, social class, rapid social change, and urbanization. Nonetheless, the intentional failure to establish rates for specific psychiatric disorders had severely limited application of previous findings to the issues of public policy and to the research in psychopharmacology, genetics, and neuropsychiatry that emerged in the 1970s.

The epidemiologic studies of the 1980s have responded to this recognition as well as to the research gaps identified by Carter's Presidential Commission on Mental Health (PCMH) in 1977. Recent convergence with the allied fields of clinical psychiatry and basic research is readily observed in the development of reliable and systematic techniques of assessment by direct interview or family history. This refined methodology is actually the legacy of the psychopharmacologic revolution, which had initiated a resurgence of interest in descriptive psychopathology as the basis for diagnostic assessment.

Clinical trials required the use of operational criteria in establishing diagnosis of a number of psychiatric disorders. This development is reflected in the publication of the Feighner criteria in 1972,[20] the RDC (Research Diagnostic Criteria) in 1978,[59] and the DSM-III in 1980.

A logical extension of the operational criteria set forth by the RDC was the development of other standardized instruments used to obtain quantitative assessment of the duration and overall intensity of the requisite symptom patterns experienced by the research subject. A structured interview, the SADS (Schedule for Affective Disorders and Schizophrenia) was designed to supplement the RDC. Its purpose was to obtain information on a patient's functioning and symptoms. It elicited details on the current episode as well as historical information.

The application of the standardized instruments in epidemiologic research proved feasible in a pilot study of 511 community residents by Weissman and Myers in 1975-1977.[66] At that time, limitations in broader applications for the intended multisite surveys prompted by the PCMH of 1977 were recognized. Namely, administration required clinically trained interviewers in order to achieve reliability, RDC and not DSM-III diagnoses were generated, and computerized scoring of the instrument had not been developed.

In response, the NIMH developed the Diagnostic Interview Schedule or DIS.[53] The DIS is a highly structured interview designed for use by lay interviewers in epidemiologic surveys. It is designed to elicit the elements of diagnosis (symptom severity, frequency, and distribution) and is capable of generating computer diagnosis in terms of DSM-III, Feighner, or RDC criteria. It has been primarily used in the NIMH-ECA program. Recent investigators in family-study research have similarly created standardized instruments for eliciting pedigree information and family psychiatric history. These are amenable to use by lay interviewers and programming for computer-assisted analysis.

Finally, it should be noted that a parallel development of a refined methodology has occurred in the United Kingdom in the form of the Present State Examination.[69] Diagnoses, set by the hierarchical rules of the ICD-9 (International Classification of Diseases, the British analogue of DSM-III are generated by computer. An "Index of Definition" (ID) establishes threshold levels for the various symptoms reported on the PSE.

EPIDEMIOLOGIC INVESTIGATIONS: PAST AND PRESENT FINDINGS

Past Findings: Prevalence Rates and Risk Factors

Many reviews, published in the early 1980s, readily acknowledged the limitations that differing case-finding techniques had imposed on properly comparing rates reported in various surveys. For example, Boyd and Weissman demonstrated that a major source of variability in rates had been the lack of standardized methodology.[7] In their review, they chose to base analyses on three groups of affective disorders—depressive symptoms, bipolar disorder, nonbipolar depression—because the international agreement for these broad categories enabled sufficient comparability between rates. Depressive symptoms were defined as a less severe form of mood disturbance in which a person may report dysphoria and symptomatology that are clearly abnormal but not pathological. Bipolar disorder was defined by a history of mania. Nonbipolar depression was recognized as a heterogeneous group, defined as any depression that was not bipolar and of sufficient intensity to warrant diagnosis. Reviewing studies that had utilized the newer diagnostic techniques, they found much greater uniformity in rates and estimated the following prevalence rates for affective disorders:

Nonbipolar depression. The point prevalence in industrialized nations was 3 percent for men and 4 percent to 9 percent for women; lifetime risk was 7 percent to 12 percent for men, 20 percent to 25 percent for women.

Bipolar depression. The lifetime risk was less than 1 percent. (The aforementioned pilot study in New Haven, 1975–1976, found a lifetime prevalence rate of 1.2 percent.)

Depressive symptoms. Point prevalence ranged from 13 percent to 20 percent of the population.

Other reviews, examining the relationship between prevalence rates and risk factors, noted other consistencies despite the methodologic shortcomings. In the following review of risk factors, the Boyd and Weissman convention has been maintained.[8] Unless specified, "depression" will refer to both depressive symptoms and nonbipolar depression.

Sociodemographic Characteristics

Gender. In almost all studies conducted in Western industrialized nations, women had shown rates approximately twice that of men for depressive symptoms as well as for nonbipolar depression. In contrast, the rates for bipolar disorder did not differ. Krauthammer and Klerman reported a range of female to male ratios as 1.3:1 to 2:1.[39] The gender differences for depression did not seem artifactually due to female help-seeking behavior as these persisted in community surveys where the majority of those reporting depressive symptoms had not sought treatment.[63] Among women, the postpartum and perimenstrual periods represented times of increased risk; menopausal women were at no greater risk for depression.

Age. A number of studies had shown that younger adults (ages 18 to 44) exhibited increased prevalence and incidence rates of all three depressive disorders. For nonbipolar depression, these rates seemed to peak in 35 to 45-year-old women and 55 to 70-year-old men. Bipolar disorder seemed to be a disease of much earlier onset and limited period of risk than nonbipolar depression. The modal age of onset was found to be 30 years and incidence rates decreased in those 50 years and older.[39]

Race. Studies had found no consistent relationships between race and affective disorder.

Social class. Studies had shown an inverse relationship between social class and report of depressive symptoms. The associations for nonbipolar depression were less pronounced. Brown et al., had reported higher rates in working-class women;[9] Weissman and Myers found rates higher in the lower social classes.[66] Bipolar disorder appeared to occur more frequently among the higher social classes, especially professionals and the highly educated.

Marital status. Previous findings had shown the highest rates of depressive symptoms in those divorced and separated. Married people seemed at least risk. Additionally, sexual differences according to marital status had been analyzed. Notably, married men reported the lowest rates, followed by married women; single and widowed women; single, widowed, divorced men; separated or divorced women. However, both Radloff and Gove had indicated highest rates of depressive symptoms in single men and married women.[50, 25] Similar analyses revealed lowest rates of nonbipolar depression among married people. Marital status did not show strong relationships with bipolar disorder.

Recent Life Events

Many studies had investigated environmental etiologies of psychiatric disorder accordant with social models of mental illness. These had been inconclusive in their findings between preexisting adversity and the onset of affective disorder. A study by Warheit supported a positive relationship between level of depressive symptoms and the number of recent life events.[60] Ilfeld analyzed the role of various "current social stressors" as marital, parental, occupational, financial, or neighborhood stressors in a Chicago community sampling of over 2000 residents.[29] Marital stressors, followed by occupational stressors for men and parental stressors for women showed the highest correlations. Ilfeld indicated that 25% of the variance in severities of depressive symptoms could be attributable to these five categories of stressors. Paykel had also noted onset of nonbipolar depression in association with "exit" events (e.g., loss of a person in the social field).[49] An equivalent increase in life events prior to the onset of bipolar disorder had been reported in most studies.

Psychosocial Variables

The above studies and others indicated that other variables must mediate the effects of environmental stress in possibly precipitating affective disorder. Investigation of the value of social support and the question of vulnerability had yielded incomplete findings but these are nonetheless worthy of consideration. For example, Brown and Harris found that women lacking an intimate, confiding relationship were four times more vulnerable to nonbipolar depression when encountering a threatening event or major difficulty.[10] In their study, three other social factors— presence of three or more children at home, loss of a mother before age 11 and unemployment—seemed to contribute to the variations in depressive disorders. All factors except unemployment tended to occur more frequently in working-class women and may have confounded the social class relationships reported earlier. The role of parental loss and other early childhood experiences had been investigated. Orvaschel, in retrospective case-control studies, found that a disruptive, negative home environment characterized by family discord and parental rejection occurred more frequently in the childhood backgrounds of depressed adults.[48] Analogous studies of bipolar disorder implied that bipolar patients often came from families of low prestige.[24, 13] It was felt that the childhood experience of these patients was one characterized by an obsessive emphasis on achievement and upward social mobility. The role of social support had not been specifically examined for bipolar disorder. Finally, studies investigating the importance of personality characteristics in predisposing to affective disorder had been inconclusive and had been unable to separate cause from consequence.

Family History

Previous studies had suggested that family history of affective disorder contributes to etiology as significantly as do those risk factors enumerated above. A role for genetic factors in affective disorders had been implicated since the 1960s. The observation that bipolar illness clusters in families had been noted by Leonhard in 1962.[41] Similar clustering of unipolar illness prompted both European and American investigators to separate the major affective disorders as two distinct entities. Subsequent studies revealed differential familial loading for each disorder. Morbid risk for either affective disorder in relatives of bipolar patients was increased relative to those of unipolar patients.

Twin and adoption studies sought to clarify the possible contributions of genetic and environmental factors to family history. A recent review by Nurnberger and Gershon estimated for bipolar disorder, a concordance rate in monozygotic twins as 65 percent compared to 14 percent in dizygotic twins.[46] The MZ/DZ ratios reported as 4.6. The situation for unipolar depression is less definitive with MZ/DZ ratios reported as 2.3.[6] Adoption studies similarly supported a familial factor.[44]

Past Findings: Health Service Utilization

In addition to identification of the above categories of risk factors, previous studies had examined help-seeking behavior as well. Studies of treatment in the US and UK had shown that a majority of patients will seek help in nonpsychiatric settings, especially by the general practitioners.[66, 10] Only about one-fifth of persons with a current psychiatric disorder had seen a mental health professional in the past year. Visits to the psychiatrist correlated with being young, female, educated, of higher SES, and having a severe disorder.[28] The above findings underscore the necessity of conducting household community surveys that seek to establish true prevalence and incidence rates in both treated and untreated populations.

The NIMH Epidemiologic Catchment Area (ECA) Program

Prompted by the desire to confirm these rates for incidence, prevalence and service use as well as the sociodemographic, environmental, and psychosocial risk factors implied from previous studies, the NIMH-ECA was initiated in the early 1980s. This epidemiologic study was designed to overcome the limitations imposed by the inconsistently applied methodology of case assessment characterizing the previous studies reviewed by Boyd and Weissman. It strove to do so in the utilization of the DIS, a standardized interview described earlier. Projected to involve at least 15,000 community and institutional residents, the program selected five university sites (Yale, Johns Hopkins, Washington University, Duke, and UCLA) to draw, respectively, random probability samples for approximately 3,000 community and 500 institutional residents. Those selected were interviewed by a lay interviewer with the DIS and service utilization questionnaire. In a longitudinal design, they were reinterviewed at least twice during the ensuing year. Furthermore, the DIS determined DSM-III disorders with reference to discrete time periods prior to interview. These included the two weeks, one month, six months, one year and entire life-time prior to interview.[88, 51]

The following discussions will present the initial three-site data based on the first wave of household interviews initiated between 1980–1982. Prevalence rates for DSM-III diagnoses of major depressive and bipolar disorders will be presented and the effects of sex and age noted. Risk factor analysis across these sites will be presented and compared to the past findings detailed in the preceding summaries.[54, 45]

Table 1 describes the NIMH-ECA three-site, Wave 1 sample characteristics.[51] Completed interviews from this initial wave had totaled over 11,500 with a completed response rate ranging from 76.6 percent to 79.1 percent. Direct refusal of the designated respondent was the major reason for noncompliance.

Table 2 details the sociodemographic characteristics of the ECA noninstitutionalized general population sample respondents. Certain sites were designated to oversample specific subpopulations. New Haven and Baltimore oversampled the elderly and St. Louis oversampled blacks.

Diagnostic assessment was based on the use of the DIS by lay interviewers. As previously described, the DIS is capable of generating computer diagnoses for the more prevalent DSM-III disorders. Respondents meet criteria for major depressive disorder if they experienced at least one depressive episode in the absence of a history of mania. Grief reactions of less than a year's duration were excluded. Bipolar disorder was diagnosed in those respondents reporting a history of at least one manic episode, with or without depressive episodes (bipolar I and bipolar II, respectively, by RDC nomenclature). Thus these two major affective disorders are mutually exclusive. The following rates that will be reported were estimated by weighting and poststratification adjustment methods to ensure comparability with the age, sex, and race distributions derived from the 1980 Census of the ECA site reference populations.

Table 3 displays the six-month and lifetime prevalence rates for DSM-III affective disorders calculated at each of the three designated sites. The rates of major depression were the highest of these DSM-III diagnoses. These rates ranged from 2.2 percent for six-month prevalence (Baltimore) to 6.7 percent for lifetime prevalence (New Haven). Rates in New Haven and St. Louis were remarkably consistent for these two time periods. Rates for bipolar disorder were considerably lower than for major depressive disorder, ranging from a six-month prevalence of 0.4 percent in Baltimore to 1.1 percent for lifetime prevalences in the other two sites. Prevalence rates were further analyzed by age and sex.

Table 4 presents the sex and age distribution for six-month prevalence rates/100 for bipolar disorder. Analysis with regression models established no significant sex differences in these rates at any site. However, rates were significantly higher in those ages 18–44 compared with ages 45–64 and older.

Table 1. NIMH Epidemiologic Catchment Area Program:
First Three-Site — Wave 1 Sample Characteristics

	Yale University, New Haven, Conn.	Johns Hopkins University, Baltimore	Washington University, St. Louis
Survey date, wave 1	1980-81	1981	1981-82
Total population size (all ages)	420,000	260,000	300,000
Adult (age 18 + yr) population size (1980 census)	300,000	175,000	277,000
Sample characteristics	Noninstitutionalized and institutionalized, urban adults	Noninstitutionalized and institutionalized, urban adults	Noninstitutionalized and institutionalized, urban adults
Sample age range, yr	18+	18+	18+
Completed interviews, household, wave 1	5,035	3,401	3,004
General population	3,058	3,020	3,004
Elderly population oversample	1,977	461	...
Completion rate, %	76.6	78	79.1

From: Regier et al., *Arch Gen Psychiatry* 1984; 41: 934-941.

Table 5 shows that six-month rates for major depressive disorder were higher in women, irrespective of age group or site. The female-to-male ratios ranged between 2.1 (New Haven) to 2.6 (St. Louis). In addition, women of 18–44 years of age seemed at significantly higher risk.

Preliminary risk factor analysis for the first three sites had been reported by Robins et al., who had investigated possible associations with race, education, and residence (urban vs. rural) in addition to age and sex.[54] They found no significant interactions between these additional variables and occurrence of affective disorder.

Subsequent analysis of the data accruing since those initial reports has implicated the following risk factors for major depression, replicable at most sites: being female; young, particularly ages 25–35; divorced, separated, or having marital discord. Married people have the lowest rates, and for divorced people who remarry, the rates return to the low rates of the married. The effects of marital status were stronger for men than women. Rates were lowest in persons 55 years of age or older. There were

Table 2. Sociodemographic Characteristics of Initial Three ECA Sites

	New Haven		Baltimore		St. Louis	
	N	%	N	%	N	%
Sex:						
Male	1292	46.5	1322	45.4	1202	46.7
Female	1766	53.5	2159	54.6	1802	53.3
Age (Yrs)						
18-24	426	16.2	504	18.6	471	18.1
25-44	1229	37.9	1212	34.6	1233	39.8
45-64	793	29.8	842	29.0	724	26.9
65 +	610	16.1	923	17.9	576	15.0
Race						
White	2593	86.6	2193	65.0	1743	77.6
Black	334	10.1	1182	31.9	1158	19.0
Hispanic	63	2.0	27	0.7	16	0.7
Other	52	1.5	79	2.4	87	2.7
Total	3058	100	3481	100	3004	100

From: Regier et al., *Arch Gen Psychiatry* 1984; 41: 934-941.

no strong relationships between current six-month prevalence of MDD and race, education, income or veteran status.

In summary, the ECA data has in large part confirmed the findings of previous epidemiologic research. Direct comparison of prevalence rates are difficult to interpret due to differing reference populations and case-finding techniques. However, prevalence rates determined by the ECA in New Haven are similar to those reported by the pilot study conducted five years earlier.[66] Moreover, the ECA has confirmed the relationships between sex and marital status as well as clarified the specific associations of social class and education to affective disorders. Lack of an intimate, confiding relationship as a risk factor for females under stress is in accord with the findings of increased rates in those encountering marital discord.

Certain challenges to the legacy of previous investigations have been suggested. Most striking is evidence that the ages of onset are decreasing and that there is a birth cohort effect, with rates notably higher in those ages 25–44. Robins had offered possible explanations including difficulty in recall and reluctance to report symptoms by the older respondents, disorder-associated mortality or institutionalization artifactually decreasing rates in the surviving and accessible older respondents, or a true historical increase in rates among the younger generations.[54]

This birth cohort trend has been duplicated in other studies as well.[26, 38] Perhaps the most appropriate examination of the temporal changes in depression is to follow up a defined population over many years. Hagnell et al. reported results of a 25-year prospective study of one such cohort existing in Lundby, Sweden.[26] The Lundby Study was initiated in 1947

Table 3. Six-Month and Lifetime Prevalence Rates/100 for DSM-III Major Affective Disorders by Site

DSM-III Disorder	New Haven (N = 3058)	Baltimore (N = 3481)	St. Louis (N = 3004)
Major Depressive Disorder			
6-month rate/100	3.5	2.2	3.2
Lifetime rate/100	6.7	3.7	5.5
Bipolar Disorder			
6-month rate/100	0.8	0.4	0.7
Lifetime rate/100	1.1	0.6	1.1

From: Robins et al., *Arch Gen Psychiatry* 1984; 41: 949-958. Myers et al., *Arch Gen Psychiatry* 1984; 41: 959-967.

Table 4. Six-Month Prevalence Rate/100 of Bipolar Disorder by Age, Sex, ECA Site

	New Haven		Baltimore		St. Louis	
	N	%	N	%	N	%
Men:						
18-24 Yrs.	176	1.3	201	0.0	191	1.4
25-44 Yrs.	542	1.0	467	1.1	505	0.7
45-64 Yrs.	337	0.0	303	0.0	288	0.8
65 + Yrs.	236	0.0	352	0.0	218	0.0
Total Men:	1291	0.6	1322	0.4	1202	0.8
Women:						
18-24 Yrs.	247	2.0	303	0.3	286	1.4
25-44 Yrs.	692	1.2	745	0.7	728	1.0
45-64 Yrs.	453	0.6	539	0.3	436	0.1
65 + Yrs.	375	0.0	572	0.0	358	0.0
Total Women:	1767	0.9	2159	0.4	1802	0.6
Sex Ratio F/M	1.5		1.0		.75	

From: Myers et al., *Arch Gen Psychiatry* 1984; 41: 959–967.

when psychiatric investigators interviewed 2550, or 99 percent of the inhabitants living in this geographically defined area. The Lundby cohort was then followed up, irrespective of relocation, in 1957 and 1975. For these times, the dropout rate was 1 percent to 3 percent. Assessments were made by field examinations, mimicking everyday psychiatrist/patient clinical contact as well as by information from relatives and agency records. Similar diagnostic criteria were used each time by similarly trained psychiatrists. Degrees of impairment—mild, moderate, severe (psychotic)—as defined were in accord with DSM-III.

Table 5. Six-Month Prevalence Rate/100
of Major Depressive Disorder by Age, Sex, ECA Site

	New Haven		Baltimore		St. Louis	
	N	%	N	%	N	%
Men:						
18-24 Yrs.	176	3.9	201	1.1	191	1.1
25-44 Yrs.	542	2.7	467	1.6	505	2.8
45-64 Yrs.	337	1.4	303	1.5	288	1.3
65+ Yrs.	236	0.5	351	0.3	218	0.1
Total Men:	1291	2.2	1322	1.3	1202	1.7
Women:						
18-24 Yrs.	247	6.1	303	3.0	280	5.2
25-44 Yrs.	692	7.4	745	4.5	728	5.2
45-64 Yrs.	453	2.2	539	2.4	436	4.9
65+ Yrs.	375	1.6	572	1.3	358	1.0
Total Women:	1767	4.6	2159	3.0	1802	4.5
Sex Ratio F/M	2.1		2.3		2.6	

From: Myers et al., *Arch Gen Psychiatry* 1984; 41: 959-967.

Incidence rates were compared between the initial ten years of follow-up (1947–1957) and the latter fifteen (1957–1972) as well as by five-year intervals. Over the 25-year period, incidence rates for depression were estimated as 8.5 percent for the men, 17 percent for the women. Analysis of rates between 1947–1957 compared to 1957–1972 showed increased probabilities for mild-moderate depression in both sexes. A considerable increase in probability was identified in young adult men, particularly ages 20–39. Depression was ten times more likely to occur in this age group during the period 1957–1972 than in 1947–1957. When five-year intervals were examined, the cumulative probability of initial manifestation of the disorder (mild-moderate) steadily increased. Again, increases in the latter intervals were more significant in the men. Investigators hypothesized that Swedish unemployment rates may have contributed to these rises, specifically affecting the less well-educated young adults more likely to be jobless. They similarly suggested that study of psychosocial factors, akin to those of Brown and Harris, be applied towards elucidating the etiology of depression in young adult males.

Klerman et al., based on data from the NIMH-Collaborative Study on the Psychobiology of Depression, noted an analogous birth cohort trend in the rates of major depression among first-degree relatives of patients with affective disorder.[38]

In their analysis, lifetime incidence of major depression was ascertained and rates compared among successive birth cohorts. Within each cohort, rates for depression were higher in females but there was evidence of a decreasing male-female difference for more recent birth cohorts, a finding consistent with the increasing rates of depression in young adult male Swedes. Klerman identified the possible artifacts noted by Robins but proposed that these do not minimize the significance of the trends supported by the family-study data. He hypothesized mediation of genetic vulnerability by environmental factors, be they biological, historical, cultural, or economic.

The ECA sought to investigate utilization of health and mental health services as well.[58] Those with affective disorders tended to overutilize treatment facilities (PMD, clinic, ER) and to perceive their mental and physical health as poor despite lack of diagnosis or treatment for a documented disorder. Indeed, among all identified with recent DIS/DSM-III disorders, those with affective disorders showed the highest rates for mental health visits. Women were more likely than men to seek help as were those ages 25–64 compared to those 18–24, 65 and older. The majority, however, do not seek help, a finding consistent with previous studies and mutual to all with a diagnosable psychiatric disorder. Furthermore, one-third of patients seeking help for mental/emotional problems did not meet DIS diagnostic criteria. The proportion of this population representing those with minor affective symptomatology had not been determined.

NIMH Collaborative Depression Study: Course and Prognosis of Affective Disorders

In addition to their yield of information on rates and risk factors, epidemiologic investigations of affective disorders can also serve to further characterize clinical psychopathology. They can study depressive and manic phenomenology and possibly identify predictors of clinical course, outcome, therapeutic response, etc.

Clinicians and researchers have long recognized that patients with affective disorders often present with chronic and/or recurrent histories. Furthermore, many patients with multiple recurrences may manifest residual symptomatology and psychosocial impairment between episodes. Indeed, the psychiatric epidemiologist has sought to establish accurate rates of chronicity and recurrence but has often been limited by the study of hospitalized and treated samples only. Thus, generalizations to the population at large are difficult. Longitudinal study of clinical course has also been complicated by the factors of variable treatment managements and patient compliance. Nonetheless, previous studies had generated prognostic information that is still worthy of the practicing clinician's consideration.

Most of the literature of the past decade has indicated a 10 percent to 15 percent rate of chronicity in patients presenting for treatment of an acute episode of depression. Chronicity in bipolar patients is more difficult to assess as only a minority of patients will have "chronic mania." In addition, lithium has altered outcome in as many as 50 percent of bipolars. However, if chronicity is defined by presence of a residual social impairment and/or symptoms, then approximately one-third of bipolar patients may be categorized as chronic. [12]

Major affective disorders also present as recurrent illnesses. Between 85 percent to 95 percent of patients with one manic episode will suffer recurrences of either depression or mania, and between 50 percent to 85 percent of patients seeking treatment for a major depressive episode will have at least one recurrence in their lifetimes. Moreover, between 10 percent to 15 percent of these depressed patients will have a subsequent manic episode and thus become bipolar. [31]

More recently, the clinical studies component of the NIMH Collaborative Depression Study has assumed the task of establishing the natural history of affective disorders by use of a rigorous methodology found lacking in earlier outcome studies. To date, this collaborative effort has generated much needed information on rates of recovery and relapse in depressed and manic patients seeking help at major research centers.

The NIMH Collaborative Depression Study is designed as a systematic, prospective, longitudinal, naturalistic study. Patients are followed up at six-month intervals using the Longitudinal Follow-up Evaluation (LIFE) instrument designed for the project. [57] A LIFE Psychiatric Status Rating Scale establishes weekly assessment with outcome measures operationalized according to the RDC. In essence, these ratings assign levels of recovery/nonrecovery in a six-point scale of symptomatic severity. Patients are considered recovered if they experience minor or no residual symptoms for at least eight consecutive weeks.

Results have shown that as many as one-fourth of the initial sample entering the study had had a major depressive episode superimposed on a low-grade chronic depression of at least two years' duration, a phenomenon called "double depression." [36] Rates of recovery and relapse for major depression in an initial 133 patient sample eligible for two-year follow-up have also been reported. [34] Of the 101 nondysthymic patients, 79 percent had recovered, 21 percent remained chronically depressed. Of the 32 "double depression" patients, 97 percent had recovered. Thirty-nine percent (N = 13) had had "full" recovery; fifty-eight percent (N = 18) had recovered from MDD only.

Most recently, Keller et al. have analyzed the persistent risk of chronicity in patients experiencing recurrence of MDD. [35] They followed an initial sample of 477 patients for a median of 18 months and estimated the 28 percent (N = 101) of patients who had relapsed into MDD before the end of the follow-up as having a 22 percent probability of chronicity at one year. This was similar to the 21 percent rate noted above.

Additional analyses have yielded cumulative probabilities of recovery and relapse as well as identification of suitable risk factors for these outcomes. [32, 33] Long duration of episode prior to study entry, inpatient hospitalization at entry, intact marriage, low family income, admitting research center and RDC unipolar/secondary subtype of MDD predicted chronic course. The major predictor of relapse was a previous history of three or more episodes of MDD. Secondary subtype of MDD and older age of onset predicted an increased probability of relapse in patients entering with their first episode.

The investigators have most recently begun similar analyses of patients with a bipolar disorder. The rate of chronicity was found to be 20 percent at 18 months follow-up. This was comparable to the rate of chronicity in depressed patients. However, rates of chronicity varied when analyzed specifically by index episode. Patients presenting in mania have a 7 percent rate of chronicity; patients presenting in depression have a 20 percent rate of chronicity; patients presenting in a mixed or cycling episode have a 35 percent rate of chronicity.

At present, the relatively small number of bipolar patients in the study has precluded meaningful analysis of clinical predictors of relapse and recovery in these bipolar patients.

Family Studies: The Genetic Epidemiology of Affective Disorders

As noted earlier, previous studies had recognized family history as a significant risk factor for affective disorder. Nurnberger and Gershon in their 1982 review described the more recent twin studies, adoption studies, and family studies that have supported a role for genetic factors in affective disorders.[46] Representative studies included those by Bertelson et al.,[6] Cadoret,[11] Mendlewicz and Rainer,[44] Winokur[70] and Gershon.[23] An updated and more thorough review is presented in a following chapter by Gershon et al.

As they report, the past decade has witnessed the use of the currently refined epidemiologic techniques for investigating family-genetic factors in affective disorders. Two major studies have been collaborative efforts, one between the NIMH and Yale University Departments of Psychiatry and Genetics and the other between the five centers involved in the NIMH-Clinical Research Branch Collaborative Program on the Psychobiology of Depression.[22, 61, 30]

The Yale-NIMH study reported that both affective and anxiety disorders occurred much more frequently in the first-degree relatives of affected probands compared to normal controls (Weissman et al., 1984). There was a two-to-threefold increase in major depression in first-degree relatives of probands (range 9.5 percent to 15 percent) compared to those of controls (5.6 percent). Major depression was also the most frequent disorder seen in all relatives, followed closely by minor depression, alcoholism, and generalized anxiety. The NIMH-CRB reported similar findings in the rates of psychiatric disorder among the first-degree relatives of their index patients. Major depression was the most frequent disorder consistently reported, again followed closely by alcoholism and then generalized anxiety disorder. They also reported that the female relatives of bipolar II patients had a higher frequency of phobic and obsessive-compulsive disorders compared to relatives of patients with bipolar I and recurrent unipolar disorders.[19]

Furthermore, relatives exhibited differential risks of specific affective disorders according to the diagnosis of the proband. Major depression, minor depression and depressive personality aggregated in the relatives of the MD proband. Major depression, bipolar-I and -II disorder, cyclothymia, hyperthymia and schizoaffective disorder aggregated in families of the bipolar-I proband. Endicott et al. reported similar results from the NIMH-CRB family studies.[19] Relatives of index patients with bipolar disorders were more apt to have major depressive, manic, or hypomanic episodes; relatives of index patients with recurrent unipolar disorder were more apt to have unipolar major depression only.

In both studies, further analysis of rates in first-degree relatives yielded sex and age effects consistent with findings of other studies.[61, 38, 52] The rates of MD were higher in female relatives whereas the sex ratios among relatives with bipolar disorder were equal. A birth-cohort trend in the rates of major depression among relatives was also noted—relatives aged 30-44 years showed the highest rates relative to their younger and older counterparts. However, this finding was not synonymous with the existence of a generation effect in first-degree relatives. In fact, the rates of all affective disorders were approximately equal in parents, siblings, and adult children.

Additional analysis of the family-genetic study data have examined the clinical heterogeneity of major affective disorders. The NIMH-Yale studies have primarily examined the subtypes of major depression, with emphasis on the prognostic importance for occurrence of major depression in relatives. The NIMH-CRB studies have primarily examined the subtypes of bipolar disorder, seeking to further characterize bipolar II disorders and the differential risks for affective disorders to first-degree relatives of bipolar I, bipolar II, and unipolar probands.

Although preliminary findings of the NIMH-Yale studies had disclosed a heterogeneity of depression that influenced the rates of depression in first-degree relatives, there tended to be overlap of these various subtypes within the depressed proband as well as for his/her relatives. Recent examinations have employed sophisticated statistical models to deal with this overlap and to best determine which criteria independently predict familial aggregation and prognostic outcome.[64] Results of these analyses have shown that only early age of onset, defined as less than thirty years of age, or the presence of anxiety or secondary alcoholism in depressed probands acted as independent predictors of increased morbid risk of major depression in first-degree relatives. The subtypes endogenous, delusional, melancholic, or autonomous depressions as well as the presence of dysthymia, suicidality, recurrence, or hospitalization did not explain the increase in morbid risk in first-degree relatives after the depressed probands' age of onset, anxiety or alcoholism were considered.

The NIMH-CRB has pursued analogous investigations for the manic syndromes. For example, preliminary analysis had indicated that bipolar II probands had first-degree relatives with significantly higher rates of bipolar II disorder compared to relatives of unipolar and bipolar I probands.[15] Relatives of the bipolar II probands evidenced intermediate risk of bipolar I disorder compared to relatives of unipolar and bipolar I probands. These relatives were at a risk for unipolar depression comparable to relatives of bipolar I probands but were at slightly higher risk for major depression associated with any of these three subtypes compared to relatives of bipolar I and unipolar probands.

Finally, bipolar II disorder seems to be clinically heterogeneous. The family-study data implies that some bipolar II patients resemble bipolar I patients, fewer resemble recurrent unipolar patients, and a majority resemble neither. Nonetheless, specificity of transmission is suggested in the relative risk rates reported by Endicott et al.[19] In comparing bipolar I, bipolar II and recurrent unipolar disorders, the relative risk for bipolar I disorder in relatives of bipolar I probands was 3.1. In bipolar II probands it was less than 1.0. The relative risk of bipolar II disorder in relatives of bipolar II probands was 2.3 compared to a risk of less than 1.0 in relatives of bipolar I probands.

Additional analyses have described the clinical history of bipolar II disorder in probands as well as in their first-degree relatives.[14, 19] For example, relatives with bipolar II disorder tended to be younger when first treated (mean age 22.2 years), to be female, to have high rates of marital discord and a history of nonserious suicide attempts and specific nonaffective syndromes, particularly schizotypal features.

High Risk Studies: Prospective Follow-Up of the Children of Patients with Affective Disorder

Recognition of affective disorders in children has increased since the previous decade, and with this interest in assessment and the possibility of prevention, investigators have begun to more systematically examine the development of affective disorder in children. Most recently, the analyses used for the adult relatives of probands with affective disorders have been extended for the children, a high risk group. In addition, family studies of children diagnosed with primary affective disorder have been pursued.

In 1980, Orvaschel, Weissman and Kidd published a timely review of the literature concerning children of parents with affective disorder.[48] These early studies presented with numerous methodological limitations, but nonetheless suggested that children of depressed parents are at higher risk of psychiatric disorder than those children of normal control parents.

In 1983, Beardslee et al. had written an updated review of 24 studies of children with parents with affective disorders who are thus considered at risk for affective disorder.[5] They noted similar conclusions regarding higher rates of impairment in these children. Again, they identified methodologic issues such as diagnostic variability, lack of blindness, absence of controls, and the limited number of children per study. They underscored the importance of future longitudinal studies in order to delineate prodromal features and differential risks for each age group. Also implied was the need for study of children of nonhospitalized parents. For example, they suggested that studies by Welner et al. and McKnew et al., which reported high rates of psychopathologic symptomatology in children may in part reflect short-lived reactions to separation from the hospitalized parent.[68, 43]

Most recently, the refined methodology employed in such family studies as the NIMH-Yale Family Study have been applied to the examination of children at high risk for depression. Initial study showed that the children (aged 6–17 years) of depressed probands had a two-to-threefold increase in rates of major depression compared to children of normal controls. The children also showed a threefold risk for any psychiatric diagnosis. Depression plus panic disorder or agoraphobia in the parents conferred an increased risk of major depression and anxiety disorders in the children.[67]

Intrigued by such findings and their implications for early detection of depression and resolution of the relationships between adult and childhood forms of depression, investigators of the Yale Family Study initiated strategies for longitudinal study of children identified at high and low risk for depression.

Due to methodologic limitations of child assessment, the original family-genetic study did not include direct interviews of children under 18 years of age. The high risk study has devised means for direct interview, supplemented by separate and independent interviews of each parent. When possible, further assessments of the children were made by other informants such as teachers and pediatricians.[67, 65, 62] Preliminary findings have included:

Relative risk, age and sex effects. The relative risk of major depression in the children of depressed parents compared to children of normal controls was 3.6. No major depression was reported in younger children but there was a notable increase at puberty in both sexes. Rates in females were not significantly higher than those in males. Rates of anxiety and alcohol/substance abuse were also increased in children of depressed parents.

Pre-perinatal and developmental history. Depressed mothers reported more illness during their pregnancies, took more medications, and experienced more birth complications. As infants, children of depressed parents were more often diagnosed with colic and considered weaker and less active than children of control parents. Compared to control children, children of depressed parents showed slight delays in bowel and bladder control and speech development; significantly more often attended nursery school or day care; and more often had poor peer relationships.

Medical history. Children of depressed parents experienced more head injuries and operations than those of normal control parents.

Impairment. Children of depressed parents were more likely to manifest difficulties with friends, siblings, and school.

Parental lack of awareness. Rates of major depression were highest when based on children's reports, lower when based on mothers' reports. Children tend to agree if their mother reports illness.

In summary, parental depression is a risk factor for childhood depression. Children of depressed parents are also at risk for medical injury and illness, school and peer difficulties, anxiety and alcohol/substance abuse disorders. These analyses are preliminary and await further differentiation of confounding factors as well as the clinical significance of these states in children for prognosis of adult disorder. However, consistent findings have been replicated in a number of other studies. For example, Beardslee et al. reported higher rates of perinatal complications as well as more frequent indications of infant stress in children of depressed mothers in a longitudinal study conducted by Sameroff and associates[56] (1984) at Rochester, New York and the initial findings concerning the comorbidity of depression and anxiety in probands and the increased risk to children for these disorders has been in part replicated in a pilot study by Livingston et al.[42]

A need for similar studies of the children of parents with bipolar disorder is indicated by the high risk patterns emerging from family study data. Gershon et al. reported age-corrected morbid risks of 9.2 for bipolar disorder and 12.3 for unipolar disorder in the parents and children of bipolar probands.[22] Affective disorder can be expected to develop in about 27 percent of those children born to at least one parent with bipolar, unipolar or schizoaffective disorder.

Other studies have observed an increased occurrence of psychopathology in children (aged 5–18) of parents with bipolar disorder.[47, 40, 17] For example, Kuyler et al. presented a preliminary study of children at risk for bipolar disorder which suggested high rates of symptomatology associated with personality disorder, adjustment reaction, and affective illness.[40]

Moreover, recent studies suggest that bipolar disorder or prodromal symptomatology may persist in large part unrecognized by clinicians.[21] Many reports have noted that onset of manic/hypomanic symptoms is rare prior to age 15. Nonetheless, recent studies of children at risk have stressed the importance of thorough assessment aimed at early intervention.

Akiskal et al. reported that in a prospective study, half of their sample of 68 referred children and siblings of adult bipolar patients manifested symptoms of bipolarity over a mean follow-up of 3 years.[1] All but two children (ages 6–14) were directly interviewed with information supplemented by parent, school, medical and psychiatric reports. Adult criteria were used to generate diagnoses of depressive, bipolar I, bipolar II, rapid cycling, dysthymic, hyperthymic, cyclothymic and polydrug use disorders. Results showed that although 44 children presenting with histories of affective symptoms had been seen by a variety of mental health professionals, none had been diagnosed with affective disorder. Alternative diagnoses had included adjustment reaction, conduct disorder, borderline personality and schizophrenia. Major reasons for referral had been bizarre (psychotic) behavior, drug-related problems, suicidal ideation/attempt and scholastic failure. The salient findings included high incidence rates of acute depressive episodes and dysthymic, cyclothymic disorders. Hypomania was noted prepubertally but all manic children were older than 13 years of age. No schizophrenic outcomes developed and of the 35 patients presenting with acute depressive/manic/mixed onset the majority had had recurrence. Significantly, 39 percent (13/33) of children initially presenting with minor mood swings and polydrug abuse progressed to bipolar disorder during the follow-up period.

CONCLUSIONS

Methodologic Limitations and Controversies

In summary, the major studies discussed had been chosen to exemplify the scope of epidemiologic investigations as pursued in the 1980s. Although use of operational criteria incorporated into structured interviews has certainly improved the diagnostic reliability of such research, limitations in methodology still persist. The seemingly insurmountable impasse of discrepancy in case assessment continues to plague ongoing research.

Such discrepancies seriously limit comparability of prevalence and incidence rates between differing nations. At present, a variety of assessment instruments have been developed. For use in community surveys, the most notable are perhaps the DIS and PSE. But there is little known about translation of these instruments into other languages as well as their suitabilities to the subtle nuances of differing sociocultural perceptions and constraints. Moreover, the differences between the diagnostic criteria of the ICD-9 and DSM-III restrict generation of corresponding diagnoses from one instrument to another.

Limitations may persist even when one classification system is employed among comparable studies, for differing interpretations of the requisite diagnostic criteria may create variations in rates of affective disorder.

In addition to limitations imposed by differing nosologies and application of criteria, other sources of variance must be considered—those of the subject's ability to recall, recognize and report symptoms. This limitation may have implications not only for determination of rates but also for identification of risk factors.

For example, Angst and Dobler-Mikola have asked whether the diagnostic criteria determine the gender differential, and have examined possible artifactual explanations for the higher rates of MDD among females.[2] They have proposed these on the basis of findings reported from their "Zurich Study," a prospective study of depressive syndromes among a young cohort of men and women, ages 19–20, who were selected from a general population in Canton of Zurich. The authors propose that such differentials may be secondary to denial and forgetting of mood disturbances that are incompatible with the male image in modern society.

There exist other controversial issues in need of further analysis. Elucidating the role of social support as a risk factor represents a major impetus to the constant reinterpretations of the Brown and Harris data on vulnerability.[10] Most studies have upheld the tenet that lack of an intimate, confiding relationship functions as a risk factor to depression. The higher rates of depression among the unmarried or in those with marital discord found in the recent ECA data supports the hypothesis. Rounsaville et al. had similarly reported marital discord as a frequently identified precipitant in women seeking treatment for depression.[55]

However, many have more thoroughly examined the role of social support. A study in Canberra, Australia had identified a key association, not with the quantitative availability of social support, but with the perceived adequacy of close relationships.[27] The degree of satisfaction/dissatisfaction with social relationship was found to be related to personality more than to the actual social environment. This finding underscores the value of disclosing independent factors. Indeed, Costello in a Canadian replication of the Brown and Harris study, proposed that the source of interaction may lie in the premorbid personalities of the women studies.[16] Vulnerability may thus possibly lie in a deficit of social skills predisposing one to both a lack of intimacy and depression.

Clinical Relevance and Implications

The preceding discussions have highlighted the major limitations and controversies present in the epidemiologic studies of depressive illnesses. Recognition of these has provided directions for future research and the need to more closely analyze the findings and assumptions of previous studies. Notwithstanding these reservations, epidemiologic investigations have still generated much needed information on the rates and risk factors of affective disorders. These indications are summarized in Table 6.

The clinical relevance of these findings is widespread in its potential applications for the treatment and management of depressive illness. The Yale-NIMH and NIMH-CRB family studies have contributed knowledge concerning the risk of psychiatric disorders in first-degree relatives of manic and depressive probands. These studies have provided contexts for testing specific genetic hypotheses. However, factors contributing to familial aggregations of affective disorders are complex and future studies must address study of environmental factors, assortative mating, sociocultural determinants, intrafamilial processes and their interactions. Prospective high risk studies of children may serve to clarify these interrelationships between genetic and environmental factors.

Community surveys have served to indicate a broader spectrum of disease than that previously recognized in the treated and hospitalized. The Zurich study had sought to study the presumed continuum of mood disturbances between sadness and depression. Others have similarly advocated adoption of a wider spectrum in manic disorders. Studies of treatment have indicated that a substantial proportion of those with milder symptomatology will seek help as well.[58] Additionally, epidemiologic study has indicated the presence of affective disorder in children and the elderly. Thus, further study of children, the elderly, and the untreated is indicated and necessary for guiding the clinician towards proper recognition of affective disorder in these populations.

Prospective studies such as the High Risk, Lundby, Zurich, and NIMH-Collaborative follow-up studies are central to the natural history of affective disorders. Closely related to these studies is the investigation of individual morbid risk. For example, analysis of risk factors for relapse and recovery in major depression has generated information essential to clinical practice and has underscored the significance of previous history and prompt treatment of depressive episodes in directing interventionary measures.

Identification of familial and sociodemographic risk factors confers additional clinical implications for prevention and early intervention. The rising rates in the young populations should alert clinicians. They should be attentive to reports of depression among children, adolescents, and young adults. For women, especially, risk periods have been identified at times of childbirth, parenting, marital discord, separation, and divorce. Moreover, these women, vulnerable to depression, are most likely to contact nonpsychiatric clinicians. Thus, these help providers must be educated to recognize manifestations of depression at these times of risk and to have knowledge of available resources in family therapy, support groups, etc. Identification of familial risk has overriding clinical relevance and implications as well. The clinician—be he or she a pediatrician, psychiatrist, internist, or gynecologist—should be aware of possible familial risk and have a

Table 6. Summary: Rates and Risk Factors in Depressive and Manic Syndromes

Rates*	Major Depression	Bipolar Disorder
Point Prevalence	2% – 3% (men) 5% – 9% (women) [2.2% – 3.5%]	0.6% – 0.9% (morbid risk) [0.4 % – 0.8%]
Life Expectancy	8% – 12% (men) 20% – 25% (women) [3.7% – 5.5%]	< 1.0% [1.1%]
Risk Factors **Sociodemographic** Sex	2:1 (women:men) women at increased risk postpartum, perimenstrually	1:1 (women:men)
Age	Young, especially 18-44 age groups	8-44 years of age; incidence rates decrease after age 50
Race	No relationship	No relationship
Social Class	No pattern	Higher social class
Marital Status	Separated/divorced; marital discord	No relationship—marital discord may be consequential
Recent Life Events	Inconclusive	
Psychosocial Social Support	Lack of intimate relationship	Not studied
Personality	Inconclusive	Inconclusive
Early Childhood	? Parental loss before age 11	Inconclusive
Family History Family History	Positive, risk increases especially with early onset MDD, Anxiety Disorder	Positive—increases risk
Familial Aggregation	MDD; depressive personality; dysthymia	MDD, BPD, schizoaffective, cyclothymic
Clinical History Previous history of 3 or more episodes	At increased risk of relapse	Not analyzed
Long duration of present episode	At increased risk of chronicity	Not studied

*Preliminary ECA 3-site, 6-month and lifetime prevalences appear bracketed.

working knowledge of the psychiatric status of significant family members. In summary, the challenges of future research will be not only in the elucidation of risk factors but also in the employment of the newly developed structured and systematic means of collecting pedigree and family psychiatric history that are amenable to use in clinical practice.

Finally, epidemiologic studies have been influential in the conceptual issues regarding diagnosis and classification of affective disorder. As indicated above, assessments in the community have fostered an awareness of and appreciation for the spectrum of affective manifestations. Furthermore, the family study data on the heterogeneity of major depression has helped to define meaningful subtypes. The associations with anxiety disorders and increased risks attendant with co-morbidity have challenged the hierarchical constructs of the DSM-III. Further research is indicated in refining nosologic distinctions, but the present findings should not go unnoticed.

In conclusion, the epidemiologic approach has much to offer to the individual clinician. The implications for social action and public health policy have not been emphasized in this chapter but they are nonetheless far-reaching and significant. An epidemiologic perspective is one that should be incorporated into clinical psychiatry. This chapter has intended to provide a working knowledge of this conceptual approach and its methods as well as to highlight the clinical relevance and future directions of the more recent investigations. In so doing, it has sought to draw the reader into the point of view of the psychiatric epidemiologist and to have generated an awareness and appreciation for the field. As a result, may the future continue to see both clinician and epidemiologist working alongside each other towards resolving the theoretical issues, defining the treatment needs, and developing the preventive and interventionary measures that will emerge from future study of depressive illness.

REFERENCES

1. Akiskal HS, Downs J, Jordan P, Watson S, Dougherty D, Pruitt DB: Affective disorders in referred children and younger siblings of manic depressives. *Arch Gen Psychiatry 1985; 42:* 996-1003.
2. Angst J, Dobler-Mikola A: Do the diagnostic criteria determine the sex ratio in depression? *J Affective Disord 1984; 7:* 189-198.
3. Angst J, Dobler-Mikola A: The Zurich study. I. The continuum from normal to pathological depressive mood swing. *Eur Arch Psychiat Neurol Sci 1984; 234:* 21-19.
4. Angst J, Dobler-Mikola A, Binder J: The Zurich study. A prospective epidemiologiccal study of depressive, neurotic and psychosomatic syndromes. *Eur Arch Psychiat Neurol Sci 1984; 234:* 13-20.
5. Beardslee WR, Bemporad J, Keller MB, Klerman GL: Children of parents with major affective disorder: A review. *Am J Psychiatry 1983; 140:* 825-832.
6. Bertelsen A, Harvald B, Hauge M: A Danish twin study of manic-depressive disorders. *Brit J Psychiatry 1977; 130:* 330-351.
7. Boyd JH, Weissman MM: Epidemiology of affective disorders: a reexamination and future directions. *Arch Gen Psychiatry 1981; 38:* 1039-1045.
8. Boyd JH, Weissman MM: Epidemiology, in Payker, E.S. (ed.): *Handbook of Affective Disorders.* Edinburgh, Churchill Livingstone, 1982, pp 109-125.

9. Brown GW, Ni Bhrolchain M, Harris TO: Social class and psychiatric disturbance among women in an urban population. *Sociology 1975; 9:* 225-254.

10. Brown GW, Harris TO: *Social Origins of Depression: A Study of Psychiatric Disorder in Women.* London, Tavistock, 1978.

11. Cadoret RJ: Evidence for genetic inheritance of primary affective disorder in adoptees. *Am J Psychiatry 1978; 135:* 463-466.

12. Clayton PJ: The epidemiology of bipolar affective disorder. *Compre Psychiatry 1981; 22:* 31-41.

13. Cohen MB, Baker G, Cohen RA, Fromm-Reichmann F, Weigert EV: An intensive study of twelve cases of manic depressive psychosis. *Psychiatry 1954: 17:* 103-137.

14. Coryell W, Endicott J, Andreasen N, Keller M: Bipolar I, bipolar II, and nonbipolar major depression among the relatives of affectively ill probands. *Am J Psychiatry 1985; 142:* 817-821.

15. Coryell W, Endicott J, Reich T, Andreasen N, Keller M: A family study of bipolar II disorder. *Brit K Psychiatry 1984; 145:* 48-54.

16. Costello CG: Social factors associated with depression: A retrospective community study. *Psychol Med 1982; 12:* 329-339.

17. Decina P, Kestenbaum CJ, Farber S, Kron L, Gargan M, Sackeim HA, Fieve RR: Clinical and psychological assessment of children of bipolar probands. *Am J Psychiatry 1983; 140:* 548-553.

18. Eaton WW, Holzer CE, VonKorff M, Anthony JC, Helzer JE, George L, Burnam A, Boyd JK, Kessler LG, Locke BZ: The design of the Epidemiologic Catchment Area Surveys. *Arch Gen Psychiatry 1984; 41:* 942-948.

19. Endicott J, Nee J, Andreasen N, Clayton P, Keller M, Coryell W: Bipolar II— Combine or keep Separate? *J Affective Disord 1985; 8:* 17-28.

20. Feighner JP, Robins E, Guze SB, Woodruff RA, Winokur G, Munoz R: Diagnostic criteria for use in psychiatric research. *Arch Gen Psychiatry 1972;* 57-63.

21. Gammon GD, John K, Rothblum ED, Mullen K, Tischler GL, Weissman MM: Use of a structured diagnostic interview to identify bipolar disorder in adolescent inpatients: Frequency and manifestations of the disorder. *Am J Psychiatry 1983; 140:* 543-547.

22. Gershon ES, Hamovit J, Guroff JJ, Dibble E, Leckman JF, Sceery W, Targum SD, Nurnberger JI, Goldin LR, Bunny WE: A family study of schizoaffective bipolar I, bipolar II, unipolar, and normal control probands. *Arch Gen Psychiatry 1982; 39:* 1157-1167.

23. Gershon ES, Mark A, Cohen N, Belizon N, Baron M, Knobe KE: Transmitted factors in the morbidity of affective disorders: A controlled study. *J Psychiat Res 1958; 21:* 71-90.

25. Gove WR: The relationship between sex role, marital status, and mental illness. *Social Forces 1972; 52:* 34-44.

26. Hagnell O, Lanke J, Rorsman B, Ojesjo L: Are we entering an age of melancholy? Depressive illnesses in a prospective epidemiological study over 25 years: The Lundby Study, Sweden. *Psychol Mes 198:* 279-289.

27. Henderson AS: Social relationships, adversity and neurosis: An analysis of pro-
    spective observations. *Brit J Psychiatry 1981; 138:* 391-198.
28. Hurry J, Tennant C, Bebbington P: The selective factors leading to psychiatric
    referral. *Acta Psychiatrica Scand Suppl 1980; 285:* 315-323.
29. Ilfeld FW: Current social stressors and symptoms of depression. *Am J Psychiatry
    1977; 134:* 161-166.
30. Katz MM, Klerman GL: Introduction: Overview of the clinical studies program.
    Am J Psychiatry 1979; 136: 49-51.
31. Keller NB: Chronic and recurrent affective disorders: incidence, course, and in-
    fluencing factors, in Kemali, D., Racagni, G., (eds.): *Chronic Treatments in
    Neuropsychiatry.* New York, Raven Press, 1985.
32. Keller MB, Klerman GL, Lavori, PW, Coryell W, Endicott J, Taylor J: Long-term
    outcome of episodes of major depression: Clinical and public health signifi-
    cance. *JAMA 1984; 252:* 799-792.
33. Keller MB, Lavori PW, Collins EL, Klerman GL: Predictors of relapse in major
    depressive disorder. *JAMA 1983; 250:* 3299-3304.
34. Keller MB, Lavori PW, Endicott J, Coryell W, Klerman GL: "Double
    Depression." Two-year follow-up. *Am J Psychiatry 1983; 140:* 689-694.
35. Keller MB, Lavori PW, Rice J, Coryell W, Hirschfeld RMA: The persistent risk
    of chronicity in recurrent episodes of nonbipolar major depressive disorder: A
    prospective follow-up. *Am J Psychiatry 1986; 143:* 24-28.
36. Keller MB, Shapiro RW: "Double Depression." Superimposition of acute de-
    pressive episodes on chronic depressive disorders. *Am J Psychiatry 1982; 139:*
    438-442.
37. Klerman GL: Affective disorders, in Armand M, Nichol MP (Eds.): *The Harvard
    Guide to Modern Psychiatry.* Cambridge, MA, Belknap Press 1978, pp. 253-281.
38. Klerman GL, Lavori PW, Rice J, Reich T, Endicott J, Andreasen NC, Keller MB,
    Hirschfeld RAM: Birth-cohort trends in rates of major depressive disorder
    among relatives of patients with affective disorder. *Arch Gen Psychiatry 1985; 42:*
    689-693.
39. Krauthammer C, Klerman GL: The epidemiology of mania, in Shopsin, B.
    (Ed.): *Manic Illness.* New York, Raven Press, 1979, pp. 11-28.
40. Kuyler PL, Rosenthal L, Igel G, Dunner DL, Fieve RR: Psychopathology among
    children of manic-depressive patients. *Biol Psychiatry 1980; 15:* 589-597.
41. Leonhard KI, Korff I, Schultz H: Die temperamente in den familien der
    monopoluren und bipolaren phasischen psychosen. *Psychiat Neurol 1962; 143:*
    416-434.
42. Livingston R, Nugent H, Rader L, Smith GR: Family histories of depressed and
    severely anxious children. *Am J Psychiatry 1985; 142:* 1497-1499.
43. McKnew DH, Cytryn L, Efron AM, Gershon ES, Bunney WE: Offspring of
    paients with affective disorders. *Brit J Psychiatry 1979; 134:* 148-152.
44. Mendlewicz J, Rainer JD: Adoption study supporting genetic transmission in
    manic-depressive illness. *Nature 1977; 268:* 327-329.
45. Myers JK, Weissman MM, Tischler GL, Holzer CE, Leaf PJ, Orvaschel H,
    Anthony JC, Boyd JH, Burke JD, Kramer M, Stoltzman R: Six-month preva-

lence of psychiatric disorders in three communities. *Arch Gen Psychiatry 1984; 41:* 959-967.

46. Nurnberger JI, Gershon ES: Genetics, in Paykel ES (Ed.): *Handbook of Affective Disorders.* Edinburgh, Churchill Livingstone, 1982, pp. 126-145.

47. O'Connell RA, Mayo JA, O'Brien JD, Mirsheidaie F: Children of bipolar manic depressives, in Mendlewicz, J., Shopsin, B. (Eds.): *Genetic Aspects of Affective Illness.* New York, Spectrum Publications, 1979, pp. 55-68.

48. Orvaschel H, Weissman MM, Kidd KK: Children and depression: The children of depressed parents; the childhood of depressed patients; depression in children. *J Affective Disord 1980; 2:* 1-16.

49. Paykel ES, Myers JK, Dienelt MN, et al.: Life events and depression: A controlled study. *Arch Gen Psychiatry 1969; 21:* 753-760.

50. Radloff LS: Sex differences in depression: The effects of occupational and marital status. *Sex Roles 1975; 1:* 249-265.

51. Regier DA, Myers JK, Kramer M, Robins LN, Blazer DG, Hough RL, Eaton WW, Locke BZ: The NIMH Epidemiologic Catchment Area Program: Historical context, major objectives, and study population characteristics. *Arch Gen Psychiatry 1984; 41:* 934-941.

52. Rice J, Reich T, Andreasen NC, Lavori PW, Endicott J, Clayton P, Keller MD, Hirschfeod RMA, Klerman GL: Sex-related differences in depression: Familial evidence. *J Affective Disord 1984; 71:* 199-210.

53. Robins LN, Helzer JE, Croughan J, Ratcliff KS: National Institute of Mental Health Diagnostic Interview Schedule. *Arch Gen Psychiatry 1981; 38:* 381-389.

54. Robins LN, Helzer JE, Weissman MM, Orvaschel H, Gruenberg E, Burke JD, Regier DA: Lifetime prevalence of specific psychiatric disorders in three sites. *Arch Gen Psychiatry 1984; 41:* 949-958.

55. Rounsaville BJ, Weissman MM, Prusoff BA, Herceg-Baron RL: Marital disputes and treatment outcomes in depressed women. *Compre Psychiatry 1979; 20:* 483-490.

56. Sameroff AJ, Barocas R, Seifer R: Rochester longitudinal study progress report, in Watt W, Rolf J, Anthony EJ (eds.): *Children at Risk for Schizophrenia.* Cambridge, Cambridge University Press, 1984, pp. 482-514.

57. Shapiro RW, Keller MB: *Longitudinal Interval Follow-up Evaluation (Life).* Massachusetts General Hospital, Boston, MA, 1979.

58. Shapiro RW, Skinner EA, VonKorff M, German PS Tischler GL, Leaf PJ, Benham L, Cottler L, Kessler LG, Regier D: Utilization of health and mental health services: Three epidemiologic catchment area sites. *Arch Gen Psychiatry 1984; 41:* 971-978.

59. Spitzer RL, Endicott J, Robins E: *Research Diagnostic Criteria.* New York, Biometrics Research Division, Evaluation Section, New York State Psychiatric Institute, 1978.

60. Warheit GJ: Life events, coping, stress and depressive symptomatology. *Am J Psychiatry 1979; 136:* 502-507.

61. Weissman MM, Gershon ES, Kidd KK, Prusoff BA, Leckman JF, Dibble E, Hamovit J, Thompson WD, Pauls DL, Guroff JJ: Psychiatric disorders in the

relatives of probands with affective disorders. *Arch Gen Psychiatry 1984; 41:* 13-21.

62. Weissman MM, John K, Merikangas KR, Prusoff BA, Wickramaratne P, Gammon GD, Angold A, Warner V: Depressed parents and their children: General health, social and psychiatric problems. *AJDC* in press.

63. Weissman MM, Klerman GL: Sex differences and the epidemiology of depression. *Arch Gen Psychiatry 1977; 34:* 98-111.

64. Weissman MM, Merikangas KR, Wickramaratne P, Kidd KK, Prusoff BA, Leckman JF, Pauls DL: Understanding the clinical heterogeneity of major depression using family data. *Arch Gen Psychiatry 1986; 43:* 430-434.

65. Weissman MM, Merikangas KR, Wickramaratne P, Prusoff BA, John K, Gammon GD: *Children at high risk for depression.* Paper read at the IVth World Congress of Biological Psychiatry. Philadelphia, PA, September 10, 1985.

66. Weissman MM, Myers JK: Affective disorders in a US urban community. *Arch Gen Psychiatry 1978; 35:* 1304-1311.

67. Weissman MM, Prusoff BA, Gammon GD, Merikangas KR, Leckman JF, Kidd KK: Psychopathology in the children (ages 6-18) of depressed and normal parents. *J Am Acad Child Psychiatry 1984; 23:* 78-84.

68. Welner Z, Welner A, McCrary MD, Leonard MA: Psychopathology in children of inpatients with depression: A controlled study. *J Nerv Ment Dis 1977; 164:* 408-413.

69. Wing JK, Cooper JE, Sartorius N: *Measurement and classification of psychiatric symptoms: An instructional manual for the PSE and CATEGO program.* New York, Cambridge University Press, 1974.

70. Winokur G, Tsuang MT, Crowe RR: The Iowa 500: Affective disorder in relatives of manic and depressed patients. *Am J Psychiatry 1982; 139:* 209-212.

Chapter 4

THE CLINICAL CLASSIFICATION
OF DEPRESSIVE DISORDERS

Martin R. Cohen, M.D.
George Winokur, M.D.

INTRODUCTION

Numerous competing classifications of depression exist. Most share overlapping categories and are all but impossible to precisely relate to each other.[1] In American psychiatry, there is now an ongoing systematic attempt to precisely define and analyze the usefulness of the most promising of these classifications. This should lead to their continuing modification and increasing validity.

CRITERIA FOR THE EVALUATION OF DEPRESSIVE CLASSIFICATIONS

A classification of depression requires, as a minimum, clearly followable rules for classifying an individual as depressed. This permits consistent diagnostic agreement (reliability) and progressive modification to increase validity. Ideally, individuals should be classified on the basis of specific etiologies and their correction or treatment.

For the purposes of this paper, we reason that patients with common preceding variables such as family history, past experience (psychological or biological events), psychiatric history or biological traits, may share a common etiology. Perhaps with less foundation, we note that patients who have similar clinical presentations, including age of onset, symptoms or signs, biological state variables, may also share a common pathogenesis.

Finally, we will evaluate suggested depressive groups as regards their ability to predict natural or treatment course (future psychosocial or psychiatric events, mortality, and the influence of treatment). In contrast to preceding variables, outcome findings have a usefulness which is independent of inferences about etiology. The clinician, once having classified the patient, should be directly aided in choosing a treatment.

From work on more completely understood medical illness, we may conclude that no simple inference can be made that shared variables directly reflect the same etiology. For example, the clinical presentation of both viral and bacterial pneumonia may be quite similar due to resulting shared pulmonary and systemic alterations. These shared secondary alterations may require similar symptomatic treatment measures such as oxygen, aspirin, etc., but their different primary etiologies require the differential use of antibiotics. However, increasing homogeneity is correlated with a higher likelihood of sharing important pathogenetic mechanisms.

In the process of developing a valid depressive classification, different classifications will be evaluated. These latter produce groups homogenous only for some variables. The fact that these variables may differ from classification to classification, might make a particular classification more useful for one purpose than another. For example, a classification that produces more homogenous preceding variables may be more useful for etiological research, whereas a classification with more predictive homogeneity may be more useful in treatment research.

Epidemiological studies, despite varying methodology and often uncertain criteria, suggest that individual lifetime risk for depression is at least 5 percent.[2,3]

There have been some more recent studies. The morbidity risk for affective disorders using research criteria in 541 relatives of psychiatrically well surgical controls was 7.6 percent to 9 percent.[4] For the diagnosis of unipolar depression, females were more likely to be affected than males regardless of which criteria were used. Morbidity risk or disease expectancy is defined as an estimate of the probability that a person will develop the disease in question at some time or another during his/her life if he/she survives the period of risk (manifestation period) for the disease.

Another recent study presents lifetime prevalence of the affective disorders.[5] The criteria which were used in this study were the DSM-III criteria.[6] The data are given in terms of lifetime risk which is the proportion of birth cohort that would be expected to have the disorder develop before a specified age, if all unaffected persons survived to that age. This material is the result of the epidemiologic catchment area study (ECA) in three separate places. The lifetime prevalence of affective disorders varied between 6.1 percent to 8.2 percent to 9.5 percent. Like the previous study, females were more likely to be affected by depression than males.

The range of clinical presentations spans the mute, withdrawn, retarded patient to the agitated, hypochondriacal patient; from the individual who is still able to work and may appear normal to the obviously ill individual who is unable to take care of even his basic biological needs for food, shelter, or rest. There may or may not be a family history of depression or other psychiatric illness. The course may be a self-limited one with complete recovery; or, more rarely, the depression may become chronic. Thus, the number and variability of patients that are to be classified, suggest that depression may be a heterogeneous illness and that a subclassification may be useful to produce more homogeneous groups.

Depressive Classification in Clinical Practice

In clinical practice, psychiatrists have diagnosed patients without clearly defined criteria. Diagnostic guides such as the *Second Diagnostic and Statistical Manual (DSM-II)*, published by the American Psychiatric Association (APA) only provided clinicians with prototypes of depressive patients. A clinician's criteria often probably reflected his personal training and experience.

The major concern of psychiatrists in diagnosing depression centered upon its differentiation from other types of mental illness (differential diagnosis) and its subclassification. This was understandable as the concern of the psychiatrist was in finding an appropriate treatment. The differentiation of depression from normality was often relegated to the patient or the community. However, even for purposes of differential diagnosis, no clear inclusion or exclusion criteria existed. This continued despite the fact that patients might present with depressive symptomatology overlapping with other diagnoses (e.g., the category schizoaffective disorder in DSM-II).

In practice, as Kendell[1] has noted, psychiatrists tended to subdivide depression into two general types. These were based upon a mixture of preceding variables, clinical presentation, and course. The terms psychotic or endogenous depression, manic-depressive illness, psychotic depressive reaction, or individual melancholia were used interchangeably to refer to a "Type 1" depression. In an analogous fashion, the terms neurotic, reactive, characterological, or exogenous depression were used to refer to a "Type 2" depression.

The prototypic "Type 1" depression was an illness with clear onset, usually without any particular precipitating event, accompanied by social and vocational incapacitation, and symptomatology that was unresponsive to the environment. Symptoms were considered severe and included psychomotor retardation, guilt, weight loss, insomnia, most typically of the late onset type (early morning awakening), and a diurnal variation of symptomatology (maximum severity of depression in the morning). Symptoms could include hallucinations and/or delusions if these could be explained in terms of the patient's depressed mood. The depression was usually considered a self-limited one with the patient making a complete recovery with or without treatment.

The prototypical "Type 2" depression began with the report of stressful life events and resulted in less impairment of everyday routine. The onset of the depression was more uncertain, but was often considered to occur in an individual who had premorbid personality difficulties and thus may have suffered from a number of psychiatric symptoms prior to the present difficulties. Symptomatology was generally considered reactive to environmental events. Symptoms generally did not include the somatic symptomatology of the "Type 1" depression and particularly did not include delusions or hallucinations. There were the additional symptoms of self-pitying, irritability, or hostility, general blaming of the environment for present difficulties and feelings of inadequacy. The course might more likely become chronic, but most patients recovered. However, it was expected that the patient would be left with the residual difficulties of a predisposing personality structure.

Numerous retrospective studies of the clinical course of hospitalized, usually "Type 1" depressives, were carried out during the first half of this century.[7,8] Unfortunately, as was the case in clinical practice, patient entry into these studies usually was based on the original chart diagnosis with no clear operational inclusion or exclusion criteria. Illness course was found to be quite variable with most of the variance unpredictable. Nevertheless, most studies concluded, at follow-ups that sometimes exceeded 25 years, that the need for a change in diagnosis was relatively infrequent. The most frequent diagnosis change would probably be to schizophrenia and this usually occurred at a rate of less than 7 percent.[7] However, again, no clear criteria were given for what would necessitate a change in diagnosis. Also, raters were not usually blind to the original diagnosis. These studies provide no absolute data as the criteria for the diagnosis of a "Type 1" depression probably changes with both time and space.[9]

For depression, diagnostic reliability in clinical practice suffers from the interaction of three factors. 1) There are no clearly defined rules for inclusion or exclusion of patients into either the "Type 1" or the "Type 2" depression. 2) Some individuals use these terms to refer to ill-defined or overlapping subdivisions of the "Type 1" or "2" depression. 3) In clinical practice and in research studies, most patients meet some of the criteria of both the "Type 1" and "Type 2" depression.

Another problem is how to assess the consistency or reliability of clinical diagnosis. The statistic kappa is perhaps agreed to as the best single quantitative measure of such because it at least corrects for chance agreement. Kappa varies from zero at chance agreement, to plus 1, perfect agreement. In a 1974 review Spitzer et al.[10] calculated the mean kappa for previous studies of the clinical diagnosis of depressive disorders. Even with the use of clinicians of similar background and training, and some specific training in diagnostic principles and the use of the same data base in some studies, the kappa for the general category of affective disorders was found to average no better than 0.41. Clinical agreement for subtypes of depression was even worse, with manic-depressive illness ("Type 1") equal to 0.33 and neurotic depression ("Type 2") 0.16.

The fact is that reliability depends on two things, 1) the systematic interview and 2) the specific criteria which are used. Using an interview called the National Institute of Mental Health Diagnostic Interview Schedule (DIS) and the DSM-III criteria, one finds kappas of .63 for depression and .69 for all DSM-III diagnoses.[11] Using different sets of criteria, i.e., the Feighner (St. Louis criteria) or the Research Diagnostic Criteria, the kappas are similar—.70 and .62 for all diagnoses and .66 and .64 for depression diagnoses.[11] Thus, though there is not perfect agreement between raters even using the same instrument and criteria, the agreement generally is satisfactory. Using a different interview, the Schedule for Affective Disorders, Schizophrenia—lifetime version (SADS-L) and the Research Diagnostic Criteria, the interclass correlation coefficient comparing initial versus consensus diagnoses for mania was .88 and for major depressive disorder .75.[12] Thus, these diagnoses are acceptably reliable.

Long-term follow-up studies suggested some validity for the clinical diagnosis of a "Type 1" depression. There was also the clinical impression that these subdivisions could somewhat predict illness course and treatment outcome. "Type 1" depressions were generally considered to respond better to ECT[13] and antidepressants[14] while "Type 2" depressions were more likely to respond to placebo. However, more recent studies have questioned even these clinical axioms.[15, 16, 17] Clearly, the state of reliability of depressive diagnosis severely limited usefulness and validity. In addition, the unclear criteria used in clinical diagnosis do not provide a basis with which to systematically modify the criteria to make them increasingly valid. Essentially, a diagnosis without operational criteria is a dead end.

Multivariate Statistical Attempts to Develop a Depressive Classification

Beginning in the early 1960s, multivariate statistical techniques were applied to the development of a depressive classification. Underlying these techniques was the assumption that subgroups homogeneous for clinical presentation might be more etiologically homogeneous and valid. Early studies were based on factor analysis, a technique designed to find symptom clusters (simply, symptoms that tend to occur together). Most studies were able to find two factors or symptom groups fairly consistently (18-21), although not all did so.[22] One factor seemed to be best considered a reflection of severity. The second, a bipolar factor, seemed to correspond to the symptomatic distinction made clinically between "Type 1" and "2" depressions. There was, of course, the possibility, as Kendell[1] has pointed out, that clinicians schooled in the diagnosis of "Type 1" and "2" depressions may have tended to unknowingly emphasize and ignore certain symptomatology in patients, confirming their own clinical impression of the patient as a "Type 1" or "2" (a halo effect). In any case, studies were not consistent as to which symptoms were important in this second factor. Also, clustering of these symptoms were not particularly impressive; that is, simply the tendency for these particular symptoms to only occur together was not strong. Thus, these studies confirmed the clinical impression of two symptomatic types of depression while clarifying the difficulties clinicians had in agreeing upon precise criteria for these two depressive types. Finally, as Kendell[1] points out, factor analysis analyzes relationships between symptoms. It does not necessarily follow that patients will be as easily grouped. Indeed, as in clinical practice where most patients seem to suffer from a mixture of both "Type 1" and "2" depressive symptomatology, most patients did not belong to one or the other end of this bipolar factor and could not easily be grouped. As a result of the above difficulties, investigators turned to the statistical technique of cluster analysis to develop a depressive classification. This was a more direct attempt to find groups of patients with similar symptomatology. Most studies were able to find a group that seemed to correspond to the clinical "Type 1" depression and usually a number of groups that seemed to correspond, perhaps to subgroups of the "Type 2" depression.[23-25] Unfortunately, the typologies, although they may have appeared somewhat similar in description, were not usually overlapping in reality.

Both factor analysis and cluster-derived typologies require advanced statistical techniques. They were not directly used to derive specific operational criteria that could be used in the ordinary diagnoses of patients or for the testing of their validity. Thus, studies of the validity of particular factors or typologies are not easily related to one another. The few studies that have attempted to evaluate their predictive validity have not had particularly impressive results. Statistically significant group differences in outcome may or may not result.[25-28] Even when present, the actual outcome variance attributable to group membership is usually small and perhaps clinically insignificant.[28]

Perhaps most devastating was the outcome in some studies when one or two clinical symptoms seemed as predictive of outcome as the statistically derived groupings. Kay et al.[26] found that retardation and somatic complaints were as predictive of good and bad outcome respectively at five- to seven-year follow-up as their factors (analytic dimensions). They suggested that the label retarded depression might be preferable to endogenous ("Type 1") depressioin. Raskin and Cook[25] found that patients who were retarded responded best to imipramine and agitated patients best to chlorpromazine. Thus, it becomes likely that differential drug effects due to group membership are more attributable to drug effects on shared secondary symptomatology. As Winokur[29] has argued, symptomatology may be a poor basis for defining etiologically important depressive subgroups since there is clear evidence that even in individual patients depressive symptomatology may vary during depressive episodes and from episode to episode. Patients may present at one time with a "Type 1" depression and at another time with a "Type 2" depression.

Statistical studies concentrated on finding appropriate subclasses for patients already considered depressed. There was little concern for the rules for establishing the patient as a depressive in the first place; this, despite the obvious influence that such criteria would have on the results and validity of any subsequent studies of the subclassification. There were some exceptions. Kendell and Gourlay[30] did attempt to use discriminant function analysis to evaluate the boundary between schizophrenia and affective psychosis ("Type 1" depression). Patients showed a normal overall distribution of factor scores, suggesting that by symptomatology no clear or natural boundary between the two disorders could be found. Still, their criteria might have been used to devise operational criteria to divide these two disorders.

Operational Criteria for a Depressive Classification

Independently in the 1960s, the Department of Psychiatry at Washington University in St. Louis began developing clear operational criteria for a depressive diagnosis based on the work of Cassidy et al.[31] This culminated in the 1972 publication by Feighner et al. of diagnostic criteria for psychiatry research.[32] This work generated for the first time for general use clearly understandable operational rules for the diagnosis of depression in a written form. Thus, although logical, clear operational criteria for a depressive diagnosis might have been derived from statistical studies of symptom and patient groups, such was not the case. A depressive disorder required the occurrence of a dysphoric mood, with a definite onset and duration of one month, and the presence of a minimum number (at least four for a probable and five for a definite diagnosis) of specific and listed accompanying symptoms. These symptoms included 1) anorexia or weight loss, 2) sleep difficulty, 3) loss of energy, 4) loss of interest in usual activities or sexual drive, 5) agitation or retardation, 6) complaints of actual thinking difficulties, 7) recurrent suicidal ideas or wishes to be dead, and 8) feelings of guilt. In addition, specific criteria were given for scoring a symptom present. In summary, the patient had either sought medical care or taken medication for the particular symptom; a symptom had been disabling enough to interfere with his usual routine; or the examiner felt the symptom was clinically important enough to count (for example, a delusional belief). All symptoms explainable by a known medical illness were not scored. Individuals undergoing a culturally acceptable grief reaction were excluded. There were vague criteria for excluding patients who might have had additional symptoms indicative of schizophrenia.

Subsequently these operational criteria have been substantially incorporated into the diagnosis of major depressive disorder in the Research Diagnostic Criteria.[33] However, the newer criteria differ on two points:

1) the diagnosis of a major depressive disorder only requires a one week period of depression for a probable diagnosis; and 2) there are clearly defined schizophrenic symptomatology which would alter the diagnosis from a major depressive disorder to one of a schizoaffective illness, depressed type. The latter criteria probably would affect less than 10 percent of patients included in a depressive classification.[7] However, the effect of the reduced requirement to only a week's period of illness may considerably increase the number of individuals diagnosed depressives. In the Feighner criteria, patients who fall short of the criteria for a depressive diagnosis remain without a particular psychiatric diagnosis. In contrast, the Research Diagnostic Criteria[33] has defined a minor depressive subclass for individuals who meet essentially many of the criteria of the major depressive disorder, but no more than three of the necessary accompanying depressive symptoms.

As one might expect, reliability is greatly enhanced for depressive diagnoses operationally defined. Helzer et al.[34] and Robins et al.,[35] report kappas for depressive diagnoses using the Feighner Criteria of 0.55, and more than 0.88 respectively. Preliminary studies of the use of the Research Diagnostic Criteria for the NIMH Collaborative Depression Study found, using multiple tests of reliability, kappas ranging from 0.76 to 0.90 for the diagnosis of major depressive disorder and 0.68 to 0.90 for minor depressive disorders.[36]

Reliability is only a necessary and not a sufficient condition for validity. Research to directly evaluate the validity of either of the above diagnostic criteria or their comparative merits is limited. It should be noted, however, that work to assess the validity of subdivisions of these depressive disorders indirectly assesses the validity of the general disorder. These studies will be reviewed subsequently.

There is no lacking for patients to meet the above criteria. In 1977 Robins et al.[37] reported on their study of consecutive admissions to a psychiatric emergency room serving the medically indigent. Using the Feighner Criteria, they found that 43 percent of some 300 patients had suffered from a depressive disorder. We can estimate that probably even more of the patients might have met the less stringent Research Diagnosis Criteria. The Feighner Criteria were not derived from statistical studies and may be considered somwhat arbitrary and unnatural boundaries for depression. Murphy et al.[38] showed that criteria almost identical to the Feighner Criteria, but with one or more depressive symptom requirement, produced a homgeneous group at five-year follow-up. However, it was apparent that many other patients with less symptoms had a similar follow-up course.

Robins et al.[39] attempted to compare classification outcome using two alternative symptom list requirements, one restricted to somatic complaints and the other to psychological symptomatology (the Feighner Criteria is a mixture of both). Essentially, all patients who met either of the two alternative criteria lists also met the Feighner Criteria. However, 40 percent of patients meeting the Feighner Criteria did not meet one of the more specific criteria sets. Ninety-six percent of those patients given a Feighner depressive diagnosis were again able to be given the same diagnosis on a blind follow-up interview at an average 18 months later. Thus, Feighner Criteria had increased coverage compared to the more restrictive criteria without any significant diagnostic instability.

Winokur[40] studied patients with primary psychiatric diagnoses other than depression (secondary depressives) and found many with a depressive affect accompanied by a number of depressive symptoms. The data suggest that any quantitative symptom requirement for the additional diagnosis of a depressive disorder may be somewhat arbitrary, since patient distribution for a number of scored depressive symptoms was unimodal.

In 1978, Weisman and Meyers[3] were able to report a preliminary community survey of affective disorders, using for the first time the Research Diagnostic Criteria. The authors reported a single point prevalence of 4.3 percent and 2.5 percent for major and minor depressive disorders, respectively. They were also able to estimate in the community a lifetime prevalence rate of 20 percent for major depression and 9.2 percent for minor depression. In contrast, Winokur,[41] using the somewhat different methodology of assessment of mental illness in families of medically hospitalized individuals, found a probable lifetime risk for a Feighner Criteria depression of 8.3 percent. This suggests that use of the Feighner versus the Research Diagnostic Criteria may lead to the study of significantly different groups.

In summary, the Feighner and Research Diagnostic Criteria are generally available depressive classifications shown to be reliable enough so as not to substantially hinder usefulness. Some work has been completed suggesting some validity to the boundaries created. For the Feighner Criteria, depressive groups show diagnostic stability. However, most importantly, these operationally defined criteria allow for their systematic modification when studies of validity suggest such.

Operational Criteria Based upon Clinical Presentation

With the development of operationally defined criteria for the diagnosis of depression, it becomes possible to derive clearly defined subclasses. Thus, subclasses of the Research Diagnostic Criteria's major depressive disorder, based upon clinical presentation, have been developed.[33] It should be noted, however, that these subdivisions may not have quite the same clinical value as the "Type 1" and "2" subdivisions appeared to have since patients in these groups must also meet the rigorous requirements for a major depressive illness.

An endogenous depression is specifically limited to a major depression with a particular number of defined symptoms. Many of these symptoms had been clinically associated with the "Type 1" depression. In contrast, a situational depression is simply defined as a major depression preceded by a clear precipitating event. Psychotic depression is restricted to patients suffering from a major depressive disorder who manifest delusions or hallucinations and yet do not meet the criteria for a schizoaffective disorder, depressed type. Finally, an incapacitating depression refers solely to the patient's inability to socially or vocationally function.

An initial study of the reliability of these subclass diagnoses, again as part of the NIMH Collaborative Depression Study, found quite respectable kappas ranging from 0.58 to 0.78.[36] Since the criteria for these groups are not mutually exclusive, it also becomes possible to study their complex relationships to one other. For example, in preliminary findings, 37 percent of endogenous patients (symptomatic characteristics of the "Type 1" depression) seem to have a clear precipitating event and thus can be considered to also suffer from a situational depression (characteristic of a "Type 2" depression). Similarly, 56 percent of endogenous depressives were considered incapacitated, in contrast to only 38 percent of the situational depressives. In brief, initial findings confirm the results of statistical studies and clinical impressions that symptoms or clusters of symptoms do occur together in patients. Most patients have a mixture of both "Type 1" and "Type 2" symptomatology.

These are newly defined by reliable depressive subclasses. There is already the suggestion that the classifications of psychotic depression, limited to the presence of hallucinations or delusions, may have some treatment validity. A number of authors have now published results of retrospective analyses[42, 43] and one prospective analysis[33] that suggest depressives with hallucinations or delusions may be less responsive to antidepressants than other depressives. However, there is at least one exception.[44]

Operational Criteria for Depressive Subclasses Based upon Preceding Variables (Primary-Secondary Depression)

Clinical and statistical subclassifications of depression tended to be based upon variation in clinical presentation. As others, as well as we, have noted, however, the results of this approach have been somewhat disappointing. It is possible that such subdivisions may prove to be more valuable now that they are operationally and reliably defined. However, the Washington University groups at St. Louis took a somewhat different approach in hopes of developing a more valid classification. They divided depressives into two types on the basis of variables preceding clinical symptomatology, reasoning that this might be more directly related to etiology. A primary depressive disorder was defined as a depression

(Feighner Criteria) in an individual who may have had a previous episode of mania or depression (operationally defined in Feighner Criteria), but no history of any other psychiatric illness (operationally defined in Feighner Criteria) or serious (incapacitating or life threatening) medical illness prior to the first episode. A secondary depressive disorder occurred in an individual who had a preexisting diagnosable nonaffective psychiatric illness prior to his first episode of depression or mania.

Robins et al.[39] have noted the possible difficulties in making the diagnostic distinction between primary and secondary. At least for research purposes, confusion should lead to classification as an undiagnosed depressive disorder. In their work, Robins et al.[39] found that only 11 of some 135 emergency room patients diagnosed with a depressive disorder were unable to be classified as either primary or secondary. At the end of an average 18-month follow-up period, second blind diagnoses on these patients revealed none of the primary depressives, only 2 percent of the secondary depressives, and only two of the original 11 patients with an uncertain depressive diagnosis were wrongly diagnosed. It should be noted, however, that these excellent results were obtained following an extensive structure diagnostic interview of each patients, which averaged four hours.

Forty-three percent of these emergency-room patients met the criteria for a depressive diagnosis. With a ratio of secondary to primary depressions of 3:2, both categories were significantly filled. However, only 17 percent of primary affective disorders occurred in men and only 1 percent in black men. This may have been a reflection of the medically indigent setting, although it may be that the primary-secondary distinction has little usefulness for black men.

On a similar basis, the Research Diagnostic Criteria also subdivides major depression into primary and secondary types.[33] However, since the Research Diagnostic Criteria for a major depressive disorder and other psychiatric illnesses differ somewhat from the Feighner Criteria, the primary and secondary depressive disorder populations defined by these two criteria may differ. As a possible example, in Weissman's community survey cited earlier,[3] primary major depressives were found to outnumber secondary depressives by some eight to one.

A preliminary comparison in the NIMH Collaborative Depression Study showed no simple relationship between these two major depressive subclasses based upon preceding variables with the clearly defined symptomatic subclassifications.[36] For example, 64 percent of primary and 45 percent of secondary depressives were considered to be endogenous depressives. Although 36 percent of the primary depressives were retarded depressives, this compared with only 6 percent of the secondary depressives. As noted previously, retardation has been associated with good outcome at a five-to-seven-year follow-up and with good response to antidepressants. Also, retardation is an important weight in statistical typologies and factor analytic studies.

The validity of any subclassification of depression is measured in the increased homgeneity of preceding, concurrent, or predictive variables produced in the subclasses, in comparison to the general class. Although the basis of the above classification is the preceding variable of psychiatric history, other preceding variables may also be assessed for increased homogeneity in the produced subclasses.

The Iowa 500 is a systematic family and follow-up study of 325 primary affective disorders, 200 schizophrenics, and 260 controls.[41] For a history of depression in first-degree relatives, a proportion of 12.1 percent was found in the families of primary depressive patients, compared to 5.4 percent in the families of schizophrenic patients and 8.3 percent in the control families. In contrast, the percentage of first-degree relatives with a history of schizophrenia was found to be only 0.8 percent in depressed families, 0.3 percent in control families, and 2.9 percent in schizophrenic families. Thus, the preceding variable of family history is clearly different for primary affective disorder than for schizophrenia or normality.

In comparison to primary depressives, secondary depressives have an increased familial incidence of psychopathology. In particular, alcoholism and, surprisingly, even perhaps affective disorders may be more common in first-degree relatives.[45, 46] This is probably the result of the required preceding psychiatric illness which is likely to be alcoholism, Briquet's disease, drug addiction or antisocial personality.[39, 45, 46] The depressions in family members of secondary depressives may themselves be secondary. There is also an increased incidence of parental divorce in the families of secondary depressives.[45] Winokur[40] presented data on the validity of the primary-secondary dichotomy. He was able to show that the occurrence of a secondary depression during the course of a psychiatric illness was not associated with an increased familial history of depression or alcoholism when the comparison was made with other patients suffering from the same psychiatric illness. This suggested an etiologically important distinction between secondary and primary depression.

The Washington University group has suggested that the validity of the primary-secondary dichotomy is also supported by the absence of a past history of mania in secondary depressives in contrast to its presence, albeit infrequently, in primary depressives.[47]

There appears to be minimal differences in presenting depressive symptomatology between secondary and primary depressives.[45, 47, 48] This might result in part from the requirement of both to meet the Feighner Criteria. Robins et al.[39] showed that changing the required depressive symptomatic criteria to include either strictly somatic or strictly psychological difficulties significantly decreased the number of patients considered depressed. It did not, however, alter the ratio of primary to secondary depressives.

In addition, although the primary psychiatric illness may begin some 10 to 15 years prior to the secondary depression, the average age of onset of secondary depression (33.5 years) is approximately the same as that in primary depression.[39] One early study of hospitalized depressives suggested only one significant depressive symptom difference between the two groups. Seventy-two percent of primary versus 28 percent of secondary depressives felt that their depression represented a change and that they were not their old self at all.[48]

In contrast to the similarity of their presenting depressive symptoms, secondary in comparison to primary depressives more commonly have a multitude of other symptoms, such as phobias, anxiety and bizarre thoughts.[45, 47] This, again, probably reflects their preceding psychiatric illness which continues during and following their depressive episodes.

Biological alterations found during the course of depression tend to validate the primary-secondary distinction. Low urinary MHPG excretion and cortisol escape from feedback suppression by the administration of dexamethasone, characterize some primary depressions, but rarely characterize a secondary depression.[49, 50] Kupfer et al.[51] have also reported that sleep abnormalities differentiate the two groups. Primary depressions have significantly shorter REM latencies (average 38.6 versus 72.3 minutes from the onset of sleep until the first REM period) and increased REM activity.

Assessment of the predictive validity of the primary-secondary dichotomy is lacking. One would suspect that the course of secondary depressives would be influenced by their psychiatric illness. Whether the course of the depressive episode itself is similarly influenced remains undetermined. The clinical treatment given for primary or secondary depression does not seem to differ.[45] More data should be forthcoming in the future.

Familial Subclasses of Primary Depression (Bipolar and Unipolar Depressions)

Most attention has been directed to what appears to be the more etiologically homogeneous disorder, primary depression. As a result, on the basis of family studies (preceding variables), Winokur and Clayton[52] were able to suggest the subdivision of primary depression into bipolar and unipolar types. A bipolar-unipolar division of depression was suggested independently by Perris and Angst.[46]

Unfortunately, presently, there is little unanimity as to how to precisely define a unipolar or bipolar depression. Patient populations studied by different authors using these categories are probably significantly different. Using a familial definition, a bipolar depression could be a primary depressive episode in an individual who has a personal or family history of mania (defined by the Feighner Criteria). As a result, a bipolar depression might occur in an individual who has not had a previous episode of mania. Studies of affectively ill relatives of individuals who have had an episode of mania show that one-half to two-thirds suffer only from depression.[46] Thus, the group of patients who may be considered bipolar by a familial definition but yet have had no personal history of mania is probably at least equal in size to the group of patients with a personal history of mania [some 10 percent of depressives[41]]. A unipolar depression is then a primary depressive disorder in an individual without a personal or family history of mania.

In contrast, the Research Diagnostic Criteria[33] divides major depression into bipolar and unipolar types on the basis of a personal history of mania and independent of the primary and secondary distinction. Finally, others would restrict the term unipolar to those individuals who have had at least three episodes of depressive illness without a history of mania. Since various studies of the validity of the bipolar-unipolar dichotomy have used varying definitions, we will try to clarify the particular definition used under our discussion of the details of each study. It might be noted that clinicians have often equated bipolar illness with "Type 1" depression. However, the proceeding NIMH Collaborative Depression Study has shown that with the use of reliably defined criteria for bipolar illness [a personal history of both mania and a major depressive disorder[36]], there is no simple relationship to clearly defined descriptive subclasses. Bipolar depressions are only sometimes incapacitating or endogenous, may involve retardation or agitation or neither and may even be situational.

The initial derivation and validity of the bipolar-unipolar dichotomy rested upon family studies. Briefly, patients who present with mania have an incidence of mania in first-degree relatives ranging from 3.7 percent to 10.8 percent (depending upon the study) compared to only 0.3 percent in first-degree relatives of patients presenting with depression. There is also a much higher incidence of a positive family history for affective disorders (63 percent versus 36 percent).[41] Studying the families of male patients with a history of mania, Winokur[46] found an apparent absence of ill fathers or father-to-son transmission. There was also a significantly increased risk of affective illness in the female relatives of manic patients. These suggested the possibility that bipolar illness might be transmitted by an X-linked dominant mechanism. This possibility was further supported by genetic studies that suggested linkage of color blindness (on the X-chromosome) with bipolar illness.[53, 54] An intensive study of 14 families with unipolar illness, selected for their ability to demonstrate linkage with the Xga blood group or forms of color blindness, could demonstrate no linkage.[53] It should be noted that other studies of bipolar illness have failed to find an absence of father-to-son transmission or evidence of genetic linkage.[55, 57] Thus, bipolar illness may be heterogenous with an X-linked mechanism of transmission important in an unknown fraction of families. In contrast, in unipolar illness X-linked transmission appears either absent or applicable to a relatively less significant fraction. More data directly comparing the symptoms, age of onset, frequency and length of only depressive episodes, in bipolars vs. unipolars might help clarify the relationship between bipolar and unipolar depression.

There is some evidence that the bipolar-unipolar distinction results in more biologically homogeneous groups. Buchsbaum[58] has suggested differences in the modulation of the visual evoked response to increasing light intensity. Low urinary MHPG excretion[49, 59] and an abnormal response to dexamethasone suppression may be more common in depression in patients with a personal history of mania than in those without.[50, 59]

The bipolar-unipolar dichotomy also seems to have some treatment validity. Lithium seems to be the clear choice for prophylaxis in bipolar patients, whereas antidepressants may be useful in unipolar patients.[60, 61] This seems to be more related to lithium's usefulness prophylactically against mania in bipolar patients rather than to any advantage lithium has in the prevention of depression in bipolars.[60, 62]

Familial Subclasses of Primary Unipolar Depression

Most recently Winokur has suggested, again on the basis of a familial paradigm, that primary unipolar depression may itself be a heterogeneous illness and best subdivided into depression spectrum disease (DSD) and pure depressive disease (PDD). DSD is a primary depression in a person who has a first-degree family member with alcoholism or antisocial personality (and may or may not have a family history of depression) but no family history of mania. In contrast, PDD is a primary depression in a person without a family history of mania, alcoholism, or antisocial personality. This may be a familial (FPDD—first-degree relative with depression), or sporadic type (SDD—no depression in a first-degree relative).

Although the classification is clearly operationally defined, no specific reliability studies have been completed. It is expected that using different methods of assessing family psychiatric illness might affect reliability. Andreasen's et al.[63] study would suggest that reliance solely on a patient-derived family history, by contrast to direct interviews with family members, probably results in considerable underreporting of psychiatric illness and false-negative histories. Thus, reliance solely on a family history taken from a proband or from a hospital chart would probably result in more diagnosed cases of SDD which upon closer family interviewing might be found to be examples of FPDD or DSD.

However, despite using the limited methodology of a chart review, Winokur et al.[29] were able to show that most primary unipolar depressives may be classified using these criteria. Of 216, 17 percent were classifiable as DSD and 50 percent PDD, of which 25 percent were familial and 32 percent sporadic. Only 25 percent had to be left undiagnosed because of such difficulties as inadequate data base in the chart or presence of alcoholism or psychosis in an extended family member. A more complete set of rules could reduce the undiagnosed in the familial subtypes to zero. Although the suggested divisions are based upon familial criteria, it is possible to further validate the classification with respect to independent familial characteristics. For example, both PDD and DSD may have depressed family members. However, in the relatives of PDD patients, depression may occur equally frequently in men and women; whereas, in DSD it is more common in female relatives.[41] In contrast, in DSD families, alcoholism and antisocial personality usually occur in the men.

Genetic studies of DSD have suggested a possible genetic linkage with α-haptoglobin or the third component of complement (C3). There is no evidence of linkage of these markers in PDD. In contrast, in PDD there is a suggested linkage with group-specific complement (Gc). Linkage studies in DSD have also tended to confirm the possibility that in DSD families, alcoholism and antisocial personality in the men may be phenotypic expression of the same genetic predisposition as depression in women.[41] These linkage studies should be considered as only suggestive. Replication would be necessary to regard them as anything but preliminary.

In a chart review of hospitalized depressives, preceding personal history differentiated between the groups. As one might expect, DSD patients had a greater incidence of interpersonal, marital, and sexual difficulties. However, these were not severe enough to label the patient with another psychiatric illness; otherwise the person would have been considered a secondary depressive.[41]

Clinical presentation also differentiated the groups. FPDD patients and DSD patients had an earlier age of onset than SDD patients (34 vs 41).[64] FPDD patients seemed to have an increased number of previous depressive episodes, an average of 1.12 vs 0.66 for the DSD patients (SDD patients lie somewhere in between).[64]

Biological studies of depression have generally not classified their unipolar patients by familial criteria. Thus, little can be conclude about the biological homogeneity of these subclasses. However, Schlesser et al.[65] showed that 23 of 28 (82 percent) FPDD patients escaped dexamethasone suppression whereas only 1 of 23 (4 percent) DSD patients, and 13 of 35 (37 percent) SDD patients did so. The mixed result for the sporadic group is what one might expect for a heterogeneous group, some of whose members on more intensive study might be given a FPDD or DSD diagnosis. Importantly, all three patient groups were equally depressed as measured by the Hamilton Depression Rating Scale. Previous attempts to explain the varying presence of this neuroendocrine versus situational depression had been much less successful. A biological abnormality homogeneous to a family grouping and unrelated to depressive symptomatology may be related to pathogenesis and implies that the group's members may share this common pathogenesis.

A recent evaluation of the dexamethasone suppression test for diagnosis by Arana et al.[66] presented an evaluation of familial subtyping of the affective disorders, unipolar type, using data from 12 separate reports.

There was a highly significant ($p < 10^{-6}$) separation between familial pure depressive disorder at a sensitivity of 46.6 percent, sporadic depressive disorder, sensitivity 38.5 percent and depression spectrum disorder sensitivity, 23.8 percent. Not all studies in the literature support a difference of dexamethasone suppression test findings between the familial subtypes, but the majority do. The major difference is between familial pure depression with a higher degree of nonsuppression and depression spectrum disease with a low degree.

We have suggested in this chapter that depressive classifications are best considered tentative hypotheses of group homogeneity. Only operationally defined criteria allow tests of those hypotheses which can result in continuing modification of the criteria to increase their usefulness and validity. One may note, for example, that results in studies of secondary depressives and DSD patients show that they have much in common. Both secondary depressives and DSD patients often come from families where alcoholism and antisocial personality may be prominent in men. They show quite similar life-styles and share quite similar depressive symptomatology. Both respond normally to dexamethasone suppression. Thus, we might postulate that more homogeneous groups would be produced if DSD patients were considered with secondary depressives. This would produce testable hypotheses.

FPDD patients show an early age of onset, more frequent episodes, and escape from dexamethasone suppression, in contrast to other primary unipolar depressives but quite similar to bipolar depressives. What percentage of these patients on intensive familial testing might be found to have an extended-family member with mania? What kinds of differential efficacy with various treatments might be associated with these subtypes? These are subjects for further study.

Finally, we might return to the concepts of "Type 1" and "Type 2" depression. As noted before the "Type 2" depression has been described in such terms as neurotic-reactive or characterological. To this we may add the concept of depression spectrum disease. Neurotic-reactive depression could be defined as a depression in a person with an unstable personality who has a tendency to react with depression, anxiety, and hostility when confronted with difficult life circumstances. These cases are associated with a family history of alcoholism in a number of studies.[67] In a sense this closes the circle. The "Type 2," or neurotic-reactive depression or characterological depression, or depression spectrum disease patient, is one who has a stormy life-style, attributes his/her illness to a life event, has lifelong personality problems and is more likely to have a family history of alcoholism. The criteria for a neurotic-reactive depression are equally as good as the criteria for an "endogenous" depression. In fact, they may be better in light of the fact that they utilize lifelong characteristics rather than evanescent symptoms.[67] Whether there are other unipolar depressions besides familial pure depressive disease (endogenous) is unknown. It is conceivable that the late onset sporadic depression may constitute a separate group but the data are not good enough to support this at the present time.

In any event, it seems clear now that diagnostic criteria such as the Feighner criteria or the RDC or the DSM-III criteria in fact do define a syndrome but they do not define diseases. There do seem to be at least two separate valid entities within the unipolar depressive group, i.e., neurotic-reactive depression (depression spectrum disease) and endogenous depression (familial pure depressive disease).

REFERENCES

1. Kendell RE: The classification of depression: A review of contemporary confusion. *Br J Psychiatry 1976; 129*: 15-28.
2. Helgason T: The frequency of depressive states in Iceland as compared with the other Scandinivian countries. *Acta Psychiatr Scand (suppl) 1961; 162*: 81-90.
3. Weisman MM, Meyers JK: Affective disorders in a United States urban community: The use of research diagnostic criteria in an epidemiological survey. *Arch Gen Psychiatry 1978; 5*: 1304-111.
4. Tsuang M, Winokur G, Crowe R: Psychiatric disorders among relatives of surgical controls. *J Clin Psycniatry 1984; 45*: 420-422.
5. Robins L, Helzer J, Weissman M, et al: Lifetime prevalence of specific psychiatric disorders in three sites. *Arch Gen Psychiatry; 42*: 949-958.
6. American Psychiatric Association Committee on Nomenclature and Statistics: *Diagnostic and Statistical Manual of Mental Disorders, Third Edition* (DSM-III), Washington DC, American Psychiatric Association, 1980.
7. Robins E, Guze S: Classification of affective disorders: The primary-secondary, the endogenous-reactive, and the neurotic-psychotic concepts, in *Recent Advances in the Psychobiology of the Depressive Illness*. Edited by Williams T, Katz M, Shield J, DHEW Pub., 1972.
8. Zis AP, Goodwin FK: Major affective disorder as recurrent illness: A critical review. *Arch Gen Psychiatry 1979; 6*: 8335-839.
9. Cooper JE, Kendal RE, Gurland BJ et al: Cross-national study of diagnosis of the mental disorders: some results from the first comparative investigation. *Am J Psychiatry 1969; 125*: 21-29.
10. Spitzer RL, Endicott J, Robins E: Research Diagnostic Critiera: rationale and reliability. *Arch Gen Psychiatry 1978; 35*: 773-782.
11. Robins L, Helzer J, Croughan J et al: National Institute of Mental Health Diagnostic Interview Schedule. Its history, characteristics, and validity. *Arch Gen Psychiatry 1981; 38*: 381-389.
12. Andreasen N, Grove W, Shapiro R et al: Reliability of lifetime diagnosis: A multi-center collaboration perspective. *Arch Gen Psychiatry 1981; 38*: 400-405.
13. Greenblatt M: Efficacy of ECT in affective and schizophrenic illness. *Am J Psychiatry 1977; 134*: 1001-1005.

14. Kiloh LG, Ball JRB, Garside RF: Prognostic factors in treatment of depressive states with imipramine. *Br Med J 1962; 1*: 1225-1227.
15. Abrams R, Fink M, Feldstein S: Prediction of clinical response to ECT. *Br J Psychiatry 1973; 112*: 457-460.
16. Simpson GM, Lee JH, Cuculic M et al: Two dosages of imipramine in hospitalized endogenous and neurotic depressives. *Arch Gen Psychiatry 1976; 3*: 1093-1102.
17. Weissman MM, Prusoff BA, DiMascio A et al: The efficacy of drugs and psychotherapy in the treatment of acute depressive episodes. *Am J Psychiatry 1979; 16*: 555-558.
18. Carney MWP, Roth M, Garside RF: The diagnosis of depressive syndromes and the prediction of ECT response. *Br J Psychiatry 1965; 111*: 659-674.
19. Kiloh LG, Andrews G, Neilson M et al: The relationship of the syndromes called endogenous and neurotic depression. *Br J Psychiatry 1972; 121*: 183-196.
20. Kiloh LG, Garside RF: The independence of neurotic depression and endogenous depression. *Br J Psychiatry 1963; 109*: 451-463.
21. Rosenthal SH, Klerman GL: Content and consistency in the endogenous depressive pattern. *Br J Psychiatry 1966; 112*: 471-484.
22. McConaghy N, Joffe AD, Murphy B: The independence of neurotic and endogenous depression. *Br J Psychiatry 1967; 113*: 479-484.
23. Overall JE, Hollister LE, Johnson M et al: Nosology of depression and differential response to drugs. *JAMA; 1966; 195*:946-948.
24. Paykel ES: Classification of depressed patients: A cluster analysis derived grouping. *Br J Psychiatry 1971; 118*: 275-288.
25. Raskin A, Crook TH: The endogenous-neurotic distinction as a predictor of response to antidepressant drugs. *Psychol Med 1976; 6*: 59-70.
26. Kay WK, Garside RF, Roy JR et al: Endogenous and neurotic syndromes of depression: A 5-to-7-year follow-up of 104 cases. *Br J Psychiatry 1969; 115*: 389-399.
27. Paykel ES, Klerman GL, Prusoff BA: Prognosis of depression and the endogenous-neurotic distinction. *Psychol Med 1974; 4*: 57-64.
28. Payel S, Prusoff BA, Klerman GL et al: clinical response to amitriptyline among depressed women. *J Nerv Ment Dis 1973; 156*: 149-165.
29. Winokur G: The types of affective disorder. *J Nerv Ment Dis 1979; 156*: 82-96.
30. Kendell RE, Gourlay J: The clinical distinction between the affective psychoses and schizophrenia. *Br J Psychiatry 1970; 117*: 261-166.
31. Cassidy WL, Flanagan NB, Spellman M et al: Clinical observations in manic-depressive disease: A quantitative study of 100 manic-depressive patients and 50 medically sick controls. *JAMA 1957; 146*: 1535-1546.
32. Feighner J, Robins E, Guze S et al: Diagnostic criteria for use in psychiatric research. *Arch Gen Psychiatry 1972; 26*: 57-63.
33. Spitzer RL, Endicott J: *Schedule for Affective Disorders and Schizophrenia* Biometric Research, New York Psychiatric Institute, New York, 1978.

34. Helzer JE, Clayton PJ, Pambakian R et al: Reliability of psychiatric diagnosis. II. The test-retest reliability of diagnostic classification. *Arch Gen Psychiatry 1977; 34:* 136-140.

35. Robins E, Gentry KA, Munoz RA et al: A contrast of the three more common illnesses with the ten less common in a study and 18-month follow-up of 314 psychiatric emergency room patients. III. Findings at follow-up. *Arch Gen Psychiatry 1977; 34:* 285-290.

36. Spitzer RL, Endicott J, Robins E: Research Diagnostic Criteria: Rationale and reliability. *Arch Gen Psychiatry 1978; 35:* 773-782.

37. Robins E, Genry KA, Munoz RA et al: A contrast of the three more common illnesses with the ten less common in a study of 18-month follow-up of 314 psychiatric emergency room patients. I. Characteristics of the sample and methods of study. *Arch Gen Psychiatry 1977; 34:* 259-265.

38. Murphy GE, Woodruff RA, Herjanic M et al: Validity of the diagnosis of primary affective disorders. A prospective study with a five year follow-up. *Arch Gen Psychiatry 1974; 30:* 751-756.

39. Robins E, Gentry KA, Munoz RA et al: A contrast of the three more common illnesses with the ten less common in a study and 18-month follow-up of 314 psychiatric emergency room patients. II. Characteristics of patients with the three more common illnesses. *Arch Gen Psychiatry 1977; 34:* 269-381.

40. Winokur G: Family history studies. VIII. Secondary depression is alive and well, and... *Dis Nerv Sys 1972; 33:* 94-99.

41. Winokur G: Linkage studies in psychiatry: Unipolar depression, in *Neurogenetics.* Edited by Breakefield, X.O., New York, Elsevier, 1979.

42. Davidson JR, McLeod MN, Kurland AA et al: Antidepressant drug therapy in psychotic depression. *Br J Psychiatry 1977; 131:* 493-496.

43. Glassman AH, Kantor SJ, Shostak M: Depression, delusions, and drug response. *Am J Psychiatry 1975; 132:* 716-719.

44. Quitkin F, Ritkin A, Klein DF: Imipramine response in deluded depressive patients. *Am J Psychiatry 1978; 135:* 806-811.

45. Andreasen NC, Winokur G: Secondary depression: Familial, clinical and research perspectives. *Am J Psychiatry 1979; 136:* 62-66.

46. Winokur G, Cadoret R: Genetic studies in depressive disorders, in *Handbook of Studies on Depression.* Edited by Burrows, G.D., Amsterdam, London, New York, *Excerpta Medica,* 1977.

47. Guze SB, Woodruff RA, Clayton PJ: Secondary affective disorder: A study of 95 cases. *Psychol Med 1971; 1:* 426-428.

48. Woodruff RA, Murphy GE, Herjanic M: The natural history of affective disorders. I. Symptoms of 72 patients at the time of index hospital admission. *J Psychiatr Res 1967; 5:* 255-263.

49. Schildkraut J, Orsulak P, Schatzberg A et al: Toward a biochemical classification of depressive disorders. I. Differences in urinary excretion of MHPG and other catecholamine metabolites in clinically defined subtypes of depression. *Arch Gen Psychiatry 1978; 46:* 1427-1433.

50. Schlesser M, Winokur G, Sherman B: Hypothalamic-pituitary-axis activity in depressive illness: Its relationship to classification. *Arch Gen Psychiatry 1980; 37*: 737-743.
51. Kupfer DJ, Foster FG, Coble P et al: The application of EEG sleep for the differential diagnosis of affective disorders. *Am J Psychiatry 1978; 135*: 69-74.
52. Winokur G, Clayton P: Family history studies. I. Two types of affective disorders separated according to genetic and clinical factors, in *Recent Advances in Biological Psychiatry*. Edited by Wortis, J., New York, Plenum Press, 1967.
53. Mendlewicz J, Fleiss JL: Linkage studies with X-chromosome markers in bipolar (manic depressive) and unipolar (depressive) illness. *Biol Psychiatry 1974; 9*: 261-194.
54. Reich T, Clayton P, Winokur G: Family history studies. V. The genetics of mania. *Am J Psychiatry 1969; 125*: 1358-1369.
55. Goetzl U, Green R, Whybrow P et al: X-linkage revisited: A further family study of manic-depressive illness. *Arch Gen Psychiatry 1974; 31*: 665-672.
56. Johnson CFS, Leeman MM: Analysis of familial factors in bipolar affective illness. *Arch Gen Psychiatry 1977; 34*: 1074-1083.
57. Loranger AW: X-linkage and manic-depressive illness. *Br J Psychiatry 1975; 217*: 482-488.
58. Buchsbaum M, Landau S, Murphy D et al: Average evoked response in bipolar and unipolar affective disorders: Relationship to sex, age of onset and monoamine oxidase. *Biol Psychiatry 1973; 7*: 199-212.
59. Carroll BJ, Curtis GC, Mendels J: Neuroendocrine regulation in depression. II. Discrimination of depressed from nondepressed patients. *Arch Gen Psychiatry 1976; 33*: 1051-1058.
60. David JM: Overview: Maintenance therapy in psychiatry. II. Affective disorders. *Am J Psychiatry 1976; 133*: 1-13.
61. Prien RF, Klett CJ, Caffey EM: Lithium carbonate and imiprame in prevention of affective episodes. *Arch Gen Psychiatry 1973; 29*: 420-425.
62. Mendels J, Ramsey TA, Dyson WL et al: Lithium as an antidepressant. *Arch Gen Psychiatry 1979; 36*: 845-846.
63. Andreasen NC, Endicott J, Spitzer RL et al: The family history method using diagnostic criteria: Reliability and validity. *Arch Gen Psychiatry 1977; 34*: 1229-1235.
64. Winokur G, Behar D, Vanvalkenburg C et al: Is a familial definition of depression both feasible and valid? *J Nerv Ment Dis 1978; 166*: 764-768.
65. Schlesser MA, Winokur G, Sherman BM: Genetic subtypes of unipolar primary depressive illness distinguished by hypothalamic-pituitary-adrenal axis activity. *Lancet 1979; 2*: 739-741.
66. Arana G, Baldessarini R, Ornsteen M: Dexamethasone suppression test for diagnosis and prognosis in psychiatry *Arch Gen Psychiatry 1985; 42*: 1193-1204.
67. Winokur G: The validity of neurotic-reactive depression: New data and reappraisal. *Arch Gen Psychiatry 1985; 22*: 1116-1122.

RECOMMENDED READING

Clayton J: A further look at secondary depression, in *Treatment of Depression: Old Controversies and New Approaches*, Edited by Clayton J, Barrett E, New York, Raven Press, 1983, pp. 169-191.

Lewis D, Winokur G: The familial classification of primary unipolar depression: Biological validation of distinct subtypes. *Compr Psychiatry, 1983; 24*: 495-501.

Winokur G: The development and validity of familial subtypes in primary unipolar depression. *The Pharmacopsychiatria, 1982; 15*: 142-146.

Winokur G: Controversies in depression, or do clinicians know something after all? In *Treatment of Depression: Old Controversies and New Approaches*, Edited by Clayton J, Barrett E, New York, Raven Press, 1983, pp 1533-168.

Chapter 5

BIPOLAR DISORDERS*

Peter E. Stokes, M.D.

INTRODUCTION

During the close of the last century and the early part of the 20th century, the identification of schizophrenia and manic-depressive illness as symptomatic disease entities was the result of Kraepelin's[34] work on classification of mental disturbances of a nonorganic type. His work ultimately united a vast group of affective disorders (the so-called "circular insanities"), uncomplicated mania, "amentias," and even "involutional melancholia" under the general domain of manic-depressive psychoses. Kraepelin's conception of manic-depressive illness was multiaxial, focusing on the identification of signs and symtoms that existed together over time and had relatively similar outcomes. The notion of an endogenous etiology was central to his classification.

The very broad interpretation of manic-depressive illness as presented by Kraepelin has been considerably narrowed over the years, as discussed elsewhere in this text.[80] British and German psychiatrists have contributed to this "narrowing" of the manic-depressive concept.[43, 39, 38] Kleist[32] and Leonhard[38] were probably the first to propose the distinction between bipolar and unipolar affective illnesses in a clear manner.

*This work was supported by a gift in memory of Florence Kan Ho. The author gratefully acknowledges the contribution of Carolyn Sikes and Maxine Greene with editorial and technical assistance in the preparation of this manuscript.

The idea of the polarity of the depressive psychoses as presented by Leonhard was extended by two other independent investigators some years later.[1, 21] These workers gave further validity to the concept of bipolar and unipolar as identifiable subtypes of major recurrent illness embodying depression. Since Leonhard's[38] first suggestion that bipolar and unipolar diseases should be separated, a large amount of data has accumulated showing differences in the genetic aspects of unipolar and bipolar disease, as well as in response to treatment, and in symptomatology and course of illness.

In this chapter, the writer will attempt to integrate his experience with many hundreds of bipolar patients with a general review of the literature.

Bipolar illness is not as common as unipolar illness,[8] but is observed fairly frequently in clinical practice. As a reflection of this, it is estimated that some 3 or 4 percent of the United States population at any given time will be suffering from a major depressive, manic-depressive, or manic episode. The fact that it is a recurrent disease furthers its prominence in clinical psychiatry.

NATURAL HISTORY

The absolute frequency of bipolar disease cannot easily be estimated in the general population since available data come from studies of hospitalized or clinical populations. A significant number of individuals who have the illness may have it at a low level of severity that never reaches the treatment stage or is never recognized and reported. Indirect estimates would suggest that a minor proportion of major depressive illness results from bipolar disease. Thus, the ratio between bipolar and unipolar illness may be as great as 1 to 10,[8] at least in populations that are reported from various centers.

Age of Onset

The literature generally attests to the fact that bipolar disease has its onset at a younger age than unipolar disease. Most investigators find that the mean age of onset of unipolar disease is in the latter portion of the third decade or perhaps the very beginning of the fourth decade,[15, 80] Kraepelin[34] and subsequently Perris,[49] found that the age of onset of bipolar disease initiated by an episode of mania or hypomania was younger than in individuals whose initial illness episode was depression. Loranger and Levine[40] reported that one out of three of their 200 bipolar patients had been hospitalized prior to age 25, and at least one out of five had had episodes of illness during adolescence. However, a few cases have been reported even as young as age 10.[34] In such cases, however, symptomatology and clinical presentation are more diverse than in adult-onset cases, and include

aggressiveness, poor appetite, poor attention span,[10] low frustration tolerance, and explosive anger,[18] as well as typical manic symptoms seen in
adults. A significant number of cases occur in the late teens.[80] The onset of
mania is extremely rare prior to puberty. However, a few cases have been
observed during the pubertal change in the early teens. One study reports
the median age of onset to be 24 years and, while this appears to be young,[2]
the use of the median data is a better estimate than the "average" age usually reported. Data by the same authors suggest there may be a bimodal
distribution. Though data at this time are not clear in this regard, it was
also reported by at least one other group.[51] A unimodal distribution has
been described in other studies.[20, 40] Some of the patients with early age of
onset of bipolar disease (especially when presenting as hypomania or
mania) may be misdiagnosed. These patients show relatively bizarre symptomatology which may be mistaken for acute psychotic reactions of an
undifferentiated type or some aspect of schizophrenic illness. Only in their
later course is it clear that they have bipolar illness. While the prevalence of
overall affective disorders is generally greater for women, there is only a
slight sex preponderance in the same direction for bipolar illness.[35, 54]

Personality

With regard to premorbid personality, there is general agreement in
the literature that bipolar patients as a group do not show clear
characterologic or personality differences during the premorbid or recovered phase as compared to non-bipolar healthy controls.

Suicide

It should be noted that major affective disorder patients have a high
suicide rate, and there is no clear sex bias in this regard.[5] Some studies[45]
have found an even higher suicide rate in bipolar as compared to unipolar
patients. There has also been reported an increased overall mortality from
all causes in bipolar patients.[60, 29] This decreased life expectancy of bipolars
as compared to unipolars was related to suicide and cardiovascular causes
of death.[47]

Illness Episodes: Number, Duration, and Frequency

In the aggregate of reports in the literature, there is generally strong
support for the concept that bipolar patients suffer more episodes of illness
than unipolar patients during their lifetime. This finding cannot be
explained by the earlier age of onset of the bipolar patients. Studies in the
1940s and 1950s[57, 9] confirmed that in a combined total cohort of about 100
bipolar patients, 8 or 9 out of 10 had two or more episodes during prolonged intervals of observation. In fact, Rennie[59] noted that during a period

longed intervals of observation. In fact, Rennie[59] noted that during a period of observation averaging a quarter of a century, most patients had "numerous attacks, with several having 20 or more in their lifetime." In another report completed before widespread use of lithium,[48] it was noted that during a mean observation interval of nearly 20 years, 8 out of 10 patients had 4 or more episodes and almost half of the patients had 7 or more episodes. In a more recent study[4] of 95 bipolar patients observed for an average of 26 years and including both retrospective and prospective phases, it was found that most individuals had more than two episodes. None of these patients received any prophylactic treatment, although acute treatment was applied as indicated. Again more than 8 out of 10 of these patients had 5 or more episodes, two-thirds of them had 7 episodes, and nearly half had 11 or more episodes. Obviously, it is essentially impossible to obtain further data on the natural history of untreated bipolar disease. Even acute treatment may alter the subsequent course.

Angst[4] divided patients into those with core illness whom he termed 'MD,' and those with major depressive episodes and minor hypomanic episodes, 'Dm.' He noted that the most frequent recurrences of illness were in the group with the nuclear form of the illness termed 'MD.' In contrast, the fewer episodes were noted in the 'Dm' pattern which is similar to the current bipolar II subcategory. Rennie[59] noted that 14 of the 66 "cyclothymic" (bipolar) cases had *only* episodes of mania or hypomania. Two of these had only single attacks and one had a persistent manic episode. The general consensus derived from the literature is that the vast majority of patients have multiple episodes. A relatively small percentage (approximately 10 percent of bipolar patients have single episodes when observed over a number of years. Almost all bipolar patients suffer recurrent depressive episodes in addition to episodes of hypomania or mania.[9, 80, 69] The experience of this writer suggests that the occurrence of manic episodes *only* must be extremely rare, at least at present. While patients occasionally first appear to have only hypomanic or manic episodes, close observations over time usually reveal some depressive episodes of a clinically detectable degree, though perhaps minor as compared to their elations.

My experience, however, may be colored by two factors. First, my exposure to bipolar patients has been in a university private practice and in clinics where I have used lithium and other drugs for acute and/or prophylactic preventive treatment. This experience, as noted before, is not necessarily generalizable to the total population of bipolar patients, though there is also no clear reason to assume that it is not. Secondly, I have seen bipolar patients only since the advent of lithium therapy, because my experience began when I started the lithium clinic at the Payne Whitney Clinic, The New York Hospital-Cornell University Medical Center in 1966.

The literature generally supports the concept that both the frequency of episodes and length of each episode increase with increasing age.[4, 59] The data from Angst's 95 bipolar patients indicate that the median first cycle length (time from onset of first episode until onset of second episode) was about four years.[4] This decreased to about two years between the second and third and fourth episodes, and then to a year before the fifth episode. Krapelin's[34] early data showed a similar decrease in cycle length as episode number increased even though he included unipolar as well as bipolar patients. However, he and later Rennie,[59] emphasized the remarkable variability of the cycle recurrence from patient to patient. While most studies indicate that episode frequency increases with time, there is also evidence relating it to the age at which the patient has his first episode. Bipolar disease onset in older individuals is associated with more frequent cycling. There is at least one report which contradicts this general concept. Dunner et al.[22] found no relationship between frequency of episodes and age at onset.

While most early studies suggested that the duration of episodes generally lengthened the longer the patient had the illness, conflicting data were presented by Lundquist,[41] who noted a shortening of later episodes. Other early studies[3, 53] indicated that episode duration remained constant over the course of the illness. Finally, there may be a confounding relationship of illness duration to age as suggested by a number of reports[41, 42, 79] which found that the initial episode was of longer duration in younger patients. This suggests that age may confound the relationship between episode number and duration of subsequent episodes.

An interesting and important point therapeutically and prophylactically is the fact that there is a long interval between the first and second episodes of illness in a large percentage of cases. This four or five year interval, often referred to as the "latency period," has important implications with regard to the initiation of prophylactic therapy in young people who have had their first episode. This will be discussed further in following sections.

Inter-episode Morbidity

More recent evidence suggests that a substantial number of individuals with bipolar illness (perhaps one out of five) have significant inter-episode morbidity. It is uncertain whether this is the result of prior episodes and the coincident disruption of social and interpersonal attachments that occur, or whether it is an integral part of the illness that does not completely resolve with cessation of the acute manic or depressive episode. Some bipolar patients suffer from a chronic dysthymic disorder between acute episodes. It also appears that the presence of other psychiatric disorders (such as alcohol abuse, alcoholism, anxiety disorder, etc.) may be associated with an increased risk of recurrence of a bipolar episode).

Bipolar disorder can, and very often does, cause considerable social and interpersonal disruption. The complications of bipolar illness are evident in increased rates of suicide attempts and completed suicides as well as increased deaths from nonpsychiatric conditions and accidents. Furthermore, there is tremendous impairment of occupational and social functioning, as well as marriage and family relationships. These are not occasional events, but are frequent as well as severe among the bipolar population. While the complications of bipolar disease have been recognized for many years, they have been detailed to a greater extent in recent times. For example, it has been shown[11] that in 30 age- and sex-matched pairs of unipolar and bipolar patients followed over time, there was a significantly ($p<.01$) greater incidence of divorce (57 percent) in the bipolar group as compared to the unipolar group (8 percent). It is further notable that these investigators found that divorce occurred after a manic attack, and *never* prior to a bipolar patient's experiencing at least one episode of mania. There was no difference in the ages at the time of marriage between the bipolar and unipolar patients. Mania and hypomania also are frequently associated with excessive use of alcohol or frank alcohol abuse.[44, 58, 80] These data suggest that the abuse of alcohol may contribute to the disruption of interpersonal ties and poor work performance frequently observed in bipolar patients during inter-episode periods. Alcohol associated with the actual hypomanic or manic episode tends to produce exacerbation of the poor judgment and behavioral impulsivity characteristic of the elated period. That is not to say that some individuals do not have a chronic alcohol abuse problem that persists during inter-episode intervals. Tsuang and colleagues[78] found that in long-term follow-up, the combined assessment of clinical status, marital status, residential and occupational status was good in two-thirds of 100 patients originally admitted for mania, and fair (14 percent) to poor (22 percent) in the remainder. The older literature suggests that in untreated manic-depressive patients there is a gradual deterioration in overall outcome and functioning. Much of this may be because of the disruption of functioning (job, family, and social ties) during the acute episodes of mania and hypomania in particular, as well as those occurring during episodes of depression.

CHARACTER OF EPISODE ONSET AND RELATION TO DEPRESSIVE EPISODES

The onset of episodes of mania, and to a lesser degree depression, in bipolar patients is usually considerably more abrupt than in unipolar patients and typically occurs over a day or a few days. The author has observed extreme instances of this in a few patients who would go from normal or one polarity to the other in a period of hours.

It has also been noted[49] that the character of the index episode of affective illness, i.e., either depression or mania, will set the stage for the most frequent type of affective episodes to recur later. Patients with an initial episode of mania have predominantly manic recurrence, and those with an initial depressive episode are said to have a predominantly depressive course of recurrences. Nearly all patients, however, show both polarities to varying degrees.

Angst[3] has reported that almost three-quarters of the affective *episodes* were in themselves unipolar, i.e., either manic (or hypomanic) or depressive. These were then followed by a symptom-free interval. A minority (10–15 percent) of patients had episodes that were biphasic with either depression preceding mania or vice versa. However, Winokur et al.[80] found that in 100 patients who were hospitalized for a manic episode, about half of them had a preceding depressive episode and the other half developed depression immediately after their manic hospitalization.

DIAGNOSIS: SYMPTOMATOLOGY AND SIGNS

Diagnosis is most secure when based on an appropriately extensive and complete medical/psychiatric history and examination with mental status. Symptoms and signs are elicited as part of this, in response to specific questions and observations.

Dunner et al.[23] stress that the unipolar/bipolar dichotomy depends on the identification of a history or presence of mania or hypomania in the proband or family. It is important to remember that some 10 percent to 15 percent of apparent recurrent unipolar depressives later develop a manic episode, and are reclassified as bipolar, and a positive family history for bipolar illness indicates this probability.

There are many similarities between bipolar and unipolar depressive episodes. However, there are several significant behavioral variables that help differentiate bipolar from unipolar depressive disorder: 1) psychomotor activity; 2) sleep disturbance patterns; 3) somatic complaints; and 4) anger.

Psychomotor activity can often provide the clearest clinical evidence to distinguish between bipolar and unipolar depressed patients. Bipolar depressives are generally much more psychomotorically retarded than are unipolars.[12, 27] Others have confirmed these clinical impressions using 24-hour behavior ratings[6] of telemetric activity recordings over 24-hour periods.[37] Unipolars were more active and agitated than bipolars. Interestingly, as depression diminishes, the bipolar depressives have a remarkable increase and the unipolars show a slight, though distinct decrease in psychomotor agitation and activity. Changes in recorded motor activity are inversely related to sleep patterns during recovery in unipolar and bipolar patients.[37]

Sleep disturbance patterns are also different in most instances of unipolar vs. bipolar depressive episodes. The latter is associated with pronounced *hyper*somnia, presenting as relatively restful lengthened sleep time (more than 8 hours per night), evident in all sleep stages. In contrast, *hypo*somnia which consists of difficulty falling asleep, frequent night and early morning awakening, or combinations of these three is characteristic of individuals with unipolar depressive illness.[21, 26, 36] The patient's report of sleep disturbances, in particular *hyper*somnia, can be verified by reports of close relatives, making this a reliable finding on interview and useful in diagnosis.

Finally, it is evident that unipolar patients have many more somatic complaints during a depressive episode than do bipolar patients who tend to be passive and show less anger towards themselves and others when depressed.[6] Bipolars often show increased food intake and weight gain, while unipolars are typically anorexic and lose weight. Cassidy[16] reported an increased incidence of complaints of disturbances in sleep, mood, and concentration among the manic-depressive group (containing both unipolar and bipolar patients) as compared to a medically sick control population.

Bipolar patients during a manic episode show as the major symptom presentation a remarkable elevation of mood. In states of hypomania this may not always be of an intrusive degree to the observer. The patient appears to be in an unusually good mood. He may be warm and friendly in a way which would be normal in an outgoing person. However, his conversation is often marked by progressively more intimate comments, uninvited familiarity, and even physical contact. When reviewed together, these convey an impression of pathology.

Hypomanic or manic speech is often described as loud, but it is less commonly loud than it is persistent, i.e., pressured. In mild cases, speech is slightly rambling and circumstantial. In the more pronounced clinical instances it can be loosened to such a degree as to be incoherent. It is often interrupted by various jokes, puns, and rhymings (so-called "clanging"). Minor events that occur during the course of a conversation many be highly distracting to the hypomanic individual. For example, a phone ringing may change the entire course of the patient's thinking. Thus, the manic patient shows remarkable distractability in speech and thinking. The patient often does not recognize the hyperactivity, rapid speech, and distractability except in a casual passing manner. Semirational or superficially rational reasons are presented for the hyperactivity.

The manic individual also does not provide the usual cues (verbal and nonverbal) that allow the other member of the dyad to understand when it is his turn to reply. This kind of "overriding" of other individuals is characteristic of the manic state, not only in speech, but in interpersonal relationships in general. Manic patients are unaware and unappreciative of the rights, needs, etc., of other individuals.

While in a manic state, the patient may write to or telephone friends whom he has not seen in many years. He may write to famous people, suggesting that he can help them with their personal affairs. Dress and personal care can change dramatically with the onset of mania. For example, women will often dress in brighter colors and wear more jewelry. Some patients use excessive makeup, occasionally to such a degree that they present a caricature of well-used cosmetic technique. Other patients will put on more than one dress or suit, one on top of the other.

The manic individual is commonly a collector, and will bring home useless items, sometimes just plain trash. His room is usually loaded with papers, periodicals, books, drawings, etc. Lists of things to do are frequent manifestations of the hypomanic and manic state.

Some manic patients I have observed will decide that it is time to clear out their domicile. This will not be done in the manner of typical "spring cleaning," but by literally emptying the contents of the house or apartment. Such patients have presented with a history of removing all their furniture or even destroying it by physical force. The same end comes to personal effects and clothing.

Unwarranted optimism and grandiose thinking are characteristic of mania. Because of the patient's poor judgment, these may lead him into business deals or interpersonal relationships that are fraught with possible damage and humiliation.

Delusions, when present, are usually grandiose in nature, with the patient "imagined" as some central figure in politics, religion, or government. Frequently, delusional misinterpretations are present so that statements on the radio or television, or overheard comments, may be interpreted by the patient as having a special meaning for him. These *ideas of reference* are generally grandiose, with the patient as the central focus. Even when the delusion contains persecutory notions, the individual often feels that these (persecutory) events are occurring because of his central importance to the overall (delusional) situation. When frank hallucinations are present (in severe mania), they tend to be mood-congruent, i.e., they fit in with the expansive attitude and inflated self-esteem of the individual. Thus, manics may hear "God's voice," or the voice of an influential religious or government personality, exhorting them to take on special projects. Typically, the manic patient is convinced that these messages come to him because he is "special," and that he is being guided or protected by various forces.

A remarkable decrease in total sleep time and sleep *need* occurs in manics. This change in sleep is a typical early symptom of the beginning of a hypomanic or manic episode, and is of diagnostic usefulness. Individuals get along on much reduced sleep and do not feel the need for more sleep or any unusual fatigue. Sleep may be reduced to an hour or two per night, and the individual awakens "feeling refreshed" and ready to go, showing the characteristic manifestation of manic activity at that time. Before the advent of adequate antimanic therapy, severely manic patients could push their hyperactivity (and lack of need of sleep) to the point where it was said that some died of exhaustion.

In so-called *mixed-manic states*, the patient shows sadness, hopelessness, and perhaps tears at one moment, stating they have a depressed mood, guilt, and self-depreciation. This will be contrasted with a sudden switch to laughter, joking, punning, rhyming, expansive mood and grandiose ideation with pressured or rapid speech, and inappropriate and unrestrained self-confidence. In this writer's experience, mixed-manic pictures are very common even in patients who are obviously within a hypomanic or manic state. Often these pictures of mixed-mania can be induced by directing the patient to particular subjects that are known from past history to result in sad, guilty, downhearted, hopeless, helpless feelings. Patients who predominantly display anger and irritability generally do *not* present with a mixed picture and tend to be more consistent in their mood. These rapid changes in mixed-mania are of interest as regards the rapid and evanescent induction of depressed mood in manics after administration of physostigmine, and suggest that central cholinergic mechanisms may be labile in such patients.[19]

DIFFERENTIAL DIAGNOSIS

A well-developed episode of manic-depressive illness as in manic or pronounced hypomanic states, is generally not difficult to diagnose. The symptoms described above are rather characteristic, and when seen in concert strongly suggest the diagnosis. While it is true that some schizophrenic individuals can present an agitated, hyperactive, delusional, and grandiose state that can be diagnostically confusing, the majority of them do not have the persistent manic good humor of a rather infectious and involving quality. In a few patients it is difficult in the acute situation to separate those who might have true manic-depressive illness from those with schizophrenia or symptomatic mixtures thereof, and these individuals may end up classified as "schizoaffective." In general, though, as Cassidy[16] has said, the majority of these individuals are relatively easily diagnosed even by nonpsychiatric physicians.

The diagnosis may be more difficult, however, when the patient is seen in a mild state of elation. Here, the key is looking for a significant *change* in the patient's behavior, mood, and affect. Consequently, history obtained from the patient and significant others can be highly useful in ascertaining whether there has been a distinct alteration in that patient's mood, behavior, activity, sleep, and thinking.

Frequently the hypomanic individual will be able to simulate a "normal," nonmanic state convincingly for a period of time. For example, a person may be under consideration for involuntary (two physician certificate) hospitalization for characteristically manic behavior; however, in front of the magistrate, he is able to "pull himself together" and present a very different picture. Here he is convincing, sincere, perhaps somewhat glib, and a bit overconfident, but not more than one might see in many apparently normal personalities. In this situation, he is alert and relatively, if not completely, appropriate. This is maintained for a long enough period that the judge concludes that the patient is not certifiable and he is dismissed.

On the other hand, *the bipolar patient in a state of depression* presents a relatively classic picture of depression similar to that seen in major depressive disorder. Here one sees the dysphoric mood typical of depression, with marked loss of interest and pleasure in all or nearly all activities. This mood state is pervasive. The typical vegetative disturbances of depression are present in terms of sleep, appetite, and psychomotor activity, with quantitative differences from the unipolar depressed patients, as previously discussed. Thus bipolar patients who are depressed tend to show *hyper*somnia and marked psychomotor retardation. There are also decreased concentration, difficulty making decisions, feelings of guilt, and frequently, thoughts about suicide. Delusions may be present and are generally consistent with the prevailing mood of depression. For example, these delusions can involve ideas of worthlessness, poverty, guilt, helplessness, and hopelessness, or less often, somatic function. Frequently, patients may feel that their current state is a retribution or punishment for past (imagined or enlarged) indiscretions and inadequacies. Hallucinations are present only in a small minority of these individuals and usually are not highly elaborated. Typically, the individual will indicate when asked that he has heard his name called in a derogatory way, or that derogatory comments have been made about him or to him. These hallucinations often may be ascertained to actually be examples of delusional misinterpretations of unrelated sounds or conversations.

Because of psychomotor retardation, and difficulties in concentration, memory, and attention, severely depressed individuals can appear demented. In these instances, the pseudo-dementia of depression must be separated from true progressive organic dementia. The characteristic clinical appearance of other depressive symptoms (or recent history of a manic episode) generally helps differentiate pseudo-dementia from true progressive dementia. One must obviously take appropriate steps to exclude organic etiology in the depressive syndrome as in the manic syndrome.

In this latter regard, one should consider the possibility of mania secondary to an organic disorder. This may be especially important in patients who present with a first manic episode in later life, and who have a negative family history for mania. Klerman and Kruthammer[35] reviewed the literature prior to 1978 to identify manic symptoms that were secondary to the ingestion of drugs, or the presence of infection, neoplasm, epilepsy, or metabolic disturbances. Subsequently, Stasiek and Zetin[73] confirmed the prior finding underscoring the necessity of a careful medical and neurological history and examination with appropriate laboratory studies. They stressed, in particular, examination of electrolytes, thyroid function tests, and syphilis serology when evaluating manic patients.

A variety of drugs have been found to be associated with secondary mania. These include bronchodilators (especially sympathomimetics), drugs of abuse (procyclidine and phencyclidine), antidepressants (in perhaps 10 percent of bipolars treated with antidepressants an episode of mania or hypomania may supervene), corticosteroids (which may produce depression, mania, psychosis, or delirium), and tolmetin (a non-steroidal, anti-inflammatory drug). It is also of note that mania may be associated with Cushing's syndrome or thyrotoxicosis, though in the latter case this is rare. These secondary manias generally, though not always, subside spontaneously when the underlying disorder is effectively removed.

TREATMENT OF BIPOLAR DISORDERS

Acute Therapy of Mania and Hypomania

Since the first report of the successful use of lithium in the treatment of acute manic illness by Cade,[14] its use has increased remarkably. Prior to 1965, lithium was rarely used in the United States, since its toxicity had resulted in a number of deaths when used as a sodium chloride substitute by individuals with hypertension. Hospitalization, sedation, and warm continuous tubs were all that were readily available, and these did not provide significant help in most cases.

Cade's original 1949 report[14] was derived from his observation that guinea pigs that had received lithium salts in other studies that he was pursuing became very lethargic and quiet. He made the large inductive leap from this observation to conclude that a trial of lithium salts in manic patients might be useful. The results were extremely encouraging in patients with mania, but not in those with schizophrenia. Noack and Trautner[46] subsequently replicated these findings. The first controlled *clinical* trials of lithium in manic-depressive illness were carried out in Denmark by Schou and colleagues.[65] However, lithium use in the acute treatment of mania was not universally accepted. In fact, in 1969 an editorial in the *Lancet*[68] concluded that no convincing evidence had been mustered to demonstrate that lithium was effective as an anti-manic substance. As late as 1970, a review article[71] appearing in the *American Journal of Psychiatry* reiterated their conclusion regarding lithium's unproven antimanic effect. Subsequently, further controlled studies in this country clearly demonstrated that lithium was a useful drug in the treatment of mania.[52, 56, 72, 76]

The widespread use of neuroleptic drugs in the late 1950s and early 1960s provided for the first time a significant degree of control of behavior in the manic or hypomanic episode, and these drugs continue to be used. However, as outlined by Davis et al.,[19] neuroleptic treatment alone seems to be less effective than lithium treatment alone in aborting manic or hypomanic attacks. Most studies reviewed by Davis show that while manic behavior is controlled by the use of neuroleptic drugs, the hyperactivity, rapid and pressured speech, and elated mood are somewhat subdued. It is almost as if the patients have been covered by a very heavy blanket or rug. If one sits and talks with these patients, it becomes obvious that the quality of their thinking, mood, and activity is not basically changed — it is merely slowed down. If one could lift up the corner of this blanket or rug of neuroleptic treatment, then underneath it one could still observe the grandiosity, hyperactivity, elation, and flight of ideas that continue to exist. Lithium, on the other hand, seems to abort the entire manic or hypomanic process in the vast majority of people who receive it over an adequate period of time in adequate dosages. Consequently, lithium remains the mainstay of treatment for acute hypomanic and manic episodes.[28]

Not only is lithium effective in diminishing or aborting the manic episode, but double-blind studies have shown that the manic picture reemerges upon substitution of a placebo for active lithium medication.[76] In addition, there is a clear dose-response relationship.[74] In fact, it appears that with increasing dosage and plasma levels (and thus increasingly tissue levels) essentially all (or nearly all) manic patients could be controlled if toxic side effects did not supervene as the dose was increased.[76] This is not to say that in the practical application of lithium treatment, all patients are efficaciously treated with lithium alone. However, in the aggregate it appears that some 80 percent or more of patients with an acute mania can be adequately returned to a euthymic state with lithium. A certain percentage of these individuals, perhaps 30 percent to 50 percent, will initially require coincident neuroleptic drugs in association with the lithium in order to control manic behavior prior to the gradual onset of the anti-manic lithium effect. The advantage of the neuroleptic drugs is their rapid onset of action as regards control of behavior. Neuroleptics can be considered almost as a chemical "straitjacket," which prevent manic patients from harming themselves through self-destructive acts until the lithium begins to work.

The administration of a particular neuroleptic should be according to the usual principles of their use, since no one drug has been found to be superior. Usual choices are high-potency (e.g., haloperidol) or sedative (e.g., chlorpromazine) drugs. Few adverse reactions have been observed with these drugs in combination with lithium, despite an earlier report.[17]

In most cases, lithium therapy can be started immediately in hypomanic and manic patients. Before instituting lithium therapy, it is important to carry out a complete psychiatric and medical history and examination. This should include identification of other diseases (especially organic diseases) that may be of significance with regard to the patient's psychiatric state. In particular, secondary causes of mania should be ruled out. A careful neurological examination and history will help eliminate the possibility of organic CNS causes of hypomania.[7] When appropriate, other neurological studies should be done, including electroencephalography, skull X rays, and computerized axial tomography scanning or magnetic resonance imaging.

Lithium can have an inhibitory effect on normal thyroid functioning and is essentially 100 percent absorbed from the gastrointestinal tract, and 100 percent excreted via the renal route. Thus, prior to initiating lithium therapy, blood tests should be obtained to assess renal and thyroid function. This should include a serum creatinine and BUN, and a thyroid profile (TSH, T4, and T3 plasma levels). During this initial period, sedative neuroleptic drugs may be used to control behavior, if indicated.

Lithium is then administered with a usual estimated starting dose of about .5 to .6 mEq/kg body weight in individuals who are not remarkably obese or underweight.[75] The total dosage is generally distributed over the day so that not more than 600 to 900 mg is given in any one dose. A period of five to seven days is required to reach a full steady-state at any one dose. It is appropriate to examine lithium levels every other day. The patient should be examined daily until he is euthymic as regards mental status, change in symptom profile, and neurological status, and emergence of significant side effects or toxic effects. The patient's clinical state is often best assessed by mental status examination and brief interview, done twice a day initially. Remarkable alterations in diurnal behavior may be noted, and their change may be a useful aid in adjusting ongoing treatment. During the manic episode it may be necessary to gradually increase the lithium dosage in a stepwise manner (usually not more often than every three days) to as high as .8 or even 1.0 mEq/kg body weight in a 24-hour period. In a 70 kg man, this would be equivalent to approximately 2400 mg of lithium carbonate per day.

It is also necessary to observe the ingestion of tablets, since sometimes manic patients will "cheek" medication and dispose of it afterwards. In this regard, it may be useful to employ liquid preparations of lithium, such as lithium citrate (Raul Pharmaceuticals), or other commercial liquid preparations. Obviously, one would not want to administer lithium intravenously due to its high toxicity. The writer has had considerable experience with intramuscular parenteral lithium (unpublished) for investigational purposes, and it is possible that this could be used in cases where it is strongly indicated. However, the vast majority of patients who need lithium therapy will take it orally.

Some hypomanic/manic episodes show significant amelioration within the first few days after the institution of lithium treatment, but the majority will require a week or two weeks to show significant response. Many are well-controlled by the end of the second week, although some persist for three weeks or longer before complete control is obtained. Some subsidence of manic behavior should start within five to seven days in most instances, or one should consider further increase in dosage.

The most common side effect in lithium therapy is the onset of a usually mild, fine intentional tremor. It can become more coarse as the lithium level increases, or as other toxic neurological signs supervene. It is necessary to be alert for the development of myoclonic jerks. These are most commonly seen in the upper extremities, especially during motions such as combing the hair or lifting a beverage from the table to the lips. Patients complain of spilling liquids and having sudden disruption of their writing by the occurrence of these jerking motions. While occasional or mild myoclonic jerks may be tolerated without progressing to further neurological toxicity, these are warning signs to go slowly and to assess plasma lithium levels regularly (daily) and repeatedly until one is certain from repeat clinical evaluations and blood lithium levels that progressive toxicity is not occurring. Mental status and neurological examination must also be assessed daily. In particular, one wants to avoid the onset of frank neurological lithium toxicity, usually presenting as an organic mental syndrome as evidenced by mild obtundation, slurred speech, mild ataxia, and increasing somnolence.

The usual effective therapeutic range of plasma lithium level in the treatment of acute mania is not far removed from the beginning level of the toxic dose (i.e., a narrow margin of safety). Some patients will begin to show a therapeutic response at lithium levels that are somewhat higher, perhaps up to 1.1 to 1.3 mEq/liter. A few patients will require even higher plasma levels.[33] It is generally recognized that one begins to enter the toxic plasma range at about 1.5 mEq/liter. However, some patients become toxic as somewhat lower levels and others will tolerate levels considerably above 1.5 mEq/liter without gross toxic symptoms. Consequently, the dose must be individualized and the patient must be observed clinically, with repeat plasma levels drawn at least every other day while adjusting lithium dosage during the acute manic episode.

In addition, studies of renal function should be obtained. Particular attention must be paid to assure that urinary output is adequate and that the BUN and creatinine are not increasing. Occasionally a brief awake EEG study will be helpful in ascertaining whether or not the patient is beginning to show toxic encephalopathy as seen by the presence of generalized slow waves and spiking.

It is generally best to start with a lithium dosage of .5 or .6 mEq/kg body weight and to observe patient tolerance, monitor plasma lithium levels, and watch for the appearance of toxic or unwanted side effects. It would be unusual to see such side effects at this dosage level. Increments in dosage can then be made as indicated after the first few days of treatment. It must be kept in mind that steady-state levels are relatively slow to

develop (five to seven days after each change in dosage level) and consequently the cumulative effects of prior increments in dosage must always
be considered during the subsequent days. This factor becomes particularly important when individuals are showing minimal neurological signs
(other than fine intention tremor) of lithium toxicity. It is the writer's experience that even if one stops all lithium at the time of detection of mild but
evident lithium-induced neurological toxicity (beyond tremor), the syndrome will probably progress significantly over the next 24 to 48 hours.
This is in part because lithium enters the CNS slowly, so plasma lithium
increments *precede* the peak lithium levels in the CNS. As mania subsides,
lithium excretion decreases and lower lithium doses should be used and
plasma levels monitored to prevent excess lithium levels and toxicity.

PROPHYLACTIC TREATMENT OF BIPOLAR DISORDER

Numerous controlled studies, as well as two decades of uncontrolled
clinical experience with lithium prophylaxis, strongly support the conclusion that bipolar patients on lithium have a significant decrease in frequency and severity of manic and depressive episodes. Eight studies
involving 761 bipolar and unipolar patients (the majority of whom were
bipolar), in which all trials were double-blind, showed there was a significant difference between relapse rate on lithium as compared to placebo.[30]
These trials support the efficacy of lithium as a prophylactic, not only in
bipolar cases, but also in unipolar cases. Three more recent American
studies which also involved large numbers of patients (unipolar and
bipolar), strongly supported the conclusion that lithium is effective in mini-
mizing or eliminating recurrent manic episodes. However, they found that
it is only moderately effective in preventing bipolar depressive
recurrences.[55] In comparison to the early studies cited above, the study by
Prien[55] did not find lithium particularly effective for preventive treatment of
recurrent unipolar depression. All three of the American studies found
that lithium carbonate was most effective in patients whose index case was
manic. The combination of lithium carbonate and imipramine showed no
advantage over lithium alone in prophylactic treatment of bipolar
patients.[55] In these studies, more than half of the imipramine-treated bipolars had a recurrent manic episode during the treatment, whereas only 11
percent in one study and 26 percent in the other study of those bipolars
receiving lithium carbonate had recurrent manic episodes. Imipramine was
not recommended for long-term prophylaxis of bipolar disorders.

One must always maintain a small but possibly significant caveat in
these intensive control studies. They were all conducted in university settings where patients were chosen for involvement in the study after having
been screened through a variety of treatment processes, not all of which
were under the control of the researchers undertaking the study. These

patients, therefore, may not be totally comparable to the pool of manic-depressive patients outside of this study group.

Who Should Be Treated Prophylactically?

This is a difficult decision in many cases. It is particularly difficult in patients who are having their initial episode. Here, if the episode has not been severe or prolonged and has not caused too many disruptions in the personal life of the individual, one might choose to slowly stop lithium treatments three or four months after the acute manic episode has subsided. One could argue for maintenance for a period of up to six months in order to cover the potential ongoing prolonged manic episode in a particular individual. If one elects to discontinue lithium after that initial and only episode, it probably should be discontinued gradually. In this manner, the individual can be observed by significant others and by the physician for possible resurgence of hypomanic symptoms. If a relapse occurs, treatment is certainly indicated for at least six more months. Then a gradual trial of cessation of lithium might again be attempted, though in some cases prophylaxis should begin. All individuals should see a physician periodically (perhaps two or three times a year) for the first one to two years after discontinuing lithium. This is because of the high relapse rate observed in double-blind discontinuation studies of lithium prophylaxis.[76] If the patient relapses a second time, this is a direct indication for prophylactic treatment.

Individuals with recurrent episodes of mania generally fall into two categories. Those who have had recurrent episodes very close together (3 in two years), and required acute treatment, are clearly in need of prophylactic treatment. Also, those who have had severe episodes requiring hospitalization or episodes that have been very disruptive to their personal lives, should in general be urged to consider prophylactic treatment more rapidly than others. The second group, about whom it is somewhat more difficult to make decisions, are those who have less frequent but recurrent episodes. For example, an individual may have had an initial episode five years ago, been treated with lithium acutely, and then been euthymic until the current episode. Here again, judgment must be used. After two episodes requiring treatment (certainly after three), even though they may have had relatively long separation (five years), most patients are willing to and should accept prophylactic treatment because of the disruption of their lives that has ensued from the disease.

Patients whose episodes are mainly depressive should be less strongly urged to start lithium prophylaxis than those who have mainly manic or severe manic episodes. One must also consider the question of whether or not the patient has tolerated lithium well during the past acute treatment. Most individuals do tolerate lithium treatment with only minor side effects, such as mild intention tremor, and perhaps the occasional tendency to looseness of the bowels. Others have essentially immediate side effects, though some complain of cognitive impairment, which in some instances can be demonstrated, at least in laboratory situations.[76]

In considering the question of initiating prophylactic treatment, it is important to include in the discussion those who are close to the patient. Their accounts can help the physician evaluate how the person tolerated the acute lithium treatment, especially *after* they were euthymic. It is also important to tell the patient that it may take one to two years to determine the efficacy of lithium prophylaxis. Patients initially on prophylaxis may continue to have some fluctuation in mood of a pathological degree (both depressive and hypomanic). Some will respond to increases in lithium dosage, others seem to gradually improve with time on the initial dosage. However, it is common to see that patients are more stable in mood several years after being on lithium than they were after one year.

Initially it is reasonable to recommend a plasma lithium level on a once-a-month basis for one to two years after the patient has been maintained on the same dosage without showing significant mood fluctuations. Thereafter, blood levels may be checked once every two months, and continued indefinitely, if the patient is stable in mood. Even though patients are on a stable lithium dose, significant fluctuations in plasma lithium level can occur. Episodes of prolonged heat with associated exercise, increased sweating, and decreased fluid intake may cause an increase in plasma lithium level and sometimes an increase in side effects, or the onset of toxic effects. One particularly insidious process occurs when patients gradually become more depressed, but do not see their physician, and continue to take their lithium while decreasing their food intake. This results in a much decreased sodium load to the kidneys and a higher percentage of reabsorption of lithium from the glomerular filtrate, causing increased lithium retention and gradually increasing plasma and tissue lithium levels, sometimes to the point of overt lithium toxicity and gross organic brain syndrome. This may also occur when individuals have prolonged gastrointestinal upset insufficient to prevent them from taking their lithium, but sufficient to prevent them from ingesting much food.

Lithium prophylactic dosage can be begun in the same way as was described under acute lithium treatment, assuming normal renal function. Adjustments up or down can be made as needed according to clinical response, and the dosage increment is proportional to the current plasma level *vs.* that desired. Alternatively, one can estimate an increase of approximately 0.22 mEq lithium per l of plasma with each additional tablet or capsule of 300 mg lithium carbonate. Most patients can be maintained prophylactically on plasma lithium levels between 0/5 and 0/9 mEq lithium. Older patients (>60) often require and tolerate only the lower ranges of these levels, or even less.

The laboratory tests to be obtained before starting lithium carbonate consist of BUN, creatinine (blood), 24-hour creatinine clearance (urine), thyroid function tests (T3, T4, and TSH), and electrolytes. A routine urinalysis is generally obtained as a baseline. It is important to recall that creatinine clearance decreases with age, especially above 50 or 60. Consequently, lithium dosage in older individuals might have to be adjusted downward from the recommended starting dose of 0.5 mEq/kg body weight for prophylactic treatment. This also can occur (as observed in a number of patients followed for 20 or more years on prophylactic treatment) as they proceed into the sixth or seventh decade of life. Naturally, before starting prophylactic lithium treatment in individuals who have not been on lithium, it is important to obtain a complete psychiatric and medical history and examinations, as well as the laboratory tests discussed in acute treatment. Thyroid function tests, BUN, and creatinine (blood and urine) should be repeated once every year, as well as when clinically indicated. The onset of lithium induced hypothyroidism is usually first signaled by an increase in TSH levels (>5.0 mu/ml) or the appearance of thyromegaly (goiter) on physical examination. Few if any classical symptoms of hypothyroidism supervene at this time of "compensated" hypothyroidism characterized by normal plasma T3 and T4 levels at the expense of excessive TSH and thyroid enlargement.

Unfortunately, although lithium is an extremely useful drug, it is not a panacea for all individuals who are on prophylactic or acute anti-manic or antidepressant treatment. About 20 percent of individuals will not do particularly well on lithium prophylactic treatment. Either they develop intolerable side effects, or they continue to have significant mood fluctuations. Some of these individuals are clearly not responsive to lithium even in large doses carefully monitored. These individuals, as well as those who have rapid mood cycling either before institution of lithium prophylaxis or after the initiation of this treatment, should be considered for additive treatment, with carbamazepine (see section on *carbamazepine*).

When Should Lithium Prophylaxis Be Discontinued?

Some patients raise the question periodically of stopping their lithium treatment. These patients usually fall into two groups. One is the group of patients that really does not (for various reasons) want to take chronic medications. These individuals are frequently poor compliers with various aspects of the prophylactic treatment, including lithium ingestion, office visits, etc. They are frequently individuals who seem to enjoy their episodes of hypomania. These are difficult individuals to treat, although this can sometimes be approached by the addition of carbamazepine as a secondary drug. The other group contains individuals who have been compliant and who have done well on lithium prophylaxis over a period of years. If they have been euthymic for a period of five years, and have had only one prior episode, then one would *consider* discontinuing their lithium treatment gradually. This step should be taken with the same caveat as described above in regard to gradual discontinuation *after* detailed discussion of the risks with the patient's significant others. Schou's[65] data showed that the majority of patients removed from lithium prophylaxis relapse within one to two years with the same intensity (or greater) as the prior episode, even if they have been continuously on lithium therapy for many years. The writer's experience strongly concurs with this.

EFFECT OF LITHIUM ON DEPRESSIVE STATES

Lithium is clearly effective in decreasing the severity and frequency of depressive episodes in bipolar patients who are prophylactically treated. Of greater controversy is the potential efficacy of lithium as an antidepressant in unipolar depressed patients. A small number of controlled studies suggest that lithium has a measurable antidepressant effect in about 40 percent of recurrent unipolar depressives.[30] Endogenous depression with a cyclic pattern seems to be controlled significantly by lithium as well as by tricyclic antidepressants, both of which are superior to placebo.[24]

Use of Lithium in Schizoaffective and Schizophreniform Illness

In general, lithium is less effective in atypical bipolars, and in schizoaffectives and schizophrenics.[70, 31] There may be some instances, however, of patients with schizophreniform illness where the administration of lithium will result in improved affective symptomatology.[25] Occasional patients with schizophrenia and marked mood fluctuations may be helped by lithium in addition to the typical antipsychotic treatment.

In general, lithium and neuroleptics appear to have different modes of action,[65, 81, 70, 31] and neuroleptics should probably be the first choice for treatment in schizoaffective illness and schizophrenia, provided the diagnostic is clear.

Pharmacology

Many mechanisms have been proposed but no single known mechanism adequately explains the therapeutic effect of lithium in affective disorder. Lithium has effects on a variety of neurotransmitters. It is thought to increase the metabolism of catecholamines and perhaps inhibit the release of these transmitters at the synapse while simultaneously decreasing postsynaptic receptor sensitivity. Lithium may also have an effect on dopaminergic systems since it can block supersensitivity of dopamine neurons observed after neuroleptic withdrawal.[13] Lithium tends to increase monoamine oxidase (MAO) activity which could further augment intraneuronal turnover of catecholamines. It has also been postulated that lithium may have an effect on cell membrane permeability because of its distribution both intra- and extracellularly in body water.

Pharmacokinetics — Pharmacodynamics

Lithium is rapidly and completely absorbed from the gastrointestinal tract in a matter of hours. Peak plasma levels occur within 1 to 2 hours after the dose. Lithium is distributed in total body water and enters the intracellular compartment more slowly, especially in fat-containing tissues such as the nervous system. Lithium is almost 100% excreted via the renal route, indicating the need for kidney function tests. The lithium clearance diminishes when sodium load is remarkably restricted. While lithium has been measured in plasma red cells, saliva, and CSF, the analysis of plasma lithium levels is the most clinically useful measure for ascertaining adequacy of dose and absence of potential toxicity.[33]

Lithium-Induced Effects on Thyroid and Kidneys

Lithium also has significant effects on thyroid function in some patients, inhibiting all forms of thyroid hormone secretion including T4, T3, and organic iodine. Consequently circulating thyroid hormone levels are lowered and an increased release of thyroid stimulating hormone (TSH) occurs. In most instances the thyroid gland can respond to the increased endogenous TSH adequately and this may lead to normalization of thyroid hormone output and in some instances to production of a goiter, even though slight. In borderline cases an augmented TSH response to administered TRH can bolster the diagnosis of sub-clinical hypothyroidism. There is some suggestion in the literature that patients who develop hypothyroidism *vs.* those that do not, show a differential response of their bipolar illness to lithium therapy. Lithium-induced hypothyroidism is completely treatable by administration of thyroid hormone, usually given as thyroxin (T4) in full replacement doses.

Lithium has a clear effect on renal function in that it reversibly inhibits normal activity of antidiuretic hormone (vasopressin), as first reported in a clinical study by Trautner.[77] This polyuria is rarely severe (>3-4 liters per day) but in perhaps 10 to 30% of patients a distinct increase in urine volume can be observed after lithium treatment is started. There is some dose relationship but, once present, even lowering the dose does not usually reverse the polyuria/polydypsia. The mechanism of this effect on renal tubular function is due to a lithium-induced refractoriness of the renal tubular to the action of antidiuretic hormone.

Lithium Toxicity

The treatment of lithium toxicity that has progressed to the presence of significant neurological disturbance, beginning organic mental syndrome or renal insufficiency (increased BUN or creatinine) must be pursued in a hospital and is beyond the scope of this chapter.

CARBAMAZEPINE AND OTHER ANTICONVULSIVE DRUGS

The potential use of carbamazepine in manic-depressive illness was first suggested by Okuma et al.[48] Since that time a number of workers in Japan and in the United States in particular have been pursuing the potential usefulness of carbamazepine in manic depressive illness. There is now a reasonably large experience in both open and controlled studies reported in the literature. Approximately two-thirds of nearly 100 patients have been reported to show improvement during carbamazepine prophylaxis. It appears that patients who are lithium-refractory and have severe, rapid-cycling persistent episodes are those most likely to benefit from carbamazepine. This drug is now being increasingly used in Europe and in the United States, in research centers, or on a physician-discretion basis in private practice. The data available at present suggest that the drug is useful both as an *acute* anti-manic drug and as a *prophylactic* preparation in individuals who are lithium nonresponsive. Both the frequency and severity of manic episodes have been reduced in patients treated with carbamazepine. Preliminary data suggest that patients who show acute antidepressant response to one night's sleep deprivation were also better responders to carbamazepine in a manner similar to those who have rapid and severe episode cycles. A distinct dose-dependent therapeutic response has been noted with carbamazepine and most individuals who are going to respond have responded to a total dose of 1600 mgs a day or less. Patients generally require at least 800 mg of carbamazepine per day for adequate response. The side effect profile of carbamazepine differs significantly from that of lithium. A 15 percent incidence of generalized pruritic rash requiring discontinuation of therapy has been reported in patients receiving this drug. Occasional minor elevations of liver function tests occur in perhaps 5 or 10 percent of patients. A serious side effect of carbamazepine, fortunately rare, is suppression of the bone marrow, which is estimated to occur in only perhaps 1 in 20,000 or more individuals. Some decrease in peripheral blood white count with administration of carbamazepine is common and this decrease is not dose-related.

Carbamazepine can produce drowsiness and some patients complain of nausea and gastrointestinal upset especially if the dose is increased too fast. Larger doses can produce dizziness, ataxia, and organic mental syndrome. It has also been found to reduce total T4, and free T4 and T3 levels in patients without substantial changes in thyroid-stimulating hormone levels. It is also of interest that preliminary data suggest that patients who show the best response (anti-manic or antidepressant) to carbamazepine also show the larger decreases in T4 during carbamazepine treatment.[61]

At present no clear understanding of the anti-manic or antidepressant effects of carbamazepine are available, although it does seem to affect noradrenergic mechanisms and GABAnergic turnover in the brain and these may be important to its anticonvulsant effects. It is of interest that carbamazepine has a structure similar to imipramine (IMI) and that some of its effects on biogenic amines are similar to those described for IMI. Currently, carbamazepine has also been noted to have effects on neuroendocrine function.[64]

Studies using other anticonvulsant medications are less encouraging but are continuing. The data on diphenylhydantoin suggest that this is not useful in psychiatric patients in spite of some older and uncontrolled data suggesting that it might be a useful antidepressant compound.

Valproic acid has been used as an anticonvulsant agent for some years. Investigations with this drug are less extensive than with carbamazepine but it does appear that it has some therapeutic effect on acute manias and as a prophylactic in a large percentage of those individuals who do not respond well to lithium and who have severe and/or rapid cycles.[57] Thus, it might be appropriate for use in the same individuals who respond best to carbamazepine. The usual dosage of valproic acid is from 900 to 1800 mgs a day. The mechanism of action of valproic acid in affective disorders is not clear at this time. The commonest side effects seem to be gastrointestinal upset and decreased appetite, especially early in the treatment or in association with rapid increases in dosage. The potentiation of neuroleptic effects during combined treatment with valproic acid requires a decrease in neuroleptic dosage.

NEUROENDOCRINE STUDIES OF MANIC PATIENTS

Neurocendocrine studies in manic patients are much less extensive than in depressed patients. Baseline cortisol levels have less frequently been found to be elevated in mania than in depression, though Platman and Fieve[52] reported mean plasma levels of 23 ug/dl for both manic and depressed patients during the second week of their hospitalization.

The HYPAC (hypothalamic-pituitary-adrenocortical) axis has been the most extensively studied neuroendocrine axis in bipolar patients, especially in depressive episodes where hyperactivity of this system is common, though in general, of less severe degree than that observed in unipolars.[75] However, moderately large numbers of manic patients have been studied as regards this axis.

Other neuroendocrine studies in manic patients are few in number though growth hormone (GH) response to insulin hypoglycemia and to L-dopa have been reported to be blunted in manics. In contrast, GH release after apomorphine was equivalent to normals in bipolar patients whether depressed or manic and was normal after L-tryptophan. Blunted TSH response to TRH, fairly common in depressives, may be similar in manics. All the above studies are on very few patients and some methodological problems exist.

Numerous other biological studies involving multiple neurotransmitter systems and various neuroendocrine axes are currently being pursued. As yet, these studies are still on relatively small numbers of patients, and though some have withstood the test of multiple replications, their clinical utility, as far as sensitivity and specificity go, leaves much to be desired. Moreover, many of these studies involve only measurements of one isolated neurotransmitter or endocrine system. Future studies must focus on multiple hormone and neurotransmitter systems, and the interaction between these systems.

CONCLUDING REMARKS

It is clear from the data presented in this chapter that the use of the bipolar-unipolar dichotomy, as developed over the past 30 or 40 years, has clinical utility in its current form. The natural history, clinical presentation, and treatment of bipolar illness as compared to unipolar disease are sufficiently distinct and crisp. Furthermore, these differences in clinical presentation of episode and response to therapy suggest possible differences in etiology and certainly in pathogenesis, though current studies of the biology of bipolar versus unipolar disease find many similarities. These combined with the shared clinical aspects, especially depression, of the two polar disorders also suggest common basic mechanisms for the underlying disorder.

A diagnosis of bipolar disorder remains a clinical one at the present time, and its identity can generally be obtained or at least labeled as highly suspect by even the non-psychiatric physician. But, it must be borne in mind that some cases are so subtle as to escape clinical detection, at least for prolonged periods, under the guise of a situational aberration or a facet of personality.

Treatment also requires numerous and ongoing clinical judgments aided and guided by constant and ongoing biological measurements. In particular, measurements of plasma lithium levels are important, not only to ensure adequate therapy and help avoid toxicity, but because, as we have shown, lower plasma lithium levels often precede the onset of mania. Adequate thyroid and renal function studies are an absolute requirement.

Informing and counseling the patient and his family when (if ever) to discontinue lithium (or carbamazepine) therapy, and how (if ever) to undertake pregnancy with its genetic implications and its hazards either off (relapse) or on (teratogenicity) lithium will then challenge the knowledge, ingenuity, and clinical and medical acumen of any well-trained physician. In fact, this illness has so many medical and psychological concomitants as to provide the physician with a rare opportunity to acquire further medical knowledge regarding behavior and its biological substrate. Past collaboration between those afflicted with this illness, their friends, and the physician involved in its identification, treatment, and study, have provided us with our current generally effective therapies. This continuing clinical collaboration bears the future promise of much improved treatment and prevention, and an enlarged understanding of the illness and its related unipolar cousin, both recognized as having high morbidity and mortality.

REFERENCES

1. Angst J: Zur Atiologie und Nosologie endogener depressiver psychosen (Toward an etiology and nosology of the endogenous depressive psychoses). *Monographier aus dem Gesamtgebiete der Neurologie and Psychiatrie*, Berlin: Springer, 1966.
2. Angst J: The course of affective disorders. II. Typology of bipolar manic-depressive illness. *Archiva Psychiatrica Nervenkrankheit 1978; 226*, 65-73.
3. Angst J: Course of affective disorders. In van Praag et al (Eds.), *Handbook of Biological Psychiatry* (pp. 225-242). New York; Marcel Dekker, 1981.
4. Angst J, Felder W, and Frey R: The course of unipolar and bipolar affective disorders. In Schou M and Stromgren E (Eds.), *Origin, Prevention and Treatment of Affective Disorders* New York, Academic Press, 1979, pp. 215-226.
5. Angst J, and Perris C: Zur Noslogie endogener Depressionen. Vergleich der Ergebnisse zweier Unterschungen. *Archiv Fur Psychiatric 1968; 210*: 373-386.
6. Beigel A, and Murphy DL: Differences in clinical characteristics accompanying depression. *Arch Gen Psychiatry 1971; 24*: 215-220.
7. Binder RL, and Dickman WA: Psychiatric manifestations of neurosyphillis in middle-aged patients. *Am J Psychiatry 1980; 137*: 741-742.
8. Boyd JH, Weissman MM: Epidemiology. In Paykel ES (Ed.), *Handbook of Affective Disorders*. New York, The Guilford Press, 1981.
9. Bratfos D, Haug JD: The course of manic-depressive psychosis. *Acta Psychiatrica Scandinavica 1981; 44*: 89-112.
10. *British Medical Journal:* Manic states in affective disorders of childhood and adolescence. *1979; 1*: 214-215. (supplement).
11. Brodie HKH, Leff MJ: Bipolar depression: A comparative study of patient characteristics. *Am J Psychiatry 1971; 127*: 1086-1090.

12. Bunney WE Jr, Murphy DL: The behavioral switch process and psychopathology. In Mendels J (Ed.) *Biological Psychiatry* (pp. 345-368). New York, Wiley-Interscience, 1973.

13. Bunney WE Jr, Pert A, Rosenblatt J, Pert CB, Gallaper D: Mode of action of lithium: Some biological considerations. *Arch Gen Psychiatry 1979; 36:* 898-901.

14. Cade JF: Lithium salts in the treatment of psychiatric excitment. *Med J Australia 1949; 2:* 349-352.

15. Carlson GA, Kotin JL, Davenport YB, et al.: Follow-up of 53 bipolar manic-depressive patients. *Br J Psychiatry 1974; 124:* 134-139.

16. Cassidy WL, Flanagan MB, Spellman M, and Cohen ME: Clinical observations in manic-depressive disease. *J Am Med Assoc 1957; 64:* 1535-1546.

17. Cohen SN, Cohen JL: Pharmacotherapeutics: Review and commentary. *Ped Clin North Am 1974; 21:* 95-101.

18. Coll PG, Bland R: Manic depressive illness in adolescence and childhood: Review and case report. *Can J Psychiatry 1979; 24:* 255-263.

19. Davis JM: Overview: Maintenance therapy in psychiatry. II. Affective disorders. *Am J Psychiatry 1976; 133:* 1-13.

20. D'Elia G, Perris C: Suicide attempts in bipolar and unipolar depressed psychotics. *Archivs fur Psychiatrie and Nervenkrankheiten 1969; 212:* 339-356.

21. Detre T, Himmelhoch J, Swartzburg M, Anderson CM, Byke R, Kupfer DJ: Hypersomnia and manic-depressive disease. *Am J Psychiatry 1972; 128:* 1303-1305.

22. Dunner DL, Gershon ES, Goodwin FK: Hertiable factors in the severity of affective illness. *Biol Psychiatry 1976; 11:* 31-42.

23. Dunner DL, Murphy D, Stallone F et al.: Episode frequency prior to lithium treatment in bipolar manic-depressive patients. *Comp Psychiatry 1979; 22:* 511-515.

24. Fieve RR, Dunner DL, Kumbarachi T, et al.: Lithium carbonate in affective disorders. IV. A double-blind study of prophylaxis in unipolar recurrent depression. *Arch Gen Psychiatry 1975; 32:* 1541-1544.

25. Garver DL, Hirschowitz J, Fleishmann R, Djuric PE: Lithium response and psychoses: A double-blind, placebo-controlled study. *Psychiatry Res 1984; 12:* 57-68.

26. Hartman E: Longitudinal studies of sleep and dream patterns in manic-depressive patients. *Arch Gen Psychiatry 1968; 33:* 1187-1188.

27. Himmelhoch JM, Coble P, Kupfer DJ, InJenito J: Agitated psychotic depression associated with severe hypomanic episodes: A rare syndrome. *Am J Psychiatry 1976; 133:* 765-771.

28. Holliston LE: *Clinical Pharmacology of Psychotherapeutic Drugs,* chapter 6. New York, Churchill Livingstone, 1983.

29. Jaaskelainen JPK: The course and prognosis of unipolar and bipolar depression. *Psychiatria Fennica Monograph 1976;* (no. 7).

30. Johnson G: Antidepressant effect of lithium. *Compr Psychiatry 1974; 15:* 43-47.

31. Johnson G, Gershon S, Hekimian, LJ: Controlled evaluation of lithium and chlorpromazine in the treatment of manic states: An interim report. *Compr Psychiatry 1968; 9:* 563-573.

32. Kleist K: Die Gliederung der neuropsychischen Erkankungen (The classification of the neuropsychological illnesses). *Monatsschrift fur Psychiatric and Neurologic 1953; 125:* 526-554.

33. Kocsis JH, Lieberman KW, Stokes PE, Van der Noot G: Case report. High dose lithium therapy. *Biol Psychiatry 1978; 13:* 759-762.

34. Kraepelin E: *Manic-Depressive Insanity and Paranoia.* Edinburgh, E.S. Livingstone, 1921.

35. Krauthammer C, Klerman GL: Secondary mania: Manic syndromes associated with antecedent physical illness or drugs. *Arch Gen Psychiatry 1978; 35:* 1333-1339.

36. Kupfer DJ, Himmelhock JM, Swartzburg M, Anderson L, Byke R, Detre TP: Hypersomnia in manic-depressive disease. *Dis Nerv Syst 1972; 33:* 720-724.

37. Kupfer DJ, Weiss BL, Foster G, Detre TP, Delgado J, McPortalnd R: Psychomotor activity in affective states. *Arch Gen Psychiatry 1974; 30:* 765-768.

38. Leonhard K: *Aufteilung der endogenen Psychosen* (Subtypes of endogenous psychoses) (ed. 104). Berlin, Akademnic, 1957-1971.

39. Lewis A: A clinical survey of depressive states. *J Ment Sci 1934; ce, 80:* 277-378.

40. Loranger AW, Levine PM: Age at onset of affective bipolar illness. *Arch Gen Psychiatry 1978; 35:* 1345-1348.

41. Lundquist G: Prognosis and course in manic-depressive psychoses. A follow-up study of 319 first admissions. *Acta Psychiatr Neur 1975; 35:* (Suppl. 1), 1-96.

42. MacDonald JB: (1918). Prognosis in manic-depressive insanity. *J Nerv Ment Dis 1918; 17:* 20-30.

43. Mapother E: Manic-depressive psychosis. *Br Med J 1926; 2:* 872-879.

44. Mayfield DC, Coleman LL: Alcohol use and affective disorder. *Dis Nerv Syst 1968; 29:* 467-474.

45. Mayo JA: (1970). Psychosocial profiles of patients on lithium treatment. *Int Pharmacopsychiatry 1970; 5:* 190-202.

46. Noack CH, Trautner EM: Lithium treatment of manic psychosis. *Med J Australia 1951; 2:* 219.

47. Norton B, Whalley LJ: Mortality of a lithium treated population. *Br J Psychiatry 1984; 145:* 277-282.

48. Okuma T, Kishimoto A, Inoue K, et al.: Anti-manic and prophylactic effects of carbamazepine on manic depressive psychosis: A preliminary report. *Folia Psychiatrica Neurol Jap 1973; 27:* 281-297.

49. Perris C: (1966). Study of bipolar (manic-depressive) and unipolar recurrent depressive psychoses. *Acta Psychiatr Scand 1966; 42:* (Suppl. 194), 68-82.

50. Perris C: (1968). The course of depressive psychoses. *Acta Psychiatr Scand 1968; 44:* 238-248.

51. Petterson V: (1977), Manic-depressive illness. *Acta Psychiatr Scand 1977; 69:* 1-93.

52. Platman SR: A comparison of lithium carbonate and chlorpromazine in mania. *Am J Psychiatry 1970; 127:* 351-353.

53. Pollock HM: Recurrence of attacks in manic-depressive psychoses. *Am J Psychiatry 1931; 11:* 568-573.

54. Pope HG, Lipinski JF Jr: Diagnosis in schizophrenia and manic-depresive illness: A reassessment of the specificity of 'schizophrenic' symptoms in the light of current research. *Arch Gen Psychiatry 1978; 35:* 811-828.
55. Prien RF, Levine J: Research and methodological issues for evaluating the therapeutic effectiveness of antidepressant drugs. *Psychopharm Bull 1984; 20:* 250-257.
56. Prien RF, Point P, Caffey EM, et al.: Comparison of lithium carbonate and chlorpromazine in the treatment of mania. *Arch Gen Psychiatry 1972; 26:* 146-153.
57. Puzynski S, Rode A, Bidzinski A, Mrozek S, Zaluska M: Failure to correlate urinary MHPG with clinical response to amytriptyline. *Psychopharm Bull 1984; 20:* 171-173.
58. Reich LH, Davies RK, Himmelhoch JM: Excessive alcohol use in manic-depressive illness. *Am J Psychiatry 1974; 131:* 83-89.
59. Rennie TAC: Prognosis in manic-depressive psychosis. *Am J Psychiatry 1942; 98:* 801-814.
60. Rorsman B: Dodligheter bland psykiatriska patienter. *Svenska Lakartidningen 1968; 65:* 149-156.
61. Roy-Byrne PP, Joffe RT, Uhde TW, Post RM: Carbamazapine and thyroid function in affectively ill patients. Clinical and theoretical implications. *Arch Gen Psychiatry 1984; 41:* 1150-1153.
62. Rorsman B: Dodligheter bland psykiatriska patienter. *Svenska Lakartidninger 1968; 65:* 149-156.
63. Roy-Byrne PP, Joffe RT, Uhde TW, Post RM: Carbamazapine and thyroid function in affectively ill patients. Clinical and theoretical implications. *Arch Gen Psychiatry 1984; 41:* 1150-1153.
64. Rubinow DR, Post RM, Gold PW, Uhde TW: Neuroendocrine and peptide effects of carbamazepine: Clinical and mechanistic implications. *Psychoparm Bull 1984; 20:* 590-594.
65. Schou M: Lithium in psychiatric therapy and prophylaxis. *Psychiatr Res 1968; 6,* 67-95.
66. Schou M, Baastrup PC, Grof P et al: Pharmacological and clinical problems of lithium prophylaxis. *Br Psychiatry 1970; 116:* 615-619.
67. Schou M, Juel-Nielson N, Stromgren E, Boldby H: The treatment of manic psychoses by administration of lithium salts. *J Neuro Neurosurg Psychiatry 1954; 17:* 250-260.
68. Serry M: Lithium retention and response. *Lancet 1969; 1:* 1267-1268.
69. Shobe FO Brien P: Long-term prognosis in manic-depressive illness. *Arch Gen Psychiatry 1971 24:* 334-337.
70. Shopsin B, Gershon S: Plasma cortisol response to dexamethasone suppression in depressed and control patients. *Arch Gen Psychiatry 1971; 24:* 320-326.
71. Shull WK, Sapira JD: *Am J Psychiatry 1970; 127:* 218-222.
72. Spring G, Schweid D, Gray C, et al: A double-blind comparison of lithium and chlorpromazine in the treatment of manic states. *Am J Psychiatry 1970; 126:* 1306-1310.
73. Stasiek C, Zetin M: Organic manic disorders. *Psychosomatics 1985; 26:* 394-402.

74. Stokes PE, Kocsis JH, Arcuni DJ: Relationship of lithium chloride dose to treatment response in acute mania. *Arch Gen Psychiatry 1976; 33:* 1081-1084.

75. Stokes PE, Stoll PM, Koslow SH, Maas JW, Davis JM, Swann AL, Robins E: Pretreatment DST and hypothalamic-pituitary-adrenocortical function in depressed patients and comparison groups. *Arch Gen Psychiatry 1984; 41:* 257-267.

76. Stokes PE, Stoll PM, Shamoian CA, Patton MJ: Efficacy of lithium as acute treatment of manic depressive illness. *Lancet 1971; I:* 1319-1325.

77. Trautner EM, Morns R, Noack CH, Gershon S: The excretion and retention of ingested lithium and its effects on the ionic balance of man. *Med J Australia 1955; 42:* 280.

78. Tsuang MT, Woolson RF, Flemming JA: Long term outcome of major psychoses. *Arch Gen Psychiatry 1979; 36:* 1295-1304.

79. Wertham TJ: A group of benign and chronic psychoses: Prolonged manic excitements. *Am J Psychiatry 1929; 9:* 17-78.

80. Winokur G, Clayton PJ, Reich T: *Manic Depressive Illness* (Chapter 7). St. Louis, C.V. Mosby, 1969.

81. Wittrig J, Anthony EJ, Lucarno HE: An asking technique for endogenous lithium in human brain and other biological tissues. *Dis Nerv Sys 1970; 31:* 408-411.

Chapter 6

CHRONIC DEPRESSION*

James H. Kocsis, M.D.
Allen J. Frances, M.D.

> The depressive temperament is characterized by a permanent gloomy
> emotional stress in all experiences of life.

Emil Kraepelin, 1921

Among the several categories that were introduced by the *Diagnostic and Statistical Manual of Mental Disorders, Third Edition, (DSM-III),*[1] Dysthymic Disorder (DD) was one of the most controversial, probably because it represented quite a radical departure from previous nosological convention. In DSM-II,[2] chronic states of depression had been subsumed under cyclothymic personality and were classified within the personality disorders section. DSM-III relabeled chronic depressions with the new designation DD and classified them within the affective disorders section. These changes were in the spirit of recent trends in American psychiatry to broaden the inclusiveness of affective disorders categorization, and reflected the notion that mild, chronic forms of depression are on a spectrum with the more florid and acute variants of affective disorder. The creation of the DD category and the choice of its specific diagnostic criteria were based on very limited empirical evidence. However, the new system has the virtue of attempting to distinguish chronic "subsyndromal" from

*Supported in part by grant MH 37103 from the National Institute of Mental Health. Parts of this material appeared in Kocsis JH, Frances AF: DSM-III Dysthymic Disorder: A commentary. *American Journal of Psychiatry.*

acute major depression and has stimulated research to determine descriptive characteristics and treatment response of chronic depression. There is accumulating evidence that chronic depressions are commonly encountered in both clinical and community samples and that they deserve increased diagnostic recognition and research attention. In this chapter we will review the history of the classification of chronic depression and summarize the empirical data that have accumulated on such states. We will offer suggestions for possible future clinical and research directions.

HISTORICAL BACKGROUND

In his classic volume, *Manic-Depressive Insanity and Paranoia*,[4] Kraepelin gave a rich clinical description of patients with chronic depressive tendencies. He termed this condition "depressive temperament" and considered it to be "a rudiment" of fully developed manic-depressive insanity. As evidence for this spectrum concept, Kraepelin pointed out similarities in the clinical characteristics between depressive temperament and episodic full-blown depression, with the latter presenting with acute symptoms that were more severe and flamboyant. He also reported that 12.1 percent of his manic-depressive cases had had a premorbid depressive temperament. The view that mild chronic states of depression represented attenuated variants of typical manic-depressive illness continued as a theme in classical European psychiatry. Kretschmer[5] described dysthymics and cyclothymics as "in the first place in the prepsychotic personalities of the psychopaths (meaning manic-depressives) themselves and then in their nearest blood-relatives." Slater and Roth[6] suggested that the true association between dysthymia and manic-depressive illness could be seen by the occasional dramatic improvement of dysthymics when they received convulsive therapies.

Schneider, on the other hand,[8] viewed "depressive psychopathy" as having a constitutional etiology, by which he meant a combination of hereditary, neonatal and early environmental influences. He pointed out a tendency for "psychopathies" (personality disorders) to fluctuate with the life cycle and to be modifiable with psychotherapy. He saw them as on a spectrum with normal personality traits and types and not related to the affective disorders. Until recently, American psychiatry has been under the predominant influence of psychodynamic schools of thought which have viewed chronic depressive and dysthymic states as character neuroses with an etiology embedded in early environmental influences. "Oral dependency," "object hunger," "superego pathology," and "pathological narcissism" have been described as character developments in such individuals, which have left them vulnerable to intermittent or chronic bouts of depressed mood and associated dysthymic symptoms.[8-10] In the second edition of the Diagnostic and Statistical Manual of the APA (DSM-II, 1968), manic depression and other affective states were classified as psychotic disorders, whereas chronic and mild forms of depression were considered to belong to the neuroses and personality disorders. Thus chronic dysthymic patients might have been diagnosed as having a subtype of cyclothymic or asthenic personality disorder or as neurasthenic neuroses. These diagnostic concepts apparently derived from the confluence of American psychoanalytic thinking and the influence of the International Classification of Diseases, which bore the stamp of Schneiderian thought.

In a subsequent classification of depressive states proposed by Schildkraut and Klein in 1975, *chronic characterological depression* was a term used to designate chronic depressions which were "an inherent part of a lifelong personality problem." These authors stated that a specific type of character pathology was not essential for the diagnosis, but that a particular constellation of symptoms and mood reactivity to environmental or interpersonal events was characteristic. They also described pharmacologic responsiveness in some subtypes of chronic charactologic depression. The same authors also delineated a second variant of chronic depression. *Demoralization* was a term used to refer to patients who showed persistent dysphoria in the face of chronic unresolved realistic life problems, including physical or mental illness.[11]

More recent systems for classifying psychiatric disorders have utilized descriptive (so-called "atheoretical") terms for classification of the chronic, "minor" depressions, e.g., *intermittent depression* in the Research Diagnostic Criteria of Spitzer et al.[12] and *dysthymic disorder* in DSM-III. However, it has been previously pointed out by one of us (AJF), that inclusion of these disorders in the affective disorder sections of these classifications does represent an important theoretical shift and a reconceptualization of their etiology, pathogenesis and treatment.[13]

Implicit in this brief review of the history of the classification of chronic depression and dysthymic states is that they have been viewed variously as inherited temperaments, acquired character tendencies, attenuated variants of classical manic-depressive disorders, or complications of other mental disorders, physical illnesses, or environmental stressors. We will now review the literature relevant to putative associations between chronic states of depression and other conditions, including studies of epidemiology, clinical characteristics, relationship to personality diagnosis, and response to antidepressant medication.

EPIDEMIOLOGY OF CHRONIC DEPRESSION IN COMMUNITY SAMPLES

Two recently conducted epidemiologic studies have investigated the prevalence of chronic depression in randomly selected community population samples. Weissman and Myers[17] found a 4.5 percent prevalence of intermittent depression (Research Diagnostic Criteria[12] term for chronic depression) in a study conducted in New Haven. The vast majority of these cases of intermittent depression (87.5 percent) were found to have one or more additional RDC diagnoses, although these were not subclassified into affective vs. nonaffective categories.

The NIMH Epidemiologic Catchment Area study recently reported on prevalences of various DSM-III diagnostic categories based on interviews conducted in random population samples in three cities.[18] The rates for dysthymia ranged from 2.1 to 3.8 percent. Prevalences of dysthymia in women ranged from 2.9 to 5.4 percent and were significantly greater than in men in two of the three sites. The ECA study methodology did not report data relevant to possible further subtyping of chronic depression, e.g., double-depression, chronic major depression, secondary chronic depression.

PREVALENCE OF CHRONIC DEPRESSION IN PSYCHIATRIC SAMPLES

Chronic depression apprears to be extemely common among patients presenting to psychiatric settings for treatment of depression. Rates of 25 percent and 36 percent have been reported in two studies which evaluated patients retrospectively using Research Diagnostic Criteria.[15, 19] Prevalences of chronicity have also been reported in prospective long-term outcome studies conducted in depressed patients.[18] Working with a predominantly inpatient sample, Keller et al.[16] reported that 21 percent of patients with major depression were not recovered after two years. When the subgroup with "double depression" was examined separately after two years, 97 percent had recovered from the superimposed MD but only 39 percent had additionally recovered from the chronic intermittent or minor depression.

Weissman and Klerman[20] have reviewed eleven follow-up studies of patients treated for depression and found that an average 15 to 20 percent of patients were reported to experience incomplete recovery and to show some intermittent fluctuating and chronic symptoms, often for years. Recent prospective studies conducted with both inpatients and outpatients support such figures.[10, 21, 22]

One recent investigation which was conducted in children referred for treatment of mood disorders by Kovacs et al.[23, 24] reported that 43 percent of 65 subjects had a history of DD (which is defined as a duration of at least one year in children). Furthermore, among children who initially presented with a DD, recovery was found to be slow, with a median time of three and a half years and 70 percent of these patients experienced at least one period of MD over a seven-year period. These studies are especially interesting because they provide validation for reports from adult samples of the onset of states of chronic depression in childhood.[26, 27]

It appears that DD may be commonly associated with other medical and psychiatric diagnoses as well, although interpretation of such associations may be complicated by problems of definitional overlap. Thus, anger or irritability, insomnia and anxiety may constitute criteria for a variety of medical or psychiatric diagnoses, including DD. For example, a study by Tan et al.[25] reported a 45 percent prevalence of DD in a sample of patients presenting for treatment of chronic insomnia.

ONSET AND COURSE OF CHRONIC DEPRESSION

RDC and DSM-III represent an important departure from other recent nosological systems, and a return to a Kraepelinian notion that the course of a psychiatric disorder can be of considerable clinical importance in classification. Thus these newer diagnostic classifications provide separate categories for chronic and acute states of depression (Intermittent Depression in RDC and DD in DSM-III). Because of their insidious onset, most clinical and research diagnostic evaluations of the course of chronic depression are based solely on patient self-reports. If the course of a disorder is to be thought of as important in a clinical classification, it follows that such self-reported data must be reasonably reliable and valid. We and other clinical researchers who have been interested in chronic depression, have wondered whether depressed patients report of chronicity represented perceptual biases in line with other known negative cognitive distortions occurring in depression.[42] We currently have a study in progress to test the reliability of patient self-reports of chronic depressive symptoms by repeating structured diagnostic interviews when patients have recovered from their depression. Furthermore, we are attempting to assess the validity of the history given by patients by interviewing close relatives or significant others. Two recent studies conducted elsewhere have investigated aspects of patients' self-reports of the longitudinal course of depression and the results have supported their reliability and validity. Kandel and Davies[40] interviewed adolescents at age 15–16 and then performed a follow-up after nine years. They found that depressive symptoms were relatively stable over time and that individuals reporting symptoms as adolescents were the most likely to do so as young adults. Furthermore, depression scores in adolescence were the most powerful predictors in a multiple regression for depressive symptoms in young adulthood. Billings and Moos[41] in a study of acute and chronic unipolar, depressed patients and their spouses, compared their agreement about reports of family environment, stressors and resources with a control group of nondepressed husbands and wives. There was as much agreement in the experimental as in the control group. They concluded that negative perceptual bias on the part of the patient did not appear to account for the excess in negative events in the depressed families.

Although much work remains to resolve questions about the value of self-reported historical data in chronic depression, the available research results lend credence to the possibility of reliable and valid information.

Three investigations known to us have evaluated the course of illness in samples of patients having chronic depression. Keller et al.[16] reported on 80 patients with "double depression." Fifty-five percent of these reported chronic depression before the first episode of MD while 41 percent reported onset with a clear-cut episode of MD. Forty-eight percent of patients reported onset before the age of 26, and 50 percent said they had been depressed for more than 10 years. The relationship between the age of onset and the type of onset was not specified in this report.

Akiskal et al.[27] studied 137 outpatients with chronic depressions. They subdivided these into three groups according to the course of illness. One group (28 percent) consisted of patients who developed chronic depression following clear-cut episodes of MD in middle or late life. A second group (36 percent) developed chronic depressions as complications of other psychiatric or chronic medical illness. The third group of so-called "characterologic depressions" consisted of "intermittent subsyndromal depression" with insidious onset in childhood or adolescence, and constituted 37 percent of the overall sample. Approximately one-third of this latter group were said to have had periods of major depression superimposed on their chronic-mild depression, a complication which was associated with a more favorable response to antidepressant medication.[14]

We have recently examined the course of illness in a sample of 39 outpatients who presented with complaints of chronic depression for longer than two years.[26] The type of onset was rated using the Newcastle scale,[28] and a structured clinical interview was administered to determine age of onset, duration of illness, and course of illness. Ninety-seven of these patients reported an insidious or indistinct onset of their depressive symptoms, 65 percent reported onset prior to age 25 and 50 percent stated that their depression had been present for more than 10 years. Because 95 percent of our subjects fulfilled DSM-III criteria for MD plus DD upon their admission to the study, we undertook systematic evaluations of the duration of individual depressive symptoms in a subsample of our study cohort. We found that 60 percent of those examined reported sufficient persistent symptomatology to meet the criteria for MD continuously for longer than two years, while the other 40 percent reported substantial increments in their symptoms within the past six months, i.e., "double-depression."

In summary, while questions remain about the reliability and validity of self-report history of chronic depressives, there is preliminary research indicating that the information given is indeed meaningful. The small numbers of studies conducted thus far which have examined the course of chronic depressive states suggest that one group exists with insidious onset of symptoms at an early age, followed by a course which may progress to intermittent or chronic depression of major proportion. A second, less well-studied group, may develop an acute period of MD at a later age, followed by an intermittent or chronic depressive course. More investigation will be necessary to clarify the course of illness in these proposed groups and much work remains to determine nosologic and treatment implications of these variations.

RELATIONSHIPS BETWEEN DYSTHYMIC DISORDERS AND PERSONALITY DISORDERS

Clinicians have long been curious about the nature of the relationship between chronic depression and character pathology,[4, 5, 7, 10, 11] Because personality disorders (PD's) and DD's appear to have a similar course and often share common symptoms or traits, it is intuitively reasonable to study the association between these two types of disorders. DSM-III has suggested that DD may be particularly associated with certain PD's (borderline, histrionic and dependent). Similarly, Akiskal et al.[14] have reported an excess of "unstable" personality traits (passive-dependent, histrionic, antisocial, or borderline) in characterologic depressions unresponsive to antidepressant medications. Therefore it is of interest to investigate whether certain PD's predispose to DD, whether PD's in general are more prevalent in DD than in other Axis I disorders and whether presence of a PD affects response of DD to treatment with medication.

Empirical studies pertinent to these questions have been few and have been hampered by methodologic problems. For example, most have been conducted as cross-sectional assessments and have failed to take into account the effects of depressed mood itself, which may confound the PD evaluations, as has been shown repeatedly for studies of PD in acute depression.[29, 30]

Several studies have been done which have demonstrated lower recovery rates from acute depression and development of chronicity when a coexistent PD or "high neuroticism" are present in depressed patients.[31, 33] The hypotheses that preexisting PD's might lead to the development of chronicity in patients who later enter an episode of MD awaits prospective longitudinal investigation for support.

We have also searched for empirical data relevant to the questions of whether PD's exist more commonly in DD patients than in other Axis I conditions, and whether certain PD's are specifically associated with DD's. Our own study has now evaluated 54 outpatients with chronic depression most of whom have fulfilled criteria for both DD and MD. Forty-one percent were diagnosed by treating clinicians as having an Axis II disorder, the most common being dependent (13 percent) and atypical, mixed (11 percent). Some of these data have been previously reported.[26] Koenigsberg et al.[34] reported a 34 percent rate of Axis II diagnoses in a sample of 68 DD patients, the most common types also being atypical, mixed (16 percent) and dependent (8 percent).

The question of whether Axis II diagnoses are more prevalent in chronic depression than in acute MD and other Axis I disorders has been addressed by studies which have provided rates of Axis II conditions in other disorders. For example, Koenigsberg et al.[34] reported rates of Axis II diagnoses of 23 percent for MD, 50 percent for panic disorders and 24 percent for generalized anxiety disorders. In two studies involving inpatients with MD, rates of Axis II diagnosis have been reported as 50 percent and 34 percent.[32, 33] We have also reported a 40 percent rate of Axis II diagnoses in a small simple of outpatients with acute MD.[26]

The currently available data are sparse but suggest that inpatients and outpatients having MD are diagnosed as having an Axis II disorder at approximately the same rate as is true for patients who have DD or "double depression," and that dependent and mixed PDs may be the most commonly diagnosed PDs in states of chronic depression. While considerable evidence suggests that presence of a PD impairs response to antidepressant medication among patients who are acutely depressed,[31, 33] to date no systematic data pertinent to this important clinical question have been reported in samples of DD or other chronic depressive conditions.

MEDICATION TREATMENT OF CHRONIC DEPRESSION

Although several reports have appeared suggesting responsiveness of some patients who have chronic forms of depression to various antidepressant medications, diagnostic criteria for entry into these studies have varied considerably, and only our own recent study was performed using a placebo control group.[35]

Ward et al.[36] treated 15 patients, all of whom met RDC for MDD with a duration longer than a year, for four weeks with doxepin. Eleven of these patients had been depressed for more than two years and three for more than ten years. Eighty percent showed marked or moderate improvement on the Clinical Global Impression Scale during this open trial of treatment.

In a double-blind comparison of amitriptyline, perphenazine and a combination for treatment of RDC major depression, Rounsaville et al.[19] included 23 patients who had an additional diagnosis of intermittent depression. Although no figures were given for responses to the three treatments separately, the overall response for patients with MD plus intermittent depression was comparable to the response of those with MD alone.

Akiskal et al.[14] treated 50 "characterologic depressives"; outpatients with chronic, mild, insidious onset depressions openly with a variety of antidepressant medications prescribed nonblindly in a clinical setting.

Forty percent were considered to be favorable responders by "global clinical criteria."

Paykel et al.[37] administered phenelzine, amitriptyline, and placebo in a randomized, double-blind trial to 131 depressed outpatients. Fifty-six of these patients were considered to have "neurotic dysphoria," a diagnosis derived from concepts of Klein and Davis[38] meaning "a pattern of long-standing or recurrent depression, without clear differentiation of episodes from personality and with evidence suggesting depressive personality." While both active drugs were superior to a placebo in the overall sample, there was a tendency for the subgroup of patients with characterologic depression to respond more poorly to phenelzine than to amitriptyline or placebo, which differed little in effectiveness from each other.

Preliminary results of our own ongoing double-blind, placebo controlled trial of imipramine for chronic depression have recently been reported.[35] Thirty patients, all of whom fulfilled DSM-III criteria for both DD and MD, completed the six-week treatment. Favorable response was defined as a final 24-item HAM-D total score of less than seven plus reduction of dysthymic symptoms such that the patient no longer met criteria for DD by the end of treatment. Fifty-five percent of imipramine-treated and 14 percent of placebo-treated subjects achieved this level of recovery (p.05 by FET). These results were particularly interesting in view of the fact that the vast majority of subjects had had previous extensive psychotherapy. Furthermore, in a "naturalistic" follow-up study of 80 "double-depressives," Keller et al.[16] reported that only 6 percent of these patients recovered from both MD + DD after eight weeks. This rate is similar to the 14 percent response rate in our chronically depressed sample following eight weeks of placebo. Thus active antidepressant medication prescribed in adequate doses for adequate duration appears to offer short-term relief for both acute and chronic symptoms of depression in a substantial percentage of cases.

In conclusion, this review of treatment studies suggests that a substantial proportion of chronically depressed patients may be helped by antidepressant medications. It seems likely that future treatment studies for chronic depression can be enhanced by discriminating subgroups according to the interaction of severity and course, thus separating chronic "minor," chronic "major," or "double" (acute major superimposed upon chronic mild) depressive subtypes. Other factors which may have an important bearing on response to antidepressant medications, such as presence of various types of Axis II diagnoses, will also have to be evaluated in these subgroups of chronic depressions. From a practical standpoint we would suggest initiating therapy with a standard tricyclic antidepressant such as imipramine, using standard doses. If an adequate trial of a TCA is not beneficial, other considerations would include use of a MAO inhibitor, lithium or a "second generation" antidepressant. It would be important for such treatment trials to be adequate and to be discontinued if unsuccessful. An unexplored area of interest would also be use of certain brief psychotherapeutic techniques such as cognitive-behavioral or interpersonal therapy.[3, 43]

PROBLEMS WITH DSM-III DYSTHYMIC DISORDER

Table 1 lists the DSM-III diagnostic criteria for DD. The accompanying DSM-III text describing DD suggests that such patients often present with an associated personality disorder; an onset that usually begins in early adult life but may occur in childhood or adolescence or in later adult life (in some cases following a major depression); an onset that is usually insidious and a course that is chronic, and; predisposing factors that include chronic physical disorder, chronic psychosocial stressors, and other Axis I or Axis II disorders that do "not completely remit and merge imperceptibly into this condition." The diagnostic criteria for DD require: at least two years duration of depressed or dysphoric mood (one year for children and adolescents); persistent symptoms with no more than a few months of remission at a time; the presence of at least 3 from a list of 13 signs and symptoms of depression: absence of psychotic features; and, when there is a preexisting mental disorder, a clear differentiation of the chronic depression from the individual's usual mood.

The several problems and inadequacies of the DSM-III definition of DD can be taken up separately under the headings of severity, age of onset, type of onset, and relationship to Axis II.

Severity

Perhaps the most important problem in the DSM-III definition of DD is that its severity criterion is so very close to the threshhold established for major depression. In order to meet the severity criterion for DD, the presence of three of thirteen depressive symptoms is required, while for MD it is necessary to have four of eight symptoms (note that six of the DD and MD defining items overlap; on the additional items, the DD list emphasizes cognitive symptoms, while the MD list emphasizes somatic symptoms). If a DD patient acquires just one more symptom, the patient now meets the additional diagnosis of major depression. This lack of distinctiveness in the severity definition of DD and MD may account for a high prevalence of "double depression"[15, 16] DD patients who become only slightly more or slightly less depressed may with each small change in symptomatology just make or just miss the criterion level for MD. The consequences of having virtually identical severity criteria for DD and MD have been obvious in our own study in which almost all chronic depressives also met the severity criteria for MD.[26] An essential element of the DD construct is that it describes a chronic subsyndromal level of depression. If all or most DD patients also meet criteria for chronic major depression or "double depression" one might just as well use the terms chronic and/or double as modifiers describing different possible courses for major depression, no separate DD category would be needed. If DD is to remain a separate category, its severity threshhold must be more distinctly differentiated from MD, either by lowering the threshhold for DD or by raising the threshhold for MD, or preferably by instituting both of these, i.e., changing the number of associated symptoms required to fulfill criteria for these diagnoses.

Age of Onset

The DSM III criteria set for DD does not specify anything about an age of onset. It requires only that symptoms be present for two years in adults (or one year in children). The resulting DSM-III definition for DD thus lumps together in one diagnostic category those chronic depressions which have an onset early in life (usually without clear-cut precipitants) and those

Table 1. DSM-III Criteria for Dysthymic Disorder

A. During the past two years (or one year for children and adolescents) the individual has been bothered most or all of the time by symptoms characteristic of the depressive syndrome that are not of sufficient severity and duration to meet the criteria for a major depressive episode.

B. The manifestations of the depressive syndrome may be relatively persistent or separated by periods of normal mood lasting a few days to a few weeks, but no more than a few months at a time.

C. During the depressive periods there is either prominent depressed mood (e.g., sad, blue, down in the dumps, low) or marked loss of interest or pleasure in all, or almost all, usual activities and pastimes.

D. During the depressive periods at least three of the following symptoms are present:
    (1) insomnia or hypersomnia
    (2) low energy level or chronic tiredness
    (3) feelings of inadequacy, loss of self-esteem, or self-depreciation
    (4) decreased effectiveness or productivity at school, work, or home
    (5) decreased attention, concentration, or ability to think clearly
    (6) social withdrawal
    (7) loss of interest in or enjoyment of pleasurable activities
    (8) irritability or excessive anger (in children, expressed toward parents or caretakers)
    (9) inability to respond with apparent pleasure to praise or rewards
    (10) less active or talkative than usual, or feels slowed down or restless
    (11) pessimistic attitude toward the future, brooding about past events, or feeling sorry for self
    (12) tearfulness or crying
    (13) recurrent thoughts of death or suicide

E. There are no psychotic features, such as delusions, hallucinations, or incoherence.

F. If the disturbance is superimposed on another mental disorder or a preexisting mental disorder, such as obsessive compulsive disorder or alcohol dependence, the depressed mood, by virtue of its intensity or effect on functioning, can be clearly distinguished from the individual's usual mood.

which begin later in life (often following in the wake of major depression, another psychiatric disorder, a chronic medical disorder, or chronic stress). Other authors have suggested,[39] and we agree, that it may be of value to distinguish early onset ("lifelong") depressions which have the same onset and time course as the personality disorders from those chronic depressions that follow unresolved major depression or appear to be secondary to major psychiatric or medical conditions or to demoralization in reaction to chronic stress. These subgroups may have differing familial patterns, prognoses and treatment responses. The DSM-III definition of DD does not make these potentially important distinctions.

Type of Onset

The DSM-III definition of DD also fails to distinguish the type of onset that often characterizes chronic as opposed to acute depressions. The available literature[10] and our own data suggest that early onset chronic depressions tend to have an insidious onset in contrast to typical episodic MD which is more likely to have fairly clear-cut and recognizable onset. This distinction has been supported by factor analytic studies in depression[28] and has been included in the Newcastle scale to distinguish endogenous from reactive depression, but it does not inform the DSM-III definition of DD.

Relationship to Personality Disorders

The DSM-III placement of DD with the Axis I affective disorders rather than with the Axis II personality disorders was controversial since it seemed to provide premature closure on the question of whether and when such conditions are part of the spectrum of affective disorders or a spectrum of character pathology, or more likely whether DD is a heterogeneous category including both sorts of patients. The major saving grace of DSM-III in this regard is the provision of Axis II on which to rate concurrent personality disorders. This provides an opportunity to determine whether the co-morbidity of an Axis II diagnosis and DD predicts differences in course, onset, and treatment responses. Of course, the uncontaminated assessment of personality disorder in the presence of a concurrent chronic affective disorder presents difficult, and perhaps insoluble, technical problems.

In summary, then, the DSM-III definition of DD fails to distinguish early and insidious onset chronic depressions ("I have been depressed all of my life") from those that appear to be secondary to psychiatric or medical illness or unhappy life situations. The major distinction in DSM-III between DD and MD rests on the severity of depression and here the difference between the syndromes is just one symptom. The DSM-III definition of DD therefore provides insufficient specificity for the different types of chronic depression and insufficient distinction between DD and MD.

CONCLUSIONS

It is important to note that research in the field of affective disorders has traditionally focused upon acute major depressive disorders treated with relatively short-term psychopharmacological interventions and studied with cross-sectional psychobiological probes. Chronicity has usually either not been evaluated systematically in drug studies or alternatively would serve as a criterion for exclusion. Thus, states of chronic depression have just recently been subjected to investigation. DSM-III Dysthymic Disorder is likely to be a heteregeneous category that will gradually become more specific as increased knowledge is gained. Future nomenclatures will likely be even more specific in distinguishing more homogenous sybtypes for future research concerning the etiology, pathogenesis and treatment of chronic depressive disorders.

In this chapter we have focused on the historical concepts which have guided clinical thinking about chronic depression, given a summary of results of empirical studies of epidemiology, course, and treatment of these conditions, which are pertinent to their understanding. Much work remains to delineate clinical, biological, and treatment aspects of chronic states of depression, but we have outlined areas where current and future research will help to clarify these important questions.

REFERENCES

1. *Diagnostic and Statistical Manual of Mental Disorders (Third Edition)* — DSM-III. American Psychiatric Association, Washington, 1980.
2. *Diagnostic and Statistical Manual of Mental Disorders (Second Edition)* — DSM-II. American Psychiatric Association. Washington, 1968.
3. Klerman GL, Weissman MM, Rounsaville BJ, Chevron ES: *Interpersonal Therapy of Depression.* New York, Basic Books; 1984.
4. Kraepelin E: *Manic-Depressive Illness and Paranoia.* E & S Livingstone, Edinburgh, 1921.
5. Kretschner E: *Physique and Character.* Harcourt, Brace and Co., New York, 1925, Ch IV.
6. Slater E, Roth M: *Clinical Psychiatry (3rd ed),* Baltimore, Williams & Wilkins, 1969.
7. Schneider K: *Clinical Psychopathology.* New York, Grune and Stratton, 1959, Ch. II.
8. Fenichel O: *The Psychoanalytic Theory of Neurosis.* New York, W.W. Norton and Co., 1945.

9. Gaylin W: (Ed.) *The Meaning of Despair*. New York, Science House, Inc., 1968.

10. Akiskal HS, Bitar AH, Puzantian VR et al: The nosological status of neurotic depression. *Arch Gen Psychiatry, 1978; 35*: 756-766.

11. Schildkraut JJ, Klein DF: The classification and treatment of depressive disorder. In Shader RI (Ed): *Manual of Psychiatric Therapeutics*, Boston, Little, Brown and Co., 1975, Ch. 3.

12. Spitzer RL, Endicott J, Robins E: *Research Diagnostic Criteria (RDC) for a Selected Group of Functional Disorders, (3rd ed)*, New York, Biometrics Research, 1978.

13. Frances AJ: The DSM III personality disorders section. *Am J Psychiatry, 1980; 137*: 1050-1055.

14. Akiskal HS, Rosenthal TL, Haykal RF et al: Characterologic depressions: clinical and sleep EEG findings separating "subaffective dysthymias" from "character spectrum disorders." *Arch Gen Psychiatry, 1980; 37*: 777-783.

15. Keller MB, Shapiro RW: "Double depression": Superimposition of actue depressive episodes on chronic depressive disorders. *Am J Psychiatry, 1982; 139*: 438-442.

16. Keller MB, Lavori PW, Endicott J et al: "Double depression": Two-year follow-up. *Am J Psychiatry, 1983; 140*: 689-694.

17. Weissman MM, Myers JK: Affective disorders in a US urban community. *Arch Gen Psychiatry, 1978; 35*: 1304-1311.

18. Robins LN, Helzer JE, Weissman MM et al: Lifetime prevalence of specific psychiatric disorders in three sites. *Arch Gen Psychiatry, 1984; 41*: 949-958.

19. Rounsaville BJ, Sholomskas D, Prusoff BA: Chronic mood disorders in depressed outpatients. *J Aff Disorders, 1980; 2*: 73-88.

20. Weissman MM, Klerman GL: The chronic depressive in the community: underrecognized and poorly treated. *Compr Psychiatry, 1977; 18*: 523-531.

21. Ceroni GB, Neri C, Pezzoli A: Chronicity in major depression: A naturalistic study. *J Aff Dis, 1984; 7*: 123-132.

22. Bronisch T, Wittchen H, Krieg C et al: Depressive neurosis. *Acta Psychiatr Scand, 1985; 71*: 237-248.

23. Kovacs M, Feinberg TL, Crouse-Novak MA et al: Depressive disorders in childhood. *Arch Gen Psychiatry, 1984; 41*: 229-237.

24. Kovacs M, Feinberg TL, Course-Novak MA et al: Depressive disorders in childhood. *Arch Gen Psychiatry, 1984; 41*: 643-649.

25. Tan T-L, Kales JD, Kales A et al: Biopsycho behavioral correlation of insomnia, IV: Diagnosis based on DSM III. *Am J Psychiatry, 1984; 141*: 357-362.

26. Kocsis JH, Voss C, Mann JJ et al: Chronic depression: demograhic and clinical characteristics. *Psychopharm Bull. 1986; 22*: 192-195.

27. Akiskal HS, King D, Rosenthal TL et al: Chronic depressions, Part 1. Clinical and familial characteristics in 137 probands. *J Aff Dis, 1981; 3*: 297-315.

28. Bech P: Rating scales for affective disorders. *Acta Psychiatr. Scand, 1981; 64: (Suppl. 295)*, 11-101.

29. Hirschfeld RMA, Klerman GL, Clayton PJ et al: Assessing personality: effects of the depressive state on trait measurement. *Am J Psychiatry, 1983; 140*: 695-699.

30. Liebowitz MR, Stallone F, Dunner DL et al: Personality features of patients with primary affective disorder. *Acta Psychiatr Scand, 1979; 60*: 214-224.

31. Zuckerman DM, Prusoff BA, Weissman MM et al: Personality as a predictor of psychotherapy and pharmacotherapy outcome for depressed patients. *J Consult Clin Psycho, 1980; 48*: 730-735.

32. Charney DS, Nelson JC, Quinlan DM: Personality traits and disorder in depression. *Am J Psychiatry, 1981; 138*: 1601-1604.

33. Pfohl B, Strangle D, Zimmerman M: The implications of DSM III personality disorders for patients with major depression. *J Aff Dis., 1984; 7*: 309-318.

34. Koenigsberg HW, Kaplan RD, Gilmore MM et al: The relationship between syndrome and personality disorder in DSM III: Experience with 2462 patients. *Am J Psychiatry, 1985; 142*: 207-212.

35. Kocsis JH, Frances AJ, Mann JJ et al: Imipramine for the treatment of chronic depression. *Psychopharm Bull, 1985; 21*: 698-700.

36. Ward NG, Bloom VL, Friedel RO: The effectiveness of tricyclic antidepressants in chronic depression. *J Clin Psychiatry, 1979; 40*: 49-52.

37. Paykel ES, Rowan PR, Parker RR et al: Response to phenelzine and amitriptyline in subtypes of depressed outpatients. *Arch Gen Psychiatry, 1982; 39*: 1041-1049.

38. Klein DE, Davis JM: *Diagnosis and Drug Treatment of Psychiatric Disorders*. Baltimore, Williams and Wilkins, 1969.

39. Akiskal HS: Dysthymic disorder: Psychopathology of proposed chronic depressive subtypes. *Am J Psychiatry, 1983; 140*: 11-20.

40. Kandel DB, Davies M: Adult sequelae of adolescent depressive symptoms. *Arch Gen Psychiatry, 1986; 43*: 255-262.

41. Billings AG, Moos RH: Chronic and nonchronic unipolar depression: the differential role of environmental stressors and resources. *JNMD 1984; 172*: 65-75.

42. Breslow R, Kocsis J, Belkin B: Contribution of the depressive personality to memory function in depression. *Am J Psychiatry, 1981; 138*: 227-230.

43. Bech AT, Rush AJ, Shaw BF, Emory G: *Cognitive Therapy of Depression*. New York, Guilford Press, 1979.

RECOMMENDED READING

Akiskal HS: Dysthymic disorder: psychopathology of proposed chronic depressive subtypes. *Am J Psychiatry, 1983*, 14011-20.

Klerman GL: Other specific affective disorders: In *Comprehensive Textbook of Psychiatry, Third Edition*, H.I. Kaplan, A.M. Freedman, B.J. Sadock (eds), Baltimore, Williams and Wilkins, 1980, Ch. 18:3.

Schildkraut JJ, Klein DF: The classification and treatment of depressive disorders; in *Manual of Psychiatric Therapeutics* R.I. Shader (Ed); Boston, Little, Brown & Co., 1975, Ch. 3.

Chapter 7

ATYPICAL DEPRESSION

Shelley Fox Aarons, M.D.

INTRODUCTION

In 1959 West and Dally[1] used the term "atypical" or "hysterical depression" in their report about a group of patients whose symptom profile differed from classical endogenous depression, and who responded well to treatment with monoamine oxidase inhibitors (MAOIs). The latter was particularly noteworthy since many of these patients had been ill for years, and were unresponsive to other treatments.

In 1986, most clinicians and researchers who have experience in the treatment of affective disorders would agree in general with West and Dally's observations, but the specific definition of atypical depression remains vague. Not only has the term been used in a variety of different but indistinct ways, many of the ways in which it has been used are themselves poorly defined.

Table 1 lists common meanings of the term atypical depression. The diagnosis has been applied to a heterogeneous group of patients that probably includes some patients with primary anxiety disorders and character disorders, as well as patients with primary affective disorders.

Labels other than atypical depression, such as hysteroid dysphoria[2] and subaffective dysthymia[3] have been used to describe patients who are in many ways similar, and this has probably contributed to the confusion about what constitutes atypical depression.

Clarifying the concept is important for two reasons. First, despite one possible connotation of atypical, i.e. rare, atypical depression is actually

Table 1. Multiple Meanings of Atypical Depression

Residual category; depression that does not meet DSM-III criteria for major depression, dysthymic disorder, or adjustment disorder with depressed mood

Nonendogenous depression

Neurotic depression

Depression with prominent anxiety symptoms

Depression *secondary* to an anxiety disorder (generalized anxiety, phobic anxiety, or panic disorder)

Mood-reactive depression

Hysterical depression

Depression with prominent characterological features

Depression with reversed neurovegetative signs

Depression with alexithymia and predominant somatic symptoms

---

extremely common, particularly in outpatient treatment settings. Secondly, the hypothesis that atypically depressed patients have particular treatment needs, specifically preferential responsivity to MAOIs[2] has yet to be either definitively demonstrated or clearly refuted.

In addition, the question of exactly which "atypical" clinical characteristics correlate with the putative preferential response of this group to MAOIs has also not been answered.

A number of controlled clinical trials have documented the efficacy of MAOIs against placebo, and more recently they have been tested against tricyclic antidepressants (TCAs) as well. These treatment studies are of great interest, but the lack of uniform criteria for the diagnosis of atypical depression imposes some limitations on attempts to synthesize the results.

Clearly, a number of important questions about both the nosology and treatment of atypical depression remain unresolved. This chapter will review available data from both of these areas and will offer some tentative conclusions pending further research. Available information about laboratory findings and characteristics of clinical course and family history will also be reviewed. Because of the lack of consensus as to the key clinical characteristics of atypical depression, data will be included for mild to moderately depressed outpatients in general, albeit variably diagnosed.

NOSOLOGY AND CLINICAL CHARACTERISTICS OF ATYPICAL DEPRESSION

DSM-III[4] defines atypical depression as a residual category for individuals with depressive symptoms who do not meet criteria for major depression with or without melancholia, dysthymic disorder, or adjustment disorder with depressed mood.

This use of the term as a diagnosis of exclusion is helpful in establishing the boundaries of the "typical" depressive disorders, but not surprisingly, the resulting group of "atypical" depressives is a very heterogeneous one. Entities with such markedly different clinical presentations and prognoses as minor depression as defined by RDC criteria[5] and postpsychotic depression would be included together. Thus, while this definition is clear, semantically correct, and consistent with the DSM-III definition of other atypical categories, because of the diversity of the resulting patient group, it is not helpful in guiding treatment, and it also does not correspond to common usage of the term.

As commonly used, the term derives from the original descriptions of West and Dally[1] (see Table 2) and Sargant[6, 7] of the iproniazid-responsive syndrome that they termed atypical or hysterical depression.

Atypical or hysterical depression was characterized by depressed mood, "overreactivity," and somatic preoccupation. Despite complaints of extreme lethargy and fatigue, these patients tended to have difficulty falling asleep at night. When diurnal variation of mood was present, it was more likely to be worse in the evening. A case illustration described increased appetite and weight gain but hyperphagia and hypersomnia were not emphasized in these early descriptions. "Typical" depressive symptoms of early morning awakening, mood worst in the morning, and self-blame, tended to be absent. The patients were described as very similar in appearance to patients with anxiety hysteria with secondary depression. In addition to generalized anxiety, phobias and panic attacks were commonly observed among these patients. Severe premenstrual tension was a frequent complaint among the women. Many of these patients had been ill for years and were unresponsive to other treatments. However, those who in addition to the above symptoms, were judged to have had lifelong inadequate personalities were not among the group of dramatic responders to iproniazid.

Table 2. Characteristics of Atypical Depression as Described by Dally, West, and Sargant

Initial insomnia

Evening worsening

Severe fatigue

Symptom variability (mood reactivity)

Somatic overreactivity including tremor, circulatory lability, and somatization

Anxiety symptoms; hysterical, phobic, generalized

Premenstrual worsening

Absence of marked self-reproach

Absence of early morning awakening

Good premorbid personality

Made worse by ECT treatment

At around the same time, Alexander and Berkeley[8] also reported treatment success with iproniazid in a group of nonclassically depressed patients. They used the term inert psychasthenic anhedonic reaction rather than atypical depression, but described similar clinical features that were associated with good response to treatment with the MAOI: anhedonia; self-pity; extreme fatigue and inertia; primary insomnia; and in some cases hypersomnia.

However, Alexander and Berkeley's description of a "joyless inhibited state" contrasts with that of West and Dally, and also with the descriptions of Klein et al.[2] in which "mood reactivity," the ability to respond to positive environmental events with a return to normal mood, is an essential feature.

Drawing on the work of Klein, Liebowitz et al.[9] have operationalized criteria for atypical despression that in addition to mood reactivity, emphasize hyperphagia, hypersomnia, and inertia. They also state that the symptom of extreme sensitivity to interpersonal rejection plays a role in the depressions of some atypical patients. These patients are termed hysteroid dysphorics, which these investigators consider a subtype of atypical depression. See Table 3.

Table 3. Criteria for Atypical Depression According to Leibowitz, Klein, and Quitkin

Nonautonomous mood (reactivity)

2/4 of the following:

Hyperphagia

Hypersomnia

Rejection sensitivity

Extreme fatigue/inertia
"leaden paralysis"

Generalized or phobic anxiety and panic attacks are not included in Klein and Liebowitz's criteria for atypical depression. On the other hand, Tyrer[10] has emphasized the importance of phobias and somatic anxiety in predicting a positive response to MAOIs.

Pollitt and Young[11] have pointed out that many of the patients they treated for anxiety disorders who responded well to MAOIs presented with neurovegetative signs in addition to their anxiety. These neurovegetative complaints were both typical (decreased sleep and appetite, worsened mood in the morning, early morning awakening) and atypical (increased sleep and appetite, worsened mood in the evening, initial insomnia.) Both the typical and atypical symptoms were quite common in the anxiety disorder patients, as well as in patients with a diagnosis of primary depression.

Nies and Robinson[12, 13] who have used the term atypical depression as essentially synonymous with nonendogenous depression also placed great emphasis on anxiety symptoms in differentiating atypical from typical forms of depression. The Diagnostic Index, a measure they developed to quantify this distinction also assigns negative (atypical) weights to other "atypical" symptoms such as initial insomnia, evening worsening, weight gain, and mood reactivity, (See Table 4). However, overall, anxiety symptoms are weighted most heavily.

Table 4. Features Distinguishing Atypical Depression in the Nies and Robinson Diagnostic Index

Psychic anxiety	Communicative suicide attempts
Somatic anxiety	Self pity
Initial insomnia	Reactivity
General somatic	Symptom fluctuation
Longstanding phobia	Hysterical personality
Weight gain	Worse p.m.
Actual loss	Situational anxiety

It is interesting that a Canadian clinician, apparently unaware of the body of work described above, wrote a report on his success using MAOIs to treat depressed patients suffering from what he termed the "too-much" syndrome.[14] He emphasized the importance of hypersomnia, hyperphagia, weight gain and possibly increased libido, but also noted the presence of psychic and somatic anxiety. His patients were almost all premenopausal women with a history of prior poor response to tricyclic antidepressants.

Thus while different investigators have emphasized different aspects of the syndrome, what does emerge from these descriptions is support for the general idea that there is a group of depressed patients who differ in clinical characteristics from classical melancholics, and who appear to benefit substantially from treatment with MAOIs. There is less support for the idea that atypical depression is one discrete or homogeneous diagnostic entity, and as will be evident in the discussion of treatment below, it is not clear that this group of depressed patients responds *only* to MAOIs, although this may be true of certain subgroups.

LABORATORY STUDIES

The focus of the above review has been on clinical description. More recently the availability of a variety of laboratory measures makes it possible to examine other parameters as well. Positive laboratory findings have most frequently been reported for melancholia. It is not yet clear whether atypically depressed patients resemble melancholics or normals or have their own characteristic laboratory profile. Because of the lack of one clear definition of atypical depression, laboratory data from nonendogenously depressed patients, anxious depressives, anxiety disorder patients with secondary depression, subaffective dysthymics, and patients with borderline personality disorder are included here.

Dexamethasone Suppression Test

The overnight dexamethasone suppression test (DST), a procedure that reflects hypothalamic pituitary-adrenal-cortical function, has been noted to be abnormal in patients with melancholia. Although the specificity of this test has been called into question by others, in the hands of Carroll and colleagues it is said to have a diagnostic confidence level of greater than 90 percent for melancholia, despite a sensitivity estimated to be only 40 to 67 percent.[15]

Nonendogenously depressed patients[16,17] do not appear to have a rate of abnormal response to dexamethasone significantly above the 4 to 15 percent rate described in normal controls.[15,18,19] In some outpatient samples higher rates have been reported[19] and this probably reflects the inclusion of some endogenously depressed patients. Even among endogenously depressed patients, outpatient status is associated with lower rates of abnormal response to dexamethasone challenge than inpatient status.

One study of patients with panic disorder reported no cases of DST nonsuppression,[20] and another found no significant difference between rates of nonsuppression for patients with primary anxiety disorder and outpatient depressives whose rate of nonsuppression was 13 percent.[21] This is similar to the rate of DST nonsuppression reported in other anxiety disorder studies.[22,23]

Among depressed patients with borderline personality disorder, some investigators have found a significant percentage of patients with abnormal escape from dexamethasone suppression[24,25,26] while others report far lower rates.[27]

Sleep EEG Studies

Shortened REM latency (number of minutes from sleep onset to the first REM period) on sleep EEG has emerged as one of the most consistent laboratory correlates of the clinical diagnosis of primary depression.[28] Akiskal and colleagues[3] found a decreased REM latency in patients with subaffective dysthymia as well as in those who were left with mild chronic residual dysphoric states after an episode of primary depression. Patients with character-spectrum disorder (defined by nonresponse to antidepressant medication) and those with chronic dysphoria secondary to a medical or other psychiatric illness had normal REM latency periods.

Quitkin and colleagues[29] have reported on the sleep of atypical depressives as defined in Table 3. above. The presence or absence of anxiety symptoms was not specified. Like the patients with endogenous depression, the atypical depressives also differed significantly from normals in having decreased REM latency periods, but did not share the sleep continuity disturbances of the endogenously depressed patients. In this way the atypical patients were similar to what has been reported by Kupfer to be true of anergic bipolar depressives.[28]

Similar sleep EEG abnormalities have also been reported in a small group of patients with panic disorder.[30]

Patients with borderline personality disorder and significant depression at the time of testing have also been found to have delayed REM latency.[31] In addition, Akiskal[32] reported shortened REM latency in a group of patients with borderline personality disorder who were not depressed.

Platelet Monoamine Oxidase Activity

Platelet monoamine oxidase activity has been measured in patients with a variety of psychiatric disorders. Results are not completely consistent, but in general platelet MAO activity has been reported to be decreased in bipolar depressives[33] and increased in both unipolar endogenous patients[34] and unipolar nonendogenous patients.[35] This increase in platelet MAO has been correlated with the presence of psychic anxiety and somatic complaints.[36] However, the specificity of these findings for depression is called into question by reports of increased platelet MAO activity in patients whose depression is secondary to an anxiety disorder[37] and in patients with primary anxiety disorder without depression.[38, 39, 40]

It is interesting in this regard that when patients with mixed states of anxiety and depression were treated with amitriptyline, a drug which has been shown to produce a minor degree of MAO inhibition, there was a significant positive correlation between the percent MAO inhibition and improvement in symptoms of anxiety, but not in symptoms of depression.[41]

The possibility that atypically depressed patients, particularly those with prominent anxiety, have higher than normal baseline levels of platelet MAO and thus respond to treatment with MAO inhibitors, and possibly to the MAO inhibiting properties of TCAs as well, is an appealing, although probably simplistic hypothesis. Nonetheless this is an area that deserves further study.

Our preliminary analysis of data from a mixed group of endogenously and nonendogenously depressed outpatients treated with the selective MAOI 1-deprenyl indicated that treatment responders did have significantly higher pretreatment levels of platelet MAO.[42] Similar results were reported by Giller and colleagues in a study of the MAOI isocarboxazid.[43] However Nies and Robinson[44] did not find levels of pretreatment monoamine oxidase activity to be correlated with response to phenelzine.

There has been an assumption underlying much of this work that levels of platelet MAO activity reflect the level of activity of MAO in the brain. The fact that the biochemical and kinetic properties of platelet MAO and central nervous system MAO B are very similar supports this view. However, a recent study directly comparing the activities of platelet MAO B with MAO B obtained from neurosurgical specimens failed to find a correlation.[45] Clearly further study of the significance of platelet MAO in general is necessary before any firm conclusions can be drawn about the significance of the enzyme in affective disorders.

Phenylethylamine Levels

Monoamine oxidase inhibitors share a structural similarity with phenylethylamine (PEA), a putative neurotransmitter that some investigators have suggested is an endogenous amphetamine.[46] Urinary concentrations of phenylethylamine and its metabolite phenylacetic acid (PAA) have been reported to be low in depressed patients.[47] The reports of these findings have been criticized on technical grounds, and clinical descriptions of the subtype of depressed patients studied have been lacking. The hypothesis that PEA is involved in the neurobiology of atypical depression[48] remains to be tested.

To generalize, it appears that some depressed patients who lack classical clinical endogenous features do in some ways resemble melancholic patients physiologically. The wide range of laboratory results may be attributed to a number of different factors. It may reflect heterogeneity of the group being studied as well as a lack of diagnostic precision, or lack of specificity of the tests themselves, all of which are still being validated as indicators of affective illness. Alternatively, it is possible that certain biological markers may actually be related to component symptom complexes such as anxiety, anergy, and/or reversed neurovegetative signs rather than to a specific diagnostic entity.

COURSE AND NATURAL HISTORY OF ATYPICAL DEPRESSION

Liebowitz et al.[9] have emphasized the chronic course of atypical depression in the absence of treatment, but this important area has received little systematic attention.

It has been suggested that whether depressive symptoms are typical or atypical in a given patient may be a function of age, with younger patients more likely to present with atypical features and older ones with typical symptoms of melancholia.[11] In support of this idea, hypersomnia has been documented in young depressives with sleep EEG.[49]

It is also possible that some patients may present initially with "atypical depression" and, if untreated, progress to typical melancholia. Support for this view comes from a prospective study of 100 patients who on initial presentation received the diagnosis of neurotic depression (a diagnosis that like atypical depression, includes a heterogeneous group of ill-defined patients). Over a three to four year follow-up period 36 percent of these patients met criteria for melancholia.[50]

Approaching the same question from a different perspective, Rounsaville and colleagues[51] reported that two-thirds of a sample of 64 outpatients presenting for treatment with major depression also suffered from an underlying low-grade chronic mood disorder. This phenomenon has been termed double depression.[52] It is not clear what proportion of patients with double depression have atypical symptoms, but the relationship of some minor or intermittent forms of depression to major affective disorders is clearly demonstrated by these reports.

FAMILY HISTORY

West and Dally[1] reported a positive family history of mental illness in 36.2 percent of their iproniazid responders. This rate was not significantly different from the 30.2 percent of typically depressed iproniazid nonresponders who had a positive family history. However, the type of mental illness in the family members was not specified. Rosenthal et al.[53] noted significant differences in the family histories of their character-spectrum patients in comparison with subaffective dysthymic patients. In the former group, a family history of alcoholism was found for 53 percent, but only 3.3 percent had a family history of depression. In contrast, 30 percent of the dysthymics had a family history of depression, and only 10 percent of alcoholism. The dysthymics not only were significantly different from the character-spectrum patients in this regard, but were similar to a group of unipolar depressed controls. The authors noted that their finding paralleled at the subsyndromal level the work of Winokur[54] on depressive-spectrum versus pure depressive disease.

Pare and Mack[55] have suggested that there are two genetically specific types of depression that respond preferentially to either MAOIs or tricyclic antidepressants. In support of this theory, they found that in depressed first-degree relatives, treatment response or nonresponse to a given class of antidepressants was similar to that of the depressed probands. It is not clear from the report whether the MAOI-responsive patients or their MAOI-responsive relatives had features of atypical depression. Even if such genetically based patterns of antidepressant response are confirmed by other investigations, it is not clear whether they could be readily differentiated on the basis of clinical characteristics.

There is some evidence from family studies to support the idea that the subgroup of patients with major depression plus panic attacks may constitute a separate diagnostic group, with a distinct course and pattern of treatment response, in addition to a characteristic family history. Leckman and colleagues[56] found that the relatives of this group of patients were more than twice as likely to have a history of major depression, panic disorder, phobia, and/or alcohol abuse as a group of patients with major depression without panic attacks.

RESPONSE TO TREATMENT

Despite the variability of specific diagnostic criteria, evidence from an increasing number of double-blind, placebo-controlled studies now exists to support earlier impressionistic clinical data that MAOIs are effective antidepressants for the subset of patients who may generally be described as nonendogenous, atypical, or neurotic.[57]

However, the specificity of MAOIs for atypical forms of depression is challenged in two ways: first by reports of efficacy of MAOIs in "typical" forms of depression,[58, 59, 60] and secondly by some reports of unexpected responsivity of atypical depression to TCAs.[61, 62, 63] It is of interest, however, that many of the "typically" depressed MAOI responders are bipolar, a category of patient in whom the presence of "atypical" neurovegetive signs such as hypersomnia, hyperphagia, and anergy have been described.[64, 65] This again suggests that there may be particular target symptoms that correlate with good response to MAOI treatment, and that while these symptoms are more common in nonendogenous or atypical depression, they also may be found in some patients with melancholia.

Although the two large-scale double-blind studies cited above[61, 62] comparing tricyclics to MAOIs for the treatment of outpatients with depression found both classes of antidepressants to be effective, with similarities outweighing the differences, both studies did clearly find that patients with prominent anxiety symptoms tended to respond better to MAOIs. Further analysis of the study of Ravaris and colleagues with an expanded patient sample[66] found that the patients with panic attacks did significantly better with treatment with phenelzine than with amitriptyline. This was true regardless of whether their depressive symptoms were typical or atypical. In addition, another separate analysis of a subgroup of patients from this study suggested that features of hysteroid dysphoria were also correlated with more favorable response to phenelzine than to amitriptyline.[67]

The findings from a study by Liebowitz and colleagues comparing phenelzine, imipramine, and placebo for the treatment of atypical depression are consistent with the above. They report a very high response rate to phenelzine in atypical depressives who also had panic attacks. Those with hysteroid dysphoria, (a smaller number) had a similar pattern of response. For the atypical patients without panic attacks or hysteroid dysphoria, treatment response was equally favorable with phenelzine and imipramine, and neither differed significantly from placebo.[68, 69]

Thus, the clinical impression that MAOIs have a special efficacy for atypical depression appears to hold true in controlled studies, but only for those patients with prominent anxiety or panic attacks, and possibly for those with hysteroid dysphoria as well.

Whether it is the combination of atypical depression and panic per se, or panic in combination with any depressive illness that dictates preferential response to MAOIs is not clear, and deserves further study.

Several investigators have noted poor response to psychopharmacological treatment in patients with depression plus panic in comparison to patients with depression alone.[70, 71] Almost all of the depressed/panic patients in these studies were treated with TCAs rather than MAOIs.

In contrast to the treatment results found with nonselective MAOIs, high levels of concomitant anxiety do not predict good response to 1-deprenyl.[72] In fact, the presence of panic attacks appears to be a predictor of non-response to 1-deprenyl in doses that are MAO B selective (10-15 mg.).[42] Unlike nonselective MAOIs, 1-deprenyl in its low dose, MAO B selective range inhibits the deamination of phenylethylamine and dopamine, but not norepinephrine and serotonin.

MAOIs may have their salutary effects on anxious depression and hysteroid dysphoria through different mechanisms, and this may reflect differences in underlying pathophysiology.

Psychotherapy is commonly prescribed for patients with atypical depression, but its efficacy has received far less systematic study than has pharmacotherapy. Liebowitz and Klein[73] have suggested that the hysteroid dysphoric subgroup may specifically benefit from combined treatment with MAOIs and psychotherapy. In their study patients who were treated after initial response in a continuation phase with placebo plus psychotherapy did not fare as well as those who continued to receive phenelzine in addition to psychotherapy.

In a group of ambulatory depressed patients whose diagnosis was major depression by DSM-III criteria but neurotic depression by DSM-II, (a group that would be likely to include atypical depressives) both short-term interpersonal psychotherapy and tricyclics were shown to be active treatments; combined treatment provided greater benefit than either treatment alone.[74] Cognitive therapy has also been reported to be as good as[75] or better than[76] tricyclic antidepressants in treating depressed outpatients, although it has not been evaluated specifically for atypical depression.

Conclusions

A number of recent papers have pointed out that the term atypical depression is a confusing one[77, 78, 79] used as it has been to describe a heterogeneous group of patients, who in fact in many outpatient treatment settings are more common than the "typical" depressions.

However, the concept of atypical depression has been an extremely useful one in targeting a group of patients some of whom obtain substantial benefit from antidepressant medication, and for whom such treatment has been underutilized.

It is clear that as currently defined atypical depression is not a single discrete or homogeneous diagnostic group, however, in one or more of its subgroups syndromal validity and preferential treatment response to MAO inhibitors may be demonstrated. Such subgroups include: patients with atypical depression plus panic attacks; patients with hysteroid dysphoria; and mild to moderately depressed patients with anergy and reversed neurovegetative signs. Many of the patients in the latter group also have histories of manic or hypomanic episodes, suggesting a link between certain forms of atypical depression and bipolar disorder.

Although a recent study using a questionnaire survey of clinicians failed to demonstrate syndromal validity for hysteroid dysphoria,[80] as Klein and Liebowitz pointed out in response, it may often be difficult to distinguish clear syndromes when they are embedded in large mixed patient groups.[81]

This has been a problem with much of the research in atypical depression generally. For definitive answers further study is needed, with careful attention to nosology, clinical, laboratory, and family history characteristics and treatment response.

References

1. West ED, Dally PJ: Effects of iproniazid in depressive syndromes. *British Medical Journal 1959; 1:* 1491-1494.
2. Klein DF, Gittleman R, Quitkin F, Rifkin A: *Diagnosis and Drug Treatment of Psychiatric Disorders.* 2nd ed. Baltimore, Williams & Wilkins, 1980.
3. Akiskal HS, Rosenthal TL, Haykal RF, Lemmi H, Rosenthal RH, Scott-Strauss A: Characterological depressions: clinical and sleep EEG findings separating "subaffective dysthymias" from "character spectrum disorders." *Arch Gen Psychiatry 1980; 37:* 77-783.
4. *Diagnostic and Statistical Manual of Mental Disorders.* 3rd ed Washington, DC: American Psychiatric Association, 1980.

5. Spitzer RL, Endicott J Robins E: *Research Diagnostic Criteria (RDC) for a Selected Group of Functional Disorders*. New York, New York State Psychiatric Institute, 1978.

6. Sargant W: Drugs in the treatment of depression. *Br Med Journal 1961; 1:* 225-227.

7. Sargant W: The treatment of anxiety states and atypical depressions by the monoamine oxidase inhibitor drugs. *J Neuropsychiatry 1962; 3:* (Suppl 1), S96-S103.

8. Alexander L, Berkeley AW: The inert psychasthenic reaction (anhedonia) as differentiated from classic depression and its response to iproniazid. *Ann NY Acad Sci 1959; 80:* 669-679.

9. Liebowitz MR, Quitkin FM, Stewart JW, McGrath PJ, Harrison W, Schwartz D, Rabkin J, Tricamo E, Klein DF: Phenelzine and imipramine in atypical depression. *Psychopharm Bull 1981; 17:* 159-161.

10. Tyrer P: Towards rational therapy with monoamine oxidase inhibitors. *Br J Psychiatry 1976; 128:* 354-360.

11. Pollitt J, Young J: Anxiety state or masked depression? a study based on the action of monoamine oxidase inhibitors. *Br J Psychiatry 1971; 119:,* 143-149.

12. Nies A, Robinson DS, Lamborn KR, Ravaris CL, Ives JO: The efficacy of the monoamine oxidase inhibitor phenelzine: dose effects and prediction of response, in Bossier JR, Hippius H, Pichot P (Eds), *Neuropsychopharmacology 1974;* Amsterdam, Excerpta Medica Press, pp 765-770.

13. Robinson DS, Nies A, Ravaris CL, Ives JO, Bartlett D: The monoamine oxidase inhibitor, phenelzine, in the treatment of depressive-anxiety states. *Arch Gen Psychiatry 1978; 29:* 407-413.

14. O'Regan B: An MAOI specific affective disorder. The "too-much" syndrome. *Orthomolecular Psychiatry 1974; 3:* 152-155.

15. Carroll BJ, Feinberg M, Greden JF, Tarika J, Albala AA, Haskett RF, James N McI, Kronfol Z, Lohr N, Steiner M, de Vigne JP, Young E : A specific laboratory test for the diagnosis of melancholia. *Arch Gen Psychiatry 1981; 38:* 15-22.

16. Carroll BJ, Feinberg M, Steiner M, Haskett RF, James N McI, Tarika J: Diagnostic application of the dexamethasone suppression test in depressed outpatients. In Mendlewicz J, van Praag HM (Eds), *Psychoneuroendocrinology and Abnormal Behavior* (pp. 107-116). Basel, Karger, 1980.

17. Rabkin JG, Quitkin FM, Stewart JW, McGrath PJ, Puig-Antich J: The dexamethasone suppression test with mildly to moderately depressed outpatients. *Am J Psychiatry 1983; 140:* 926-927.

18. Amsterdam JD, Winokur A, Caroff SN, Conn J: The dexahethasone suppression test in outpatients with primary affective disorder and healthy control subjects. *Am J Psychiatry 1982; 139(3):* 287-291.

19. Peslow ED, Goldring N, Fieve RR, Wright: The dexamethasone suppression test in depressed outpatients and normal control subjects. *Am J Psychiatry 1983; 140:,* 245-247.

20. Lieberman JA, Brenner R, Lesser M, Coccaro E, Borenstein M, Kane JM: Dexamethasone suppression tests in patients with panic disorder. *Am J Psychiatry 1983; 140:* 917-919.

21. Avery DH, Osgood TB, Ishiki MD, Wilson LG, Kenny M, Dunner DL: The DST in psychiatric outpatients with generalized anxiety disorder, panic disorder, or primary affective disorder. *Am J Psychiatry 1985; 142:* 844-848.

22. Sheehan DV, Claycomb JB, Surnman OS, Baer L, Coleman J, Gelles L: Panic attacks and the dexamethasone suppression test. *Am J Psychiatry 1983; 140:* 1063-1064.

23. Peterson GA, Ballenger JC, Cox DP, Hucek A, Lydiard BR, Laraia MT, Trockman C: The dexamethasone suppression test in agoraphobia. *J Clin Psychopharmacology 1985; 5:* 100-102.

24. Beeber AR, Kline MD, Pies RW, Manring JM: Dexamethasone suppression test in hospitalized depressed patients with borderline personality disorder. *J Nerv Ment Dis 1984; 172(5):* 301-303.

25. Carroll BJ, Greden JF, Feinberg M, Lohr N, James N McI, Steiner M, Haskett RF, Albala AA, DeVigne JP, Tarika J: Neuroendocrine evaluation of depression in borderline patients. *Psych Clin N Am 1981; 4(1):* 89-99.

26. Krishnan KRR, Davidson JRT, Rayasam K, Shope F: The dexamethasone suppression test in borderline personality disorder. *Biol Psychiatry 1984; 19:* 1149-1153.

27. Soloff PH, George A, Nathan RS: The dexamethasone suppression test in patients with borderline personalities. *Am J Psychiatry 1982; 139:* 1621-1623.

28. Kupfer JD: REM latency: a psychobiologic marker for primary depressive disease. *Biol Psychiatry 1976; 11:* 159-174.

29. Quitkin FM, Rabkin JG, Stewart JW, McGrath PJ, Harrison W, Davies M, Goetz R, Puig-Antich J: Sleep of atypical depressives. *J Aff Disorders 1985; 8:* 61-67.

30. Roy-Burne PP, Uhde TW: Panic disorder and major depression: Biological relationships. *Psychopharm Bull 1985; 21:* 551-554.

31. McNamara E, Reynolds CF, Soloff PH, Mathias R, Rossi A, Spiker D, Coble PA, Kupfer DJ: EEG sleep evaluation of depression in borderline patients. *Am J Psychiatry 1984; 141* 182-186.

32. Akiskal HS: Subaffective disorders: dysthymic, cyclothymic, and bipolar II disorders in the "borderline" realm. *Psychiatr Clin N Am 1981; 4(1):* 25-46.

33. Murphy DL, Weiss R: Reduced monoamine oxidase activity in blood platelets from bipolar depressed patients. *Am J Psychiatry 1972; 128:* 1351-1357.

34. Mann J: Altered platelet monoamine oxidase activity in affective disorders. *Psychol Med 1979; 9:* 729-736.

35. White K, Shih J, Fong T, Young H, Gelfand R, Boyd J, Simpson G, Sloane RB: Elevated platelet monoamine oxidase activity in patients with nonendogenous depression. *Am J Psychiatry 1980; 137* 1258-1259.

36. Gudeman JE, Schatzberg AF, Samson JA, Orsulak PJ, Cole JO, Schildkraut JJ: Toward a biochemical classification of depressive disorders, VI: platelet MAO activity and clinical symptoms in depressed patients. *Am J Psychiatry 1982; 139:* 630-633.

37. Davidson JRT, McLeod MN, Turnbull CD, White HL, Feuer EJ: Platelet monoamine oxidase activity and the classification of depression. *Arch Gen Psychiatry 1980; 37:* 771-773.

38. Flaskos J, George AJ, Theophilopoulos N: Symptoms of agoraphobia in relation to monoamine oxidase activity. *Clin Neuropharm; 7* (Suppl. 1), 180-181.

39. Mathew RJ, Beng TH, Kralik P, Taylor D, Claghorn JL: MAO, DBH, and COMT: The effect of anxiety. *J Clin Psychiatry1980; 41:* 25-28.

40. Yu PH, Bowen RC, Davis BA, Boulton AA: A study of the catabolism of trace amines in mentally disordered individuals with particular reference to agoraphobic patients with panic attacks. *Prog Neuropsychopharm Biol Psychiatry 1983; 7:* 611-615.

41. Davidson J, Linnoila M, Raft D, Turnbull CD: MAO inhibition and control of anxiety following amitriptyline therapy. *Acta Psychiatr Scand 1981; 63:* 147-152.

42. Aarons SF, Mann JJ, Brown RP, Young RB, Frances A: Antidepressant efficacy of 1-deprenyl:clinical and biochemical correlates. In Burrows GD, Norman TR (Eds.), *Clinical and Pharmacological Studies in Psychiatric Disorders 1985.* London, John Libbey, pp. 33-36.

43. Giller E, Bialos D, Harkness L, Riddle M: Assessing treatment response to the monoamine oxidase inhibitor isocarboxazid. *J Clin Psychiatry 1984; 45(7,Sec.2):* 44-48.

44. Nies A, Robinson DS: Monoamine oxidase inhibitors, in Paykel ES (Ed.), *Handbook of Affective Disorders 1982.* New York, Guilford, pp. 246-261.

45. Young WF, Laws ER, Sharbrough FW, Weinshilboum RM: Human monoamine oxidase: lack of brain and platelet correlation. *Arch Gen Psychiatry 1986; 43:* 604-609.

46. Sabelli HC, Mosnaim AD: Phenylethylamine hypothesis of affective behavior. *Am J Psychiatry 1974; 131:* 695-699.

47. Sabelli HC, Fawcett J, Gusovsky F, Javaid JJ, Wynn P, Edwards J, Jeffries H, Kravitz H: Clinical studies on the phenylethylamine hypothesis of affective disorder: urine and blood phenylacetic acid and phenylalanine dietary supplements. *J Clin Psychiatry 1986; 47:* 66-70.

48. Klein DF: Pathophysiology of depressive syndromes. *Biol Psychiatry 1974; 8:* 119-120.

49. Hawkins DR, Taub JM, Van de Castle RL: Extended sleep (hypersomnia) in young depressed patients. *Am J Psychiatry 1985; 142:* 905-910.

50. Akiskal HS, Bitar AH, Puzantian VR, Rosenthal TL, Parks WW: The nosological status of neurotic depression. *Arch Gen Psychiatry 1978; 35:,* 756-766.

51. Rounsaville BJ, Sholomskas D, Prusoff BA: Chronic mood disorders in depressed outpatients. *J Aff Disorders 1980; 2:* 73-88.

52. Keller MB, Shapiro RW: "Double depression": superimposition of acute depressive episodes on chronic depressive disorders. *Am J Psychiatry 1982; 139:* 438-442.

53. Rosenthal TL, Akiskal HS, Scott-Strauss A, Rosenthal RH, David M : Familial and developmental factors in characterological depressions. *J Aff Dis 1981; 3:* 183-192.

54. Winokur G: Unipolar depression: is it divisible into autonomous subtypes? *Arch Gen Psychiatry 1979; 36:* 47-52.
55. Pare CMB, Mack JW: Differentiation of two genetically specific types of depression by the response to antidepressant drugs. *J Med Gen 1971; 8:* 306-309.
56. Leckman JF, Weissman MM, Merikangas KR, Pauls DL, Prusoff BA: Panic disorder and major depression. *Arch Gen Psychiatry 1983; 40:* 1055-1060.
57. Quitkin FM, Rifkin A, Klein DF: Monoamine oxidase inhibitors: a review of antidepressant effectiveness. *Arch Genl Psychiatry; 36:* 749-760.
58. Himmelhoch JM, Thase ME, Mallinger AG, Fuchs CZ: *Tranylcypromine versus imipramine in manic depression.* Washington D.C., APA, New Research, 1986.
59. McGrath PJ, Quitkin FM, Harrison W, Stewart JW: Treatment of melancholia with tranylcypromine. *Am J Psychiatry 1984; 141:* 288-289.
60. Quitkin FM, McGrath P, Liebowitz MR, Stewart J, Howard A: Monoamine oxidase inhibitors in bipolar endogenous depressives. *J Clin Psychopharmacology 1981; 1:* 70-74.
61. Ravaris CL, Robinson DS, Ives JO, Nies A, Bartlett D: Phenelzine and amitriptyline in the treatment of depression. *Arch Gen Psychiatry 1980; 37* 1075-1080.
62. Rowan PR, Paykel ES, Parker RR, Gatehouse JM, Rao BM : Tricyclic antidepressant and MAO inhibitor: are there differential effects? In Youdim MBH, Paykel ES (Eds), *Monoamine Oxidase Inhibitors: The State of The Art.* New York: John Wiley & Sons 1981, pp. 125-138.
63. Sovner RD: The clinical characteristics and treatment of atypical depression. *J Clin Psychiatry 1981; 42:* 285-289.
64. Detre T, Himmelhoch J, Swartzberg M, Anderson CM, Byck R, Kupfer DJ: Hypersomnia and manic-depressive disease. *Am J Psychiatry 1972; 128:* 1303-1305.
65. Mallinger AG, Himmelhoch JM, Neil JF: Anergic depression accompanied by increased intracellular sodium and lithium. *J Clin Psychiatry 1981; 42:* 83-86.
66. Robinson DS, Kayser A, Corcella J, Laux D, Yingling K, Howard D : Panic attacks in outpatients with depression: response to antidepressant treatment. *Psychopharm Bull 1985; 21:* 562-567.
67. Kayser A, Robinson DS, Nies A, Howard D: Response to phenelzine among depressed patients with features of hysteroid dysphoria. *Am J Psychiatry 1985; 142:* 486-488.
68. Liebowitz MR, Quitkin FM, Stewart JW, McGrath PJ, Harrison W, Rabkin J, Tricamo E, Markowitz JS, Klein DF: Phenelzine v imipramine in atypical depression. *Arch Gen Psychiatry 1984; 41:* 669-677.
69. Liebowitz MR, Quitkin FM, Stewart JW, McGrath PJ, Harrison W, Rabkin J, Tricamo E, Markowitz JS, Klein DF: Effect of panic attacks on the treatment of atypical depressives. *Psychopharm Bull 1985; 21:* 558-561.
70. Grunhaus L, Rabin D, Greden JF: Simultaneous panic and depressive disorder: response to antidepressant treatments. *J Clin Psychiatry 1986; 47(1):* 4-7.

71. VanValkenburg C, Akiskal HS, Puzantian V, Rosenthal T : Anxious depressions. Clinical, family history, and naturalistic outcome — comparisons with panic and major depressive disorders. *J Aff Dis 1984; 6:* 67-82.

72. Quitkin FM, Liebowitz MR, Stewart JW, McGrath PJ, Harrison W, Rabkin JG, Markowitz J, Davies SO: L-deprenyl in atypical depressives, *Arch Gen Psychiatry 1984; 41:* 777-781.

73. Liebowitz MR, Klein DF: Interrelationship of hysteroid dysphoria and borderline personality disorder. *Psychiatric Clin North Am 1981; 4:* 67-87.

74. Weissman MM, Prusoff BA, DiMascio A, Neu C, Goklaney M, Klerman GL: The efficacy of drugs and psychotherapy in the treatment of acute depressive episodes. *Am J Psychiatry 1979; 136:* 555-558.

75. Murphy GE, Simons AD, Wetzel RD, Lustman PJ: Cognitive therapy and pharmacotherapy singly and together in the treatment of depression. *Arch Gen Psychiatry 1984; 41:* 33-41.

76. Rush AJ, Beck AT, Kovacs M, Hollon S: Comparative efficacy of cognitive therapy and pharmacotherapy in the treatment of depressed outpatients. *Cog Ther Res 1977; 1:* 17-37.

77. Aarons SF, Frances AJ, Mann JJ: Atypical depression: a review of diagnosis and treatment. *Hosp Com Psychiatry 1985; 36:* 275-282.

78. Davidson JRT, Miller RD, Turnbull CD, Sullivan JL: Atypical depression. *Arch Gen Psychiatry 1982; 39:* 527-534.

79. Paykel ES, Rowan PR, Rao BM, Bhat A: Atypical depression: Nosology and response to antidepressants. In Clayton PJ, Barrett JE (Eds), *Treatment of Depression: Old Controversies and New Approaches.* New York: Raven Press, 1983, pp. 237-252.

80. Spitzer RL, Williams JBW: Hysteroid dysphoria: An unsuccessful attempt to demonstrate its syndromal validity. *Am J Psychiatry 1982; 139:* 1286-1291.

81. Klein DF, Liebowitz MR: Hysteroid dysphoria. *Am J Psychiatry 1982; 139:* 1520-1521.

Recommended Reading

Aarons SF, Frances AJ, Mann JJ: Atypical depression: A review of diagnosis and treatment. *Hosp Com Psychiatry 1985; 36:* 275-282.

Davidson JRT, Miller RD, Turnbul, CD, Sullivan JL: Atypical depression. *Arch Gen Psychiatry 1982; 39:* 527-534.

Paykel ES, Rowan PR, Rao BM, Bhat A: Atypical depression: Nosology and response to antidepressants. In Clayton PJ, Barrett JE (Eds), *Treatment of Depression: Old Controversies and New Approaches.* New York: Raven Press, pp. 237-252.

Chapter 8

DELUSIONAL DEPRESSION

Richard P. Brown, M.D.

Several reasons warrant a separate discussion of delusional depression, even though it remains controversial whether it is a distinct diagnostic entity. It is relatively frequent in inpatients: at least five percent of admissions to acute care hospitals are delusionally depressed.[1] For example, we have found that approximately 30 percent of admissions for depression to Payne Whitney Clinic are delusionally depressed patients (Brown et al., unpublished data). Furthermore, since these patients have a poor response to standard pharmacologic treatments during the acute episode, and prolonged recovery after discharge, the illness involves substantial costs to patients, families, and society. Such patients present a diagnostic and therapeutic challenge. The nature and severity of their symptoms are of theoretical and practical importance. Study of the underlying mechanisms may clarify the cause of nondelusional depression.

Many writers choose to use the term "delusional depression" because there is confusion surrounding the term "psychotic depression." Until the stricter definitions of the Research Diagnostic Criteria (RDC) and DSM-III, the term "psychotic depression" was often used to mean a severe depression or the presence of extreme feelings of hopelessness and worthlessness. The RDC demand the presence of delusions, hallucinations, or stupor for diagnosis of psychotic depression. A delusion is defined operationally as a belief held by the patient that can be tested against a known reality, is clearly false, and is not shared by other members of the patient's family or social group. Hallucinations and stupor meet RDC criteria for delusional depression, but since these symptoms occur in a minority of delusional depressed patients, and always in association with delusions, most writers prefer the term "delusional depression."

The phenomenology, differential diagnosis, course, family history, physiology, and treatment of this syndrome will be discussed in this chapter.

PHENOMENOLOGY

Melancholia

The typical delusional depressed patient meets DSM-III criteria for melancholia or RDC for endogenous subtype. Since DSM-III requires a choice between melancholic or psychotic symptoms in coding major depressive disorder and not all researchers in this area specify whether they require melancholia to diagnose delusional depression,[2] this may account for differences in clinical diagnosis and selection of research samples. More than the report of anhedonia should be required in order to confirm the presence of melancholia. The observed absence of reactivity of mood while on the impatient ward for one week is optimal.

Pervasive Cognitive and Psychomotor Disturbance

Compared to nondelusional patients, we and others have found that delusional depressives are more guilty,[3,4] ruminative, referential and agitated.[4,5,6,7] Glassman and Roose[8] noted more psychomotor retardation. Nelson and Bowers[9] noted more psychomotor disturbance when agitation and retardation were combined, but not when each was considered in isolation.

Further support for the symptom cluster of delusions, agitation and excessive guilt comes from two factor analytic studies. Overall[10] found a group of severely depressed patients with high scores for unusual thought content, suspiciousness, hostility, depressed mood, tension including agitation, guilt, and anxiety. Raskin and Crook[11] described an agitated cluster with marked thought disorder, paranoia, guilt, helplessness, worthlessness, and suicidal ideation. Therefore, marked agitation or motor retardation, excessive guilt and suspiciousness with or without outright paranoia should lead the clinician to suspect the presence of delusional depression and to inquire specifically about the presence of delusions.

Types of Delusional Ideas and Their Frequencies

Psychotic symptoms may involve delusions of guilt and sin, persecution and ideas of reference, nihilism, somatic disease, poverty, or multiple ideas without a single theme. Typical examples of such delusions follow. A patient refused to eat or drink since she believed her bowels and bladder had rotted and the food would run out on the floor. Another patient believed his family was starving because he was such a poor provider, even though his wife constantly reassured him they were well off financially. A patient believed the staff had a secret plan to send her to a chronic hospital for the rest of her life because she was such a terrible person. One patient believed that news of her past sexual affairs were being broadcast in radio, TV, and newspaper and the police were after her.

Paranoid ideas may therefore involve persecution or accusation because the patient believes she has committed a terrible sin. It may not be easy to elicit whether the patient thinks the persecution is to punish sin or from an external malevolent force. Although it should be obvious that the former idea is a mood-congruent delusion and the latter idea is a mood-incongruent delusion, this distinction may not be easy to make in practice. This might account in part for differences in reported rates of kinds of psychotic symptoms. The following tables will illustrate this point.

Problems in Classification of Mood-Congruence of Delusions

Study of the significance of mood-congruent or mood incongruent ideas may be further complicated because a patient may have both kinds of delusions or mood-congruent hallucinations and mood-incongruent delusions.[13] This is not merely a theoretical point since congruence of delusion may related to treatment response and prognosis.[14] The following table demonstrates that a significant proportion of delusionally depressed patients have both mood-congruent and incongruent delusions.

Some researchers will classify a patient as delusionally depressed only if the paranoid ideas are mood-congruent.[2,8] However, Winokur[15] makes the convincing case that there is no real reason to believe that mood-incongruent delusions in a person with unequivocal concomitant episodic depression are meaningfully different from mood-congruent psychotic features.

Coryell et al.[16] suggested that patients with mood-incongruent psychotic symptoms and major depression show more disturbed family history and short-term outcome than in affective disorder and less severity than in schizophrenic patients and that such mood-incongruent patients are a heterogeneous group. However this was probably related to difficulties in diagnosis rather than an actual difference, because schizoaffective or schizophrenic patients may have been included in their sample of mood-incongruent psychotic depressives. Abrams and Taylor could not find important differences between melancholic major depressives with mood-congruent or incongruent psychosis on any important variable.[17]

Future studies in delusional depression must carefully study mood-congruent, mood-incongruent, and mixed delusions in relation to biochemistry, course, family history, and treatment response. Until further study, the patient with mood-incongruent delusions and unequivocal concomitant episodic depression should be considered delusionally depressed.

Severity of Illness

Delusional depressives are among the most severely ill depressed patients. Severity of illness measured by the Hamilton Depression Scale, even subtracting items related to psychosis, is greater in these patients.[3, 4] However the relationship of severity to delusions is complicated since differences in severity do not account for poor responses to tricyclic antidepressants.[8, 18] Therefore, it is unclear whether delusions are merely a marker of severity or represent a separate trait. Conflicting data on this issue are best explained by the hypothesis that delusions emerge in the vulnerable

Table 1. Frequencies of Delusional Ideas

Type of Idea	Study	
	Kupfer et al.[12] (N = 29)	Frangos et al.[5] (N = 136)
Guilt and Sin	55%	43%
Somatic	34%	29%
Persecution	28%	44%
Nihilistic	Not Reported	44%
Poverty	Not Reported	7%
Multiple Ideas	21%	Not Reported

patient only when depression becomes more severe. Why some patients are vulnerable and others are not remains unknown at present. The question can only be resolved by further study of the pathophysiology and prospective analysis of the relationship of delusions to other symptoms over time and with treatment.

RELATIONSHIP TO AGE

Delusional depressives tend to be older.[19] Since increasing age is associated with poorer response to tricyclic antidepressants,[20] this is a confounding factor in studies of medication response.

**Table 2. Reported Frequencies of Mood-Congruent,
Mood Incongruent, and Mixed Delusions**

Study	Type of Delusion		
	Mood-Congruent	Mood-Incongruent	Mixed
Kupfer et al.[12] (N = 29)	34%	66%	Not Reported
Frangos et al.[5] (N-136)	85%	15%	Not Reported
Minter and Mandel[14] (N = 54)	22%	78%	Not Reported
Brown et al. (unpublished data, N = 28)	57%	11%	32%

The above studies suggest a typical profile of the patient with delusional depression: an older, melancholic, severely depressed patient who is irrationally guilty, markedly agitated, suspicious, self-referential, and with paranoid delusions. Hypochondriacal delusions, most often about gastrointestinal function, are common.

DIFFERENTIAL DIAGNOSIS

Other diagnoses that must be ruled out in a patient with depression and delusions are schizoaffective disorder, organic brain syndromes, major depression with melancholia and without delusions, and schizophrenia with secondary or postpsychotic depression.

Schizoaffective Disorder

The existence of schizoaffective disorder separate from depression and schizophrenia is controversial and unique among DSM-III diagnoses in not having a defining set of criteria. If a patient has grossly bizarre delusions, hallucinations of multiple voices conversing, severe thought disorder, and particularly the presence of psychotic symptoms occurring between episodes and unrelated to depression, the diagnosis of schizoaffective disorder should be made. The distinction may be difficult to make as shown by disagreement among the experts about the diagnosis in a recent case study.[21]

Organic Brain Syndromes

Physical illness causing depression and delusions must be aggressively ruled out, especially in patients presenting with a first episode in mid or late life and those who only meet criteria for major depression but not melancholia. We have recently seen two such patients who despite careful initial evaluation and positive response to medication could only be diagnosed as having meningioma and multi infarct dementia on follow-up one year later. Endocrine, neoplastic or other conditions may precipitate or exacerbate depression in the vulnerable individual.

Melancholic Major Depression

Since the severity and fixity of an unusual belief may fluctuate from day to day and patients may be poorly communicative due to guardedness, hostility or motor agitation or retardation, it is not always easy to distinguish delusional from nondelusional depression.

Schizophrenia

The combination of bizarre thought disorder, chronic deterioration in functioning, and multiple auditory hallucinations developing *prior to* onset of depressive symptoms indicates a diagnosis of schizophrenia. However, in a paranoid patient who is a poor historian, these symptoms and the chronology of their onset may be difficult to elicit at times.

Course of Illness

It appears that delusional and nondelusional depressives have a similar number of prior episodes at time of index admission[3, 5, 13] although one study[22] found more frequent hospitalizations (twice as often) but these may have been required due to the presence of psychosis. Nelson and Bowers[9] noted more prior episodes but Glassman and Roose[8] noted a trend for fewer. Overall, it seems there is no difference in number of prior episodes between delusional and nondelusional patients.

Glassman and Roose showed that delusional depressives are essentially unresponsive to placebo, including the "milder" patients with total Hamilton scores as low as 20. They also discussed data from the era before ECT or drug treatment which suggested that nonrecovery in untreated major depression was limited to delusional patients. Delusionally depressed patients therefore do not show improvement with placebo nor do they show early (1–2 week) response to medications.

Clinical experience suggests that as a recurrent depression becomes more severe and agitation grows, delusions emerge. This is consistent with the experience of Frangos et al.[5] and Nelson and Bowers.[9] Nelson et al.[23] further suggest that delusions disappear before the depressed mood resolves during acute treatment.

Coryell and Tsuang[24] and Winokur[15] presented evidence that delusional depressives were more ill compared to nondelusional depressives at time of discharge from index admission to hospital and on short-term follow-up. Coryell and Tsuang found no difference for patients with mood-congruent delusions on 40-year follow-up although this was not true for the group with mood-incongruent delusions.[24, 25]

STABILITY OF SYMPTOMS OVER TIME IN RECURRENT DELUSIONAL DEPRESSION

What is the stability of psychotic symptoms over time in recurrent depressions? It has been hypothesized that a psychotic depressive will almost always have only psychotic symptoms during recurrent depressions if psychotic depression is a separate diagnostic entity. Charney and Nelson[4] found more previous psychotic depressions in patients who had index admissions for psychotic depressions than those admitted for nonpsychotic depression. Helms and Smith[26] in a retrospective study of stability of diagnosis found that 92 percent of psychotic depressives with recurrent illness had another admission for psychotic depression. They also noted that readmission for nonpsychotic depression was rare after the index psychotic admission. However, Winokur et al.[13] found a striking decrease in psychotic symptoms over time. Price et al.[2] point out the problem of accuracy of retrospective reporting of psychotic symptoms by patients and family members. It also appears that delusionally depressed patients have recurrences of nondelusional as well as delusional depression but that they and their families are less likely to seek hospitalization for nondelusional episodes. They are better able to tolerate the symptoms of depression without psychosis. The issue will only be resolved when long-term prospective follow-up studies are completed. When delusions do recur, they are strikingly similar to previous delusions.

FAMILY HISTORY

There is little evidence for a difference in rates of affective illness in first-degree relatives of delusional and nondelusional depressives. Three studies[2, 3, 5] using large numbers of patients found no differences in rates of affected relatives in contrast to the only study which found more family history of depression in a small sample of delusional patients and nondelusional patients.[23]

Two studies reported no increase in rate of psychotic illness in relatives of delusional depressives.[2, 13, 27]

Winokur was unable to find evidence to separate bipolar from unipolar psychotic depressives[15] on the basis of clinical or demographic variables. However one study suggested a greatly increased rate of bipolar illness in relatives of delusional depressives compared to nondelusional patients.[28]

PHYSIOLOGY

Monoaminergic Biochemistry

Meltzer and associates[29-31] reported that delusional patients had increased serum creatinine phosphokinase and aldolase, skeletal muscle abnormalities, and lower serum dopamine beta-hydroxylase. Sweeney et al.[32] reported higher cerebrospinal (CSF) fluid homovanillic acid (HVA), a dopamine metabolite, and lower urine 3-methoxy-4-hydroxyphenethylene glycol (MHPG) in seven psychotic depressives compared to five nonpsychotic depressives. DeLeon-Jones et al. reported lower levels of urinary MHPG in psychotic depressives.[33] Mendels et al.[34] reported decreased CSF 5 hydroxy- indolacetic acid (5-HIAA), a serotonin metabolite, and a trend to higher HVA in psychotic depression. Spiker et al.[35] found that five delusional depressives had lower levels of all three CSF monoamine metabolites (HVA, MHPG, 5-HIAA) though not significantly lower compared to five nondelusional patients. (These findings were related to increased cortisol production and sleep onset rapid eye movement (REM) in the delusionals). Banki et al. showed a positive though not statistically significant relationship between paranoid beliefs and increased CSF HVA levels.[36] Using cortisol response to oral 5-hydroxytryptophan (5-HTP) as a measure of central serotonin function, Meltzer et al.[37] found that psychotic symptoms were associated with a decreased cortisol response which is consistent with blunted serotonin function. Our own unpublished preliminary data suggest increased CSF HVA.

Further advances in this area may partly depend upon further evidence from basic science research of the interactions between monoaminergic systems. Antelman and Caggiula[38] reviewed data from animal studies on the reciprocal interaction of noradrenergic and dopamine systems. Such data could be consistent with an hypothesis that when noradrenergic tracts reach a low enough threshold, dopaminergic tracts become disinhibited and hyperactive. Future studies to test this theory in delusional depressive patients must use multiple measures of monoaminergic function obtained at different points during the development of symptoms. If this hypothesis is correct, it would predict that as depression develops, there is an associated decrease in noradrenergic and/or serotonergic function and that this decrease results in increased dopaminergic activity and the onset of delusions.

NEUROENDOCRINE ABNORMALITIES

The most frequently studied hormonal abnormality in delusional depression has been adrenocortical dysfunction. Although there are considerable differences between studies in rates of nonsuppression on the dexamethasone suppression test (DST) and plasma cortisol levels pre- and post-dexamethasone, the majority of studies find higher rates of DST nonsuppression and cortisol levels in delusional depressives. However we have recently reviewed the literature and our own data and found that the confounding variables of agitation and melancholia explained most of the variance in cortisol levels in 93 depressed patients (Brown et al., unpublished manuscript). There was considerable overlap in cortisol values between delusional and nondelusional patients. DST suppression predicted the absence of psychosis but DST nonsuppression was only 24 percent better than chance at predicting presence of psychosis. Therefore, normal DST results make delusional depression an unlikely diagnosis, but abnormal results, even with very high cortisol levels, are not diagnostic of delusional depression.

It is unclear whether any changes in thyroid or growth hormone axes are specific to delusional depression. Sweeney et al. reported that 6 of 15 delusional depressives compared to 43 of 87 nondelusional patients had an abnormal response to thyrotropin releasing hormone (TRH), a nonsignificant difference.[39]

We have recently presented evidence that the nocturnal melatonin hyposecretion found in major depressed patients is correlated with a factor of reality disturbance derived from the Hamilton Depression Scale.[40]

Previously we noted further evidence of an association between delusional depression and inappropriate antidiuretic hormone secretion, first described by Raskind et al.,[41] which could be interpreted as evidence of central dopaminergic hyperactivity.

A major problem with most neuroendocrine studies in delusional depression is that abnormalities in any axis are not as yet proven to be specific to disturbance in one particular transmitter system. Abnormal neuroendocrine results must therefore be considered nonspecific, though tantalizing, evidence of disturbed physiology in delusional depressives. The above studies can only suggest that there may be noradrenergic/serotonergic hypofunction and dopaminergic hyperfunction involved in some endogenous depressives including those with delusions.

EEG Sleep Changes

Mendels et al.[42] found decreased stage 4, REM sleep, and total sleep in psychotically depressed patients compared to neurotically depressed patients. Kupfer et al.[12] showed that guilty delusions were associated with much decreased total sleep while somatic delusions were associated with a tendency for high REM activity early in the night as in nondelusional depressives. Kupfer and Thase[19] reported further data suggesting that the combination of long duration of illness, agitation, and relatively older age, was associated with sleep onset REM periods and that delusional patients with more recent onset of psychotic symptoms had decreased REM time which was not explained by age, severity or agitation. The latter disturbances of sleep continuity are more like the findings in acute schizophrenia and schizoaffective disorder than nondelusional depression.[12, 43]

Therefore, sleep EEG study is a promising research tool to distinguish clinical and biological characteristics of delusional depressives who should receive tricyclic antidepressants alone as initial treatment from delusional depressives who should receive antipsychotic and antidepressant medication or electroconvulsive therapy as initial treatment.

Brain Imaging

Targum et al. noted enlarged cerebral ventricles in 8 of 36 delusional depressives compared to 1 of 39 nondelusional depressives, a significant difference.[44]

The above studies suggest that: 1) there are as yet nonspecific biological differences between delusional and nondelusional depressives; 2) that there are likely clinical subgroups of delusional patients with particular physiologic abnormalities; and 3) future studies must combine multiple biological measures and careful clinical assessment.

TREATMENT RESPONSE

Standard Treatments

The three most common treatments for delusional depression are tricyclic antidepressants alone, a combined regimen of antipsychotic and antidepressant medicine, and electroconvulsive therapy (ECT). Results for each of these are summarized in the tables of major studies and text below.

It is clear from the above studies that delusional depressives have a poor response to antidepressants alone ranging from about 15 to 40 percent. Differences in response rates among studies are probably related to differences in populations (age, mood incongruence or kinds of delusions) or dosage of antidepressants. The response rate of nondelusional depressives ranges from 65 to 90 percent. These are high rates for nondelusional patients which suggest very adequate treatment trials in patients likely to benefit from TCAs. Delusional depressives fare better with other treatments described below.

Delusional depressives have a rate of response to tricyclic antidepressants and antipsychotics (TCA/AP) ranging from 40 to 100 percent. However, rate of response to ECT ranges from 80 to 100 percent.

ECT seems superior to TCA/AP although both are better than TCA alone. Markowitz et al. (unpublished manuscript) and Perry et al.[54] noted a nearly two-week earlier response in the group treated with ECT. However, a trial of TCA/AP may be warranted in many cases since these patients tend to have recurrent episodes and medication may offer an advantage for prophylaxis. TCA/AP may also be more acceptable than ECT to some patients.

Why are there differences in rates of response obtained in the above studies? Differences in age of the populations, what criteria for delusional depression are used and how they are applied, and different criteria for adequacy of a treatment trial are probably major factors.

Most of the above studies were retrospective. Prospective controlled trials[55] are required to determine the relative efficacy of the TCA/AP combination versus ECT.

Alternative Treatments

Nelson and Jatlow[56] showed that addition of an AP to desipramine (DMI) raised TCA levels to twice the levels for those receiving DMI alone. Since exposure to AP could lead to tardive dyskinesia (TD) and since older, female depressed patients may be more vulnerable to TD, we studied the effect of higher plasma levels of TCA alone in the treatment of elderly delusional depressives. The results of treatment were poor, however.[57] In fact, several patients worsened on TCA, which is consistant with an earlier report of three similar cases by Nelson et al.[58]

Other treatments have been tried in delusional depression. AP drugs alone produced a poor response rate: 19 percent for Spiker et al.,[1] 31 percent for Charney and Nelson,[4] and 33 percent for Kaskey et al.[51] Falk et al.[59] reported preliminary results for an open label study of amoxapine which has both antidepressant and antipsychotic properties. Only two of six patients improved while the other four had treatment discontinued due to lack of efficacy or side effects.

There are at least five reported cases of delusional depression responsive to tranylcypromine and unresponsive to ECT in one case, TCA/AP in another case, and TCA in three cases.[60, 61] We have recently observed three patients unresponsive to TCA/AP and ECT but responsive to phenelzine. Therefore monoamine oxidase inhibitors should be considered in patients who have failed TCA/AP and ECT.

In patients with a family history of bipolar affective disorder, addition of lithium to TCA/AP has an extremely good chance of converting nonresponse to response.[62]

Maintenance Phase

There are essentially no research data to guide the clinician on maintenance treatment of delusional depression. Important treatment decisions must still be made, though. When should AP and/or TCA be reduced or stopped in the patient who has responded? One rule of thumb is to attempt to reduce and discontinue AP but not the TCA after the patient has

**Table 3. Comparison of Response to Tricyclic Antidepressants
in Delusional and Nondelusional Depressives**

Study	% Response (N) Delusional		Nondelusional		Comment
Friedman[45]	0	(5)	—		Imipramine (IMI)
Hordern et al.[46]	0	(17)	75	(51)	Imipramine
	40	(10)	88	(59)	Amitriptyline (AMI)
Decarolis et al.[47, 48]	40	(181)	—		Imipramine
Glassman et al.[49]	23	(13)	67	(21)	IMI, 200 mg per day
Minter and Mandel	27	(11)	—		All 3 responders had somatic delusions
Brown et al.[50]	17	(18)	74	(23)	
Kaskey et al.[51]	30	(10)	—		
Moradi et al.[52]	0	(7)	—		
Charney and Nelson[4]	22	(9)	80	(40)	
Spiker et al.[1]	41	(17)	—		
Quitkin et al.[53]	No significant difference. They recommend higher doses for longer. However their patient sample is not comparable to those of other studies since delusions and hallucinations were not prominent. They used a perceptual distortion scale score to define psychosis. Their sample also tended to be younger.				

been in remission for one month (with the vigilance and cooperation of the family as an aid). In many cases this has been successful. The TCA often needs to be continued in higher doses and for a longer time than in nondelusional depressives. Sometimes it must be continued indefinitely in this highly recurrent group.

What regimen should be used to prevent relapse after a successful course of ECT? TCA/AP is a conservative approach although TCA alone is adequate in many cases. Lithium alone or in combination with a TCA might be considered in a patient with a personal or family history of bipolar illness. A very small subgroup of the most severely ill, clinically and biochemically, only stay in remission with maintenance ECT.

Table 4. Comparison of Response to Tricyclic Antidepressants and Antipsychotics (TCA/AP) in Delusional and Nondelusional Depressives

	% Response (N)		
Study	*Delusional*	*Nondelusional*	*Comment*
Nelson and Bowers[9]	92 (13)		
Moradi et al.[52]	92 (13)		When AP added to TCA
Minter and Mandel[14]	100 (16)		
Brown et al.[50]	62 (8)	90 (10)	When AP added to TCA
Charney and Nelson[4]	68 (37)		
Kaskey et al.[51]	100 (7)		
Spiker et al.[1]	78 (18)		
Perry et al.[54]	42 (12)		

Table 5. Response to Electroconvulsive Therapy in Delusional Depression

Study	*Delusional*
Decarolis et al.[47, 48]	83 (108)
Glassman et al.[49]	90 (10)
Minter and Mandel[14]	100 (11)
Brown et al.[50]	93 (15)
Charney and Nelson[4]	82 (11)
Kaskey et al.[51]	100 (5)
Perry et al.[54]	86 (14)

<h2 style="text-align:center">SUMMARY</h2>

Clinical

Since management of delusional depression is a clinically challenging process which requires many decisions in diagnosis and treatment, an algorithm summarizing the clinical material of this chapter was developed.

This algorithm begins with the presenting symptoms of delusions and major depression and leads the reader through the differential diagnosis of delusional depression. Once the diagnosis of delusional depression is made, the kind of delusions, age, physical illness, and psychosocial factors are raised as issues to consider in treatment selection. Alternatives when first treatment choices fail are outlined. Finally, selection of maintenance somatic treatments must be made. Boxes contain events or symptoms whereas circles contain clinical choices.

ALGORITHM FOR MANAGEMENT OF DELUSIONAL DEPRESSION

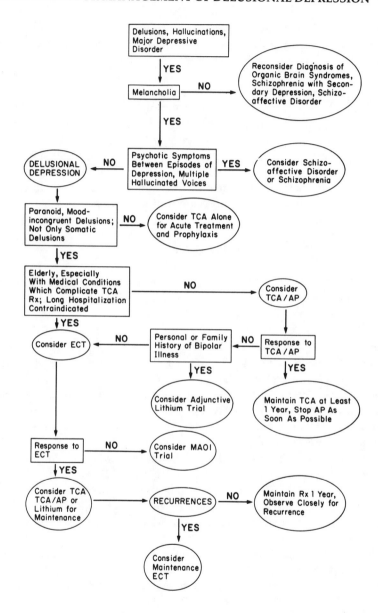

Theoretical

Is delusional depression a separate diagnostic entity? The only major differences in delusional depressives compared to nondelusional patients are in treatment response and in pathophysiology. Clinical and demographic variables do not distinguish these groups from other major depressive disorders. Delusional depression may be a severe variant of nondelusional depression in a vulnerable individual, in which a certain threshold is reached that triggers other disturbances not usually seen. For example, severe disturbance of noradrenergic or serotonergic systems may lead to hypercortisolism, dopaminergic hyperactivity and delusions.

The poor treatment response of these patients warrants their separate discussion. Study of their biological abnormalities is likely to yield clues to the pathophysiology of both depression and psychosis.

REFERENCES

1. Spiker DG, Cofsky Weiss J, Dealy RS, Griffin SJ, Hanin I, Neil JF, Perel JM, Rossi AJ, Soloff PH: The pharmacological treatment of delusional depression. *Am J Psychiatry 1985; 142*: 430-436.
2. Price IH, Nelson JC, Charney DS, Quinlan DM: Family history in delusional depression. *J Aff Dis 1984; 6*: 109-114.
3. Frances A, Brown RP, Kocsis JH, Mann JJ: Psychotic depression: a separate entity? *Am J Psychiatry 1981; 138*: 831-833.
4. Charney DS, Nelson JC: Delusional and nondelusional unipolar depression: further evidence for distinct subtypes. *Am J Psychiatry 1981; 138*: 328-333.
5. Frangos E, Athanassenas G, Tsitourides S, Psilolignos P, Katsanou N: Psychotic depressive disorder. *J Aff Dis 1983; 5*: 259-265.
6. Coryell W, Pfohl B, Zimmerman M: The clinical and neuroendocrine features of psychotic depression. *J Nerv Ment Disease 1984; 172*: 521-528.
7. Carroll BJ, Davies B: Clinical association of II hydroxycorticosteroid suppression and nonsuppression in severe depressive illness. *Br Med J 1970; 1*: 789-791.
8. Glassman AH, Roose SP: Delusional depression. *Arch Gen Psychiatry 1981; 38*: 424-427.
9. Nelson JC, Bowers MB: Delusional unipolar depression: Description and drug response. *Arch Gen Psychiatry 1978; 35*: 1321-1328.
10. Overall JE: The brief psychiatric rating scale in psychopharmacology research. *Mo Prob Pharmacopsychiatry 1974; 7*: 67-78.
11. Raskin A, Crook TA: The endogenous-neurotic distinction as a predictor of response to antidepressant drugs. *Psychol Med 1976; 6*: 59-70.
12. Kupfer DJ, Broudy D, Coble PA, Spiker DG: EEG sleep and affective psychosis. *J Aff Dis 1980; 2*: 17-25.
13. Winokur G, Scharfetter C, Angst J: Stability of psychotic symptomatology (delusions, hallucinations), affective syndromes, and schizophrenic symptoms

(thought disorder, incongruent affect) over episodes in remitting psychoses. *Eur Arch Psychiatr Neurol Sci 1985; 234*: 303-307.

14. Minter RE, Mandel MR: The treatment of psychotic major depressive disorder with drugs and electroconvulsive therapy. *J Nerv Ment Dis 1979; 167*: 726-733.

15. Winokur G: Psychosis in bipolar and unipolar affective illness with special reference to schizo-affective disorder. *Brit J. Psychiatry 1984; 145*: 236-242.

16. Coryell W, Tsuang MT, McDaniel J: Psychotic features in major depression. *J Aff Dis 1982; 4*: 227-236.

17. Abrams R, Taylor MA: The importance of mood-congruent psychotic symptoms in melancholia. *J Aff Dis 1983; 5*: 179 181.

18. Brown RP, Frances A, Kocsis JH, Mann JJ: Psychotic vs nonpsychotic depression: comparison of treatment response. *J Nerv Ment Dis 1982; 170*: 635-637.

19. Kupfer DJ, Thase ME: Psychobiologic aspects of delusional depression. *J Clin Psych Monograph 1985; 3*(1): 4-7.

20. Brown RP, Sweeney J, Frances A, Kocsis JH, Loutech E: Age as a predictor of treatment response in endogenous depression. *J Clin Psychopharm 1983; 3*: 176-178.

21. Spitzer RL, Skodol AE, Gibbon M, Williams JBW: 38 year-old mother with psychotic symptoms and affective disorder. In: DSM-III Case Studies. Frances, A.F. (Editor). *Hosp Comm Psychiatry 1981; 32*: 243-244.

22. Guze SB, Woodruff RA, Clayton PJ: The significance of psychotic affective disorders. *Arch Gen Psychiatry 1975; 32*: 1147-1150.

23. Nelson WH, Khan A, Orr WW: Phenomenology, neuroendocrine function, and tricyclic antidepressant response. *J Aff Dis 1984; 6*: 297-306.

24. Coryell W, Tsuang MT: Primary unipolar depression and the prognostic importance of delusions. *Arch Gen Psychiatry 1982; 39*: 1181-1184.

25. Coryell W, Tsuang MT: Major depression with mood-congruent or mood-incongruent psychotic features: outcome after 40 years. *Am J Psychiatry 1985; 142*: 479-482.

26. Helms PM, Smith RE: Recurrent psychotic depression. *J Aff Dis 1983; 5*: 51-54.

27. Winokur G, Scharfetter C, Angst J: A family study of psychotic symptomatology in schizophrenia, schizoaffective disorder, unipolar depression and bipolar disorder. *Eur Arch Psychiatr Neurol Sci 1985; 234*: 295-298.

28. Weissman MM, Prusoff BA, Merikangas KR: Is delusional depression related to bipolar disorder? *Am J Psychiatry 1984; 141*: 892-893.

29. Meltzer HY: Skeletal muscle abnormalities in patients with affective disorders. *J Psychiat Res 1973; 10*: 43-57.

30. Meltzer HY, Hyong WC, Carroll BJ, Russo P: Serum dopamine-B- hydroxylase activity in the affective psychoses and schizophrenia. *Arch Gen Psychiat 1976; 33*: 585-591.

31. Meltzer HY: *Decreased serum dopamine-B-hydroxylase activity in unipolar psychotically depressed patients*. Presented at the APA Annual Meeting, May, 1979, Chicago, IL.

32. Sweeney D, Nelson C, Bowers M et al. Delusional vs nondelusional depression: neurochemical differences. *Lancet 1978; 2*: 100-101.

33. DeLeon-Jones F, Maas JW, Dekirmenjian H: Diagnostic subgroups of affective disorders and their urinary excretion of catecholamine metabolites. *Am J Psychiatry 1975; 132:* 1141 1148.

34. Mendels J, Frazer A, Fitzgerald RG, Ramsey TA, Stokes JW: Biogenic amine metabolites in cerebrospinal fluid of depressed and manic patients. *Science 1972; 175:* 1380-1382.

35. Spiker DG, Berger PA, Dealy RS, Faull KF, Griffin SJ, Jarrett DB, Kupfer DJ: *The psychobiology of delusional depression: A preliminary report.* In *Proceedings of the IV World Congress of Biological Psychiatry,* Shagass C et al (Editors), New York, Elsevier, in press.

36. Banki CM, Molnar G, Vojnik M: Cerebrospinal fluid amine metabolites, tryptophan and clinical parameters in depression. *J Aff Dis 1981; 3:* 91-99.

37. Meltzer HY, Perline R, Tricou BJ, Lowy M, Robertson A: Effects of 5-hydroxytryptophan on serum cortisol levels in major affective disorders: II. Relation to suicide, psychosis and depressive symptoms. *Arch Gen Psych 1984; 41:* 379-387.

38. Antelman SM, Caggiula AR: Norepinephrine-dopamine interactions and behavior. *Science 1977; 195:* 646-651.

39. Sweeney DR, Extein IL, Pottash ALC, Gold M, Sternbach A: *Neuroendocrine responses in delusional depression.* Presentation number 78, May 20, 135 Annual Meeting of the American Psychiatric Association 1982.

40. Brown RP, Kocsis JH, Caroff S, Amsterdam J, WinokuFrazer F: *Depressed mood and reality disturbance correlate with decreased nocturnal melatonin in depressed patients.* Presented at the May 1986 meeting of the Society of Biological Psychiatry.

41. Brown RP, Kocsis JH, Cohen SK: Delusional depression and inappropriate antidiuretic hormone secretion. *Biol Psychiatry 1983; 18:* 1059-1063.

42. Mendels J, Hawkins DR: Sleep and depression. *Arch Gen Psychiat 1968; 19:* 445-452.

43. Kupfer DJ, Broudy D, Spiker DG, Neil JF, Coble PA: EEG sleep and affective psychoses: I. Schizoaffective disorders. *Psychiatry Res 1979; 1:* 173-178.

44. Targum SD, Rosen LN, Citrin CM: Delusional symptoms associated with enlarged cerebral ventricles in depressed patients. *Southern Med J 1983; 76:* 985-987.

45. Friedman C, DeMowbray MS, Hamilton V: Imipramine (Tofranil) in depressives states. *J Ment Sci 1961; 107:* 948 953.

46. Hordern A, Holt NF, Curt C et al: Amitriptyline in depressive states. Phenomenology and prognostic considerations. *Br J Psychiatry, 1963; 109:* 815-825.

47. DeCarolis V, Giberti F, Roccatagliata G et al: Imipramine and electroshock in the treatment of depression: a clinical statistical analysis of 437 cases. *Nerv Sist 1964; 16:* 29.

48. Avery D, Lubrano A: Depression treated with imipramine and ECT; The De Carolis study reconsidered. *Am J Psychiatry 1979; 136:* 559-562.

49. Glassman AH, Kantor SJ, Shostak M: Depression, delusions and drug response. *Am J Psychiatry 1975; 132*: 716 719.

50. Brown RP, Frances A, Kocsis JH, Mann JJ: Psychotic vs nonpsychotic depression: comparison of treatment response. *J Nerv Ment Dis 1982; 170*: 635-637.

51. Kaskey GB, Nasr S, Meltzer HY: Drug treatment in delusional depression. *Psychiatr Res 1980; 1*: 267-277.

52. Moradi SR, Muniz CE, Belar CD: Male delusional depressed patients: response to treatment. *Br J Psychiatry 1979; 135*: 136-138.

53. Quitkin F, Rifkin A, Klein DF: Imipramine response in deluded depressive patients. *Am J Psychiatry 1978; 135*: 806 810.

54. Perry PJ, Morgan DE, Smith RE, Tsuang MT: Treatment of unipolar depression accompanied by delusions: ECT versus tricyclic antidepressant- antipsychotic combinations. *J Aff Dis 1982; 4*: 195-200.

55. Minter RE, Mandel MR: A prospective study of the treatment of psychotic depression. *Am J Psychiatry 1979; 136*: 1470-1472.

56. Nelson NC, Jatlow PI: Neuroleptic effect on desipramine steady state plasma concentrations. *Am J Psychiatry 1980; 137*: 1332-1333.

57. Brown RP, Kocsis JH, Glick ID, Dhar AK: Efficacy and feasibility of high dose tricyclic antidepressant treatment in elderly delusional depressions. *J Clin Psychopharm 1984; 4*: 311-315.

58. Nelson JC, Bowers MB, Sweeney DR: Exacerbation of psychosis by tricyclic antidepressants in delusional depression. *Am J Psychiatry 1979; 136*: 574-576.

59. Falk WE, Gelenberg AJ, Wojcik JD: Amoxapine for the treatment of psychotically depressed subjects. *J Nerv Ment Dis 1985; 173*: 90-93.

60. Lieb J, Collins C: Treatment of delusional depression with tranylcypromine. *J Nerv Ment Dis 1978; 166*: 805-808.

61. Minter RE, Verdugo N, Mandel MR: The treatment of delusional depression with tranylcypromine: a case report. *J Clin Psych, 1980; 41*: 178.

62. Price LH, Cornwell Y, Nelson JC: Lithium augmentation of combined neuroleptitricyclic treatment in delusional depression. *Am J Psychiatry 1983; 140*: 318-322.

RECOMMENDED READING

Charney DS, Nelson JC: Delusional and nondelusional unipolar depression: Further evidence for distinct subtypes, *Am J Psychiatry, 1981; 138*: 328-333.

Kupfer DJ, Thase ME: Psychobiologic aspects of delusional depression. *J Clin Psych Monograph 1985; 3(1)*: 4-7.

Minter RE, Mandel MR: A prospective study of the treatment of psychotic depression. *Am J Psychiatry 1979; 136*: 1470-1472.

Spiker DG, Cofsky Weiss J, Delay RS, Griffing SJ, Hannin I, Neil JF, Perel JM, Rossi AJ, Soloff PH: The pharmacological treatment of delusional depression. *Am J Psychiatry 1985; 142*: 430-436.

AFFECTIVE DISORDERS IN CHILDHOOD
AND ADOLESCENCE

P. Anne McBride, M.D.
Theodore Shapiro, M.D.

INTRODUCTION

During the past decade, there has been significant progress in efforts to establish affective disorders as valid diagnostic entities in childhood and adolescence.[1-5] Several studies support the hypothesis that the core phenomenonology of major depressive disorder is similar whether the onset of symptoms occurs in prepuberty, adolescence, or adulthood.[3-11] Studies of family aggregation, natural history, neuroendocrine function, psychosocial correlates, and response to treatment in children and adolescents suggest that similar processes may be important in the pathogenesis of affective disorders in both pediatric and adult age groups.[1,2] However, the impact of developmental and maturational processes upon symptomatology, course of illness, and physiological variables remains a subject of active inquiry.

Historically, there has been considerable speculation and debate not only about the role of developmental factors in the symptomatic expression of depressed mood in children, but about the actual capacity of prepubertal children to experience depression as a state distinct from sadness or grief. Elaborating upon classical psychoanalytic theories concerning dynamic mechanisms responsible for the onset of melancholia,[12-14] Finch[15] and Rie[16] argued that depressive disorders could not occur prior to adolescence due to the intrapsychic immaturity of the prepubertal child, particularly the lack of a well-internalized superego. During the 1960s and 70s, there was increasing acceptance of the idea that children could experience depression, but that the symptomatic expression of depressed mood was generally "masked." Toolan,[17] Glaser,[18] and Cytryn and McKnew[19] maintained that behaviors or symptoms including hyperactivity, aggressiveness, delinquency, phobias, enuresis, anxiety, social withdrawal, somatic complaints, and poor school performance were "depressive equivalents," suggesting the presence of depression even in the absence of objective evidence of a mood disturbance. In the past decade, the use of "masked depression" as a diagnostic term has been discredited,[2, 5, 20-23] although it has been noted that many of the above symptoms are common presenting complaints in children and adolescents meeting adult criteria for affective disorders, and that such symptoms can distract the clinician from carefully evaluating for the presence of depression.[20, 22, 24] Despite a growing consensus that the clinical presentation of major depression is similar in children and adults, uncertainties remain concerning the degree to which essential and associated features may differ between age groups.[1, 4, 5, 25, 26]

This chapter will consider studies of the phenomenology, epidemiology, and pathogenesis of affective disorders in children and adolescents, and summarize current approaches to evaluation and treatment. Particular emphasis will be placed on findings suggestive of continuities or differences between affective disorders with onset in childhood versus adulthood.

PHENOMENOLOGY

Diagnostic Criteria

Recognition of the necessity of reliably defining homogeneous groups in studies of childhood affective disorders[1, 27-29] has led to the use of DSM-III criteria[30] and Research Diagnostic Criteria (RDC),[31] formulated for adults, in the assessment of mood disturbances in children and adolescents. Both sets of criteria for major depressive disorder require a distinct period of dysphoric mood and/or anhedonia, lasting at least two weeks, accompanied by four or five of the following symptoms: significant change in appetite or weight; sleep disturbance; loss of energy; loss of interest or pleasure; self-reproach or inappropriate guilt; diminished concentration; suicidal tendencies; and psychomotor aggitation or retardation. DSM-III states that depressed children may have age-specific associated features, most notably separation anxiety in prepubertal children and negativistic or antisocial behavior in adolescent boys.

Although the extent to which developmental processes may influence the expression of affective disorders has yet to be well-established, several studies have confirmed the feasibility of using RDC or DSM-III criteria in the diagnosis of affective disorders in school-age children and adolescents.

Significant numbers of children presenting for psychiatric treatment meet RDC or DSM-III criteria for major depressive disorder. Robbins et al.[28] reported that 27 percent of 33 adolescents admitted to an inpatient psychiatric service met RDC criteria for major depression. Likewise, Carlson and Cantwell[32] found that DSM-III criteria were fulfilled by 27 percent of 102 randomly selected youngsters, ages 7 to 17 years, from inpatient and outpatient settings. Furthermore, Strober and colleagues[5] have shown that the eight RDC subtypes of major depressive disorder can be diagnosed in adolescents with only slightly less inter-rater reliability than in adults. DSM-III and/or RDC criteria have also been successfully applied to the diagnosis of: bipolar disorder in adolescents[33]; and psychotic depression,[6, 8] dysthymic disorder, and adjustment disorder with depressed mood[3, 4] in school-age children.

During the 1970s, Ling,[34] Weinberg,[35] Cytryn and McKnew,[19] Malmquist,[36] Petti,[37] and Poznanski[38] each proposed diagnostic criteria or classificatory systems for childhood affective disorders which incorporated a developmental perspective in delineating essential clinical features. Weinberg's criteria, modified from the Feighner adult diagnostic criteria,[39] have been most extensively applied. Weinberg criteria require both dysphoric mood and self-deprecatory ideation, but the presence of only two of eight additional symptoms, including several not specific to a diagnosis of depression in adults: aggressive behavior; change in school performance; diminished socialization; change in attitude towards school; and somatic complaints. Carlson and Cantwell[32] demonstrated that Weinberg and DSM-III criteria for major depression do not necessarily identify the same children. Of 28 children ages 7 to 17 years with DSM-III diagnoses of major depression, 78.4 percent met Weinberg criteria; the converse was true in only 57.8 percent of 38 children diagnosed as acutely depressed by Weinberg criteria. Children meeting both DSM-III and Weinberg criteria for depression had significantly higher scores on the Children's Depression Inventory (CDI) and more frequent family histories of depression than children meeting Weinberg criteria alone, suggesting that Weinberg criteria are less specific for a diagnosis of depression than DSM-III criteria.[25]

While the preponderance of evidence supports the validity of employing DSM-III and RDC criteria to diagnose affective disorders presenting in childhood and adolescence, several authors[1, 3, 27] have questioned whether criteria established for adults are reliable in identifying children with less severe forms of depressive disorder. Kovacs[3] has also commented that questions concerning diagnostic precision are raised by the high prevalence of coexisting psychiatric disorders among school-age children meeting DSM-III criteria for affective disorders. While DSM-III criteria for major depression have been applied to preschool children,[7, 40] the suitability of adult criteria for use in this age group has not been adequately assessed.[7, 27, 40]

Clinical Presentation

Several investigators[5, 9, 10, 41, 42] have reported frequencies of specific symptoms in school-age children and adolescents presenting with DSM-III diagnoses of major depression. Symptoms seen in greater than 50 percent of patients in a majority of these studies included: depressed mood; depressed appearance; loss of interest or pleasure; diminished concentration; suicidal tendencies; decreased appetite; some form of insomnia; lowered self-esteem or worthlessness; indecisiveness; self-reproach or inappropriate guilt; decreased energy; and somatic complaints. Psychomotor retardation[5, 41, 42] and diurnal variation[5, 41] were relatively infrequent symptoms. Carlson and Cantwell[10] demonstrated that the following symptoms were significantly more common in children and adolescents with affective disorders than in a comparison group with other psychiatric diagnoses: dysphoric mood; low self-esteem; poor school performance; anhedonia; tiredness; insomnia; somatic complaints; suicidal ideation; and hopelessness. Similar rates for 33 symptoms of affective disorder were found in Carlson and Strober's group of 28 hospitalized depressed adolescents and two populations of adults with major depression studied by others.[41]

Strober and colleagues[5] have reported incidences of the eight RDC subtypes of major depressive disorder in a study of 40 adolescents hospitalized for treatment of depression. Primary depression was diagnosed in 75 percent of cases, endogenous in 33 percent, and psychotic in 13 percent. The authors compared incidences of the eight subtypes in their adolescent population with those reported in adults by Spitzer et al., and found that the endogenous and incapacitating types were significantly less frequent in the adolescent group.

Significant percentages of depressed school-age children have also been shown to meet RDC criteria for the endogenous and/or psychotic subtypes of disorder.[6, 8, 43] Chambers et al.[8] found that 50 percent of 58 prepubertal children who fulfilled RDC criteria for major depression belonged to the endogenous subtype. Forty-eight percent of endogenously depressed children and 24 percent of youngsters with nonendogenous depression described auditory hallucinations consisting of one or more words other than their names, which occurred during a state of clear sensorium. Command hallucinations were most frequent, and often reflected suicidal tendencies. Most auditory hallucinations were judged to be mood-congruent. Sixteen percent of the total sample of 58 children reported visual or tactile hallucinations, and 7 percent had delusional ideas. The authors pointed out that although hallucinations and delusions described by prepubertal children were similar in character to those reported by psychotically depressed adolescents and adults, the pattern of occurrence was different. Auditory hallucinations were significantly more common in their sample of prepubertal children than in adolescent and adult populations studied by others, while delusions were less prevalent among the children than adults.

The symptom constellation designated as atypical depressive disorder by Liebowitz and Klein[44] in adults has also been described in adolescents.[45] These youngsters are chronically reactive to environmental stimuli, exquisitely sensitive to rejection, have pronounced difficulties with interpersonal relationships, and overeat and oversleep during depressive episodes.

Several case reports have described school-age children and adolescents with symptoms typical of mania in adults.[46-48] However, rigorous studies of bipolar disorder in these age groups are lacking. Puig-Antich[49] has summarized anecdotal findings from more than a dozen case reports to present a "composite picture." He relates that the prepubertal child with bipolar disorder characteristically exhibits frequent and rapid swings between full-fledged manic and depressive episodes, as well as some symptom-free periods. The duration of episodes and the cycle period gradually increase as the child moves into adolescence and adulthood. Quite rare in prepuberty, bipolar disorder becomes increasingly prevalent during adolescence. Marked depressive symptomatology often precedes the first manic episode in adolescents.[33]

Knowledge of affective disorders presenting in the preschool years is currently limited. Kashani has reported case histories of two children who met DSM-III criteria for major depression,[7,40] and of an additional three with diagnoses of "possible or definite" dysthymic disorder.[7] Frank suicidal behavior has been described in preschool children.[50,51] Rosenthal and Rosenthal[51] studied 16 children ages two and one-half to five years who had attempted or succeeded in harming themselves with evidence of suicidal intent, and found that nine met Weinberg criteria for depression versus two in a comparison group of 16 nonsuicidal preschool children with behavioral problems. None of the children met DSM-III criteria for major depression. In the 1940s, Spitz[52] described a condition termed "anaclytic depression" in infants separated from consistent nurturing caretakers after six months of age. The symptoms, which included sad and immobile faces, apathy, weeping, appetite and sleep disturbances, decreased motor movements, and decreased reactivity to stimuli, are similar to those listed as criteria for major depression in DSM-III. However, the relationship between depressive-like states arising in emotionally deprived infants and frank affective disorders occurring in later childhood and adulthood has not been established.

Natural History

Several longitudinal studies[3,4,11,33,53-55] have examined the course of affective disorders in children and adolescents. Kovacs et al.,[3,4] in the most extensive of the studies, followed prospectively 65 children who originally presented between the ages of 8 and 13 years with DSM-III diagnoses of major depressive disorder, dysthymic disorder, or adjustment disorder with depressed mood. Only three of the children received pharmacotherapy. Children with major depression had index episodes lasting a mean of 32 weeks, and recovered within one and one-half years of the onset of symptoms in 92 percent of cases. On the other hand, index episodes of children with dysthymic disorder lasted an average of three years, and the maximal recovery rate of 89 percent was reached only after six years had elapsed. Children with adjustment disorder with depressed mood had the shortest mean duration of illness (25 weeks), and 90 percent had recovered within nine months of diagnosis. The younger the age of the child at the time of onset of major depressive disorder or dysthymic disorder, the more protracted was the duration of the index episode. The median age of onset for dysthymic disorder was significantly earlier than that for major depression or adjustment disorder with depressed mood.[3]

The Kovacs study has demonstrated not only the lengthy duration of index episodes of major depressive disorder in school-age children, but the recurrent course of the disorder. The cumulative risk for a second episode of major depression was 40 percent during the first two years following recovery from the presenting episode, and 72 percent within five years of initial diagnosis. Children with diagnoses of both major depression and dysthymic disorder were at greater risk for a recurrent episode of major depression than children with major depression alone,[4] although underlying dysthymia did not alter the duration of depressive episodes.[3] Furthermore, 69 percent of children with primary diagnoses of dysthymic disorder had a full-fledged episode of major depression within five years of the onset of symptoms.[4]

From the foregoing findings, Kovacs[4] concluded that major depressive disorder and dysthymic disorder presenting in childhood are diagnostically distinct but closely related entities. In contrast, adjustment disorder with depressed mood does not appear to be closely associated with either major depressive disorder or dysthymic disorder in children. None of the children originally carrying a diagnosis of adjustment disorder developed major depressive disorder.

Several other studies have documented the long-term morbidity associated with affective disorders originating in childhood. In the 1970s, Poznanski et al.[11] reevaluated 10 adolescents and young adults by clinical psychiatric interview an average of six and one-half years after they had presented with symptoms of depression, and found that 50 percent continued to have significant chronic depressive symptomatology; all had poor peer relationships and low productivity at work or school. The authors felt that the children began to resemble adult depressives as they approached adulthood, with greater dependency needs and less aggressive behavior. Eastgate and Gilmore[53] obtained clinical data on 19 young adults who had met Weinberg criteria for depression as school-age children, and reported that 50 percent of the group had been moderately to severely disabled by psychiatric disorders during the five-year period directly preceding follow-up. Final diagnoses included depressive and/or anxiety disorders, marked personality disorders, and in one case, schizophrenia. As part of the New York Longitudinal Study, Chess and colleagues[54] followed from birth to adulthood two children who developed major depressive disorder and four children who developed dysthymic disorder, as defined by DSM-III criteria, in early to mid-adolescence. Both individuals with major depression had multiple recurrent episodes throughout adolescence and early adulthood, interspersed with periods of better functioning; those with dysthymic disorder tended to exhibit chronic poor functioning, as well as evidence of associated personality disorders with increasing age. Of interest, Chess did not find a consistent association between the quality of mood in the first five years of life and the subsequent development of a depressive disorder.

Strober and Carlson[33] have reported that 20 percent of a cohort of 60 adolescents hospitalized with RDC diagnoses of major depressive disorder between the ages of 13 and 16 years developed frank bipolar disorder by the time of follow-up three to four years later. A bipolar outcome was predicted by the following: 1) a symptom cluster during the index episode of major depressive disorder consisting of rapid onset, psychomotor retardation, and mood-congruent psychotic features; 2) a family history of bipolar disorder, the presence of three or more family members with affective disorders, and/or a history of affective disorder in three successive generations of the pedigree; 3) pharmacologically-induced hypomania. The symptom cluster of rapid onset, psychomotor retardation, and psychotic features during the index depressive episode characterized 67 percent of 12 adolescents who ultimately developed bipolar disorder, but only 4 percent of 48 patients with a history of unipolar disorder at follow-up.

In a study of prepubertal children, Puig-Antich and colleagues[55] found that effective treatment of the index episode of major depressive disorder did not necessarily result in normalization of psychosocial functioning. Twenty-one children were reevaluated at least four months following sustained recovery from their depressive episodes, and at least one month following cessation of treatment with antidepressant medications. While the children's school performance had improved considerably, and was no longer significantly different from that of a control group of normal children, relationships with parents, siblings, and peers showed only partial improvement. When compared with normal children from families with comparable family constellations and parental marital relationships, recovered depressives exhibited less amount and depth of communication, less warmth, and greater hostility in relationships with their parents. They were also less likely to have a best friend or to socialize with peers; clinicians view impaired peer relationships as a sign of significant maladaptive functioning in children.

In summary, longitudinal studies have supported the presence of continuities between affective disorders occurring in children and adults. Affective disorders presenting in childhood and adolescence are typically chronic conditions, with symptoms frequently persisting into adulthood. Furthermore, Kovacs and colleagues[4] have demonstrated that major depressive disorder has a relapsing and remitting course in children as well as in adults. Dysthymic disorder characteristically persists for several years in both age groups. However, Kovacs[4] has described some apparent differences in the course of affective disorders in children versus adults. The duration of symptom-free periods may be shorter in children than in adults with major depression, while children may be more likely to ultimately experience remission of dysthymic disorder. Additional prospective longitudinal studies should clarify the impact of maturational processes upon the course of affective disorders across the life span.

Associated Conditions

Children and adolescents with affective disorders frequently meet criteria for other psychiatric disorders. For example, Kovacs et al.[3,4] found that close to half of their cohort of school-age children with diagnoses of major depressive disorder and/or dysthymic disorder fulfilled DSM-III criteria for additional diagnoses.

Listed in DSM-III as an age-specific associated feature of major depression in adolescent boys, antisocial behavior has been reported in a sizable percentage of depressed school-age children as well as adolescents by a number of investigators.[3, 21, 42, 54, 56, 57] Puig-Antich[56] found that one-third of 43 prepubertal boys who met RDC criteria for major depressive disorder also fulfilled DSM-III criteria for a conduct disorder, although none of the girls in the same sample exhibited antisocial behavior. The symptoms of major depression were not significantly different in boys with conduct disorders and appeared to precede the onset of behavioral difficulties in 87 percent of cases. Successful treatment of the affective disorder with imipramine was followed by a substantial decrease in antisocial behavior in a majority of the children. Geller et al.[57] found that antisocial behavior was evident in 11 percent of 36 prepubertal children and 35 percent of 23 adolescents with DSM-III diagnoses of major depression. However, they did not find significant differences in prevalence rates between the genders. Puig-Antich has hypothesized that boys who develop a secondary conduct disorder during an episode of major depression may later be identified as adults with antisocial personality disorder or alcoholism in family pedigrees characterized by depressive spectrum disease.[56]

Several studies[3, 43, 57-59] have also justified the inclusion of separation anxiety as an age-specific associated feature of major depressive disorder in children. Separation anxiety was present in each of 13 prepubertal children with major depression evaluated by Puig-Antich[43] and in 81 percent of both prepubertal children and adolescents in a study by Geller.[57] In all cases, separation anxiety developed after the onset of major depressive disorder. Hershberg and colleagues[58] reported that 68 percent of 28 school-age children and adolescents with depressive disorders described significant generalized anxiety, and 39 percent situation-specific anxiety. However, they found that few of their depressed children met full DSM-III criteria for anxiety disorders. Conversely, significant depressive symptomatology is common in children presenting with school phobia.[59, 60]

Associations between depression and other DSM-III diagnoses have been more variably described. Several studies[3, 20, 42] have identified attention deficit disorder as among the most common coexisting psychiatric disorders in children with depressive disorders. Puig-Antich and associates,[45] though, did not find a specific association between attention deficit disorder and major depression; they cautioned that poor concentration and psychomotor agitation occurring in the context of a depressive episode can be mistaken for hyperactivity. It is unclear whether specific developmental disorders are associated with affective disorders. A diagnosis of specific developmental disorder (arithmetic, reading, or language) was made in 62 percent of Kashani et al.'s[42] sample of children with major depression but in only 22 percent of children presenting to the same mental health clinic with nonaffective disorders. On the other hand, Puig-Antich and colleagues found that significant deficits in reading, spelling, and arithmetic noted during depressive episodes in prepubertal children[61] resolved with successful treatment of the depression.[55] Adolescents with anorexia nervosa frequently present with concurrent affective disorders,[62-64] and in one study, one-third of patients treated for anorexia nervosa later met criteria for an affective disorder at follow-up.[62]

Prominent somatic complaints have been described in significant numbers of depressed children and adolescents by several investigators.[9, 10, 41, 42] Somatic delusions have been reported in prepubertal children with psychotic depression.[8] Furthermore, high percentages of children presenting to pediatric services with complaints of chest pain[65] or gastrointestinal disturbances[66] meet DSM- III criteria for major depression. Kashani and colleagues[65] have suggested that somatic complaints should be added to the DSM-III description of age-related associated features of major depression specific to children.

DIFFERENTIAL DIAGNOSIS

Since DSM-III diagnostic criteria are used for both children and adults, the differential diagnosis of affective disorders is similar in both age groups. Nonetheless, some questions concerning diagnostic distinctions appear to arise more frequently with children and/or adolescents than with older patients. For instance, it is often necessary with adolescents to distinguish between a period of unhappiness or misery and true affective disorder. In their study of 14- to 15-year-olds residing on the Isle of Wight, Rutter and colleagues[67] found that 42 percent of boys and 48 percent of girls in a random sample of 194 youngsters reported feeling miserable or depressed when asked during clinical interviews. Significant difficulty falling or staying asleep and early morning awakening were each described on a self-report malaise inventory by approximately 20 percent of the sample. In a survey of 4,204 American high school students and their parents conducted by Kandel and Davies,[68] 20 percent of adolescents versus 6.5 percent of their parents indicated feeling "much bothered or troubled" by "feeling sad or depressed in the past year." Offer[69] found that 71 of 73 adolescents described mild to moderate depressive symptomatology at two-year follow-up in a longitudinal study of middle- class high school students in whom serious psychiatric disturbance had been ruled out at the time of induction. However, the vast majority of adolescents in the foregoing studies would not have fulfilled DSM-III criteria for affective disorders. Rutter made diagnoses of depressive disorders in only 1.5 percent of the 2,303 14- to 15-year-olds residing on the Isle of Wight.

While a positive correlation has been described between the severity of depressive symptomatology and the intensity of suicidal ideation in children and adolescents,[70] youngsters with suicidal ideation or behavior are often not clinically depressed, and frequently meet criteria for nonaffective psychiatric diagnoses.[70,71] Pfeffer et al.[71] reported that borderline personality disorder was the most common diagnosis in a group of hospitalized school-age children with both suicidal and assaultive tendencies. These children typically exhibited ego deficits, had frequent episodes of rage, and had been exposed to parental violence and/or suicidal behavior. Although the most frequent diagnoses, affective disorders were present in only 45 percent of a second group of children with suicidal, but not assaultive tendencies. Many of these youngsters had developed overt depressive symptomatology during a period of extreme environmental stress. Carlson and Cantwell[70] found that history of a suicide attempt was not correlated with a diagnosis of depression or with the severity of suicidal ideation in children and adolescents. Youngsters whose suicide attempts had not resulted in psychiatric hospitalization often denied a history of pervasive depressive symptomatology and had a pattern of antisocial behavior. On the other hand, children hospitalized following generally more lethal suicide attempts met criteria for major depressive disorder in approximately 75 percent of cases.

Although an association between affective disorders and conduct disorders has been found in children and adolescents,[56,57] the typical child with a conduct disorder experiences only brief periods of depressed mood or anhedonia, usually coinciding with punishment for antisocial behavior.[45] A diagnosis of an affective disorder is warranted in these children only if full criteria are met.

Organic affective syndromes must be considered as potential diagnoses in children presenting with depressive symptomatology. Neurologic, endocrine, and other medical illnesses,[72] as well as use of various illicit and prescription drugs, can cause disturbances of affect in pediatric age groups. Conversely, primary affective disorders may be mistaken for organic affective syndromes or adjustment disorder with depressed mood in some children with debilitating medical diseases.[72]

In short, the clinician must establish the presence of a constellation of symptoms before a diagnosis of affective disorder is made. While symptoms such as dysphoric mood and suicidal behavior may suggest an affective disorder, they lack diagnostic specificity. Organic causes of affective instability must be born in mind in children as well as adults.

EPIDEMIOLOGY

Very few studies employing DSM-III criteria and rigorous methodologies have been undertaken to determine the prevalences of affective disorders among children and adolescents in general populations. In a study of 103 healthy school-age children recruited from medical settings in Missouri, Kashani and Simonds[73] found two boys who met DSM-III criteria for major depressive disorder. Diagnoses were made on the basis of interviews of both the children and their mothers by a child psychiatrist. Kashani and colleagues[74] conducted a more extensive longitudinal study in a metropolitan area in New Zealand, and found that the point prevalences of DSM-III diagnoses of major depressive disorder and dysthymic disorder among 9-year-old children were approximately 1.8 percent and 2.5 percent, respectively. Prevalences were estimated from clinical interviews of 94 potentially depressed and 95 randomly-selected children drawn from a sample of 641 children assessed by self-report and parental questionnaires for past or present history of depression. Seventeen of 189 children interviewed had a history of past, but not present depressive disorders.

Studies relying solely upon self-report diagnostic instruments have tended to overestimate the prevalences of depressive disorders in pediatric age groups.[75] For instance, Albert and Beck[76] reported that one-third of 31 children attending 7th and 8th grades at a parochial school were moderately to severely depressed according to their responses on the short form of the Beck Depression Inventory (BDI). Also using the BDI, Kaplan and associates[77] found that 8.6 percent of 385 American junior and senior high school students were moderately to severely depressed as defined by scores of ≥ 16. The prevalence of presumed depressive disorders in the latter study is similar to the point prevalence of major and minor depressive disorders among adults in general population studies.[78, 79]

Although rigorous studies are lacking, there is evidence to suggest that prevalences of affective disorders increase significantly at puberty. In the Isle of Wight study, only three of approximately 2,000 10-year-old children were felt to warrant diagnoses of depressive disorders, while 35 were given diagnoses of affective disorders at follow-up at age 14 years.[67] Kaplan et al.[77] found that 11- to 13-year-olds had significantly less depressive symptomatology than 14- to 16- and 17- to 18-year-olds. While some studies have suggested that adolescent girls are somewhat more likely than boys to to report depressed mood,[67, 68] Kaplan et al.[77] did not find a significant correlation between gender and total scores on the BDI in their adolescent population. Furthermore, Kashani et al.[74] failed to identify an association between gender and DSM-III diagnoses of depressive disorders at age nine. In the Kaplan study, depression was positively correlated with lower socioeconomic status. In contrast, no association between depressive disorders and socioeconomic status was found in the school-age population of Kashani et al.[74] Definitive studies of the epidemiology of affective disorders in children and adolescents should not only establish prevalence rates, but clarify to what extent interactions between variables such as age, pubertal status, gender, and socioeconomic class contribute to morbid risk.

ETIOLOGIC MODELS

While etiologic models of affective disorders are generally classified by conceptual framework, there has been increasing acceptance of the view that physiological and psychological approaches are not exclusive of one another. Akiskal and McKinney[80] were among the first to present a model of depressive disorders in adults integrating psychoanalytic, behavioral, sociological, and biological schools of thought. In recent years, several authors have emphasized the necessity of characterizing relationships between multiple factors which may contribute to the etiology of childhood depression.[81-83] It has been hypothesized that the interplay between physiological and environmental factors may be particularly important in early childhood because psychological trauma may be more likely to result in permanent biochemical alterations in the immature central nervous system.[83-85] Conversely, children presenting with depressive disorders may have a physiologically based vulnerability to environmental stress.[83] With the need for an integrated approach acknowledged, biological, genetic, and psychological models pertaining to the etiology of major depressive disorder in children will be reviewed.

Biological Models

While numerous studies have revealed alterations in the function of neurotransmitters in adults with affective disorders, comparable studies have yet to be reported in children and adolescents. Biologically-oriented studies in pediatric age groups have focused on assessment of neuroendocrine function and sleep architecture. Puig-Antich[2, 49, 86] and

Cantwell[1] have noted that a number of biological correlates of major depressive disorder in adults are also found in depressed children, which suggests the possibility that biological models for affective disorders in adults may ultimately be applied to children.

Neuroendocrine studies. Several investigators[49, 87-95] have described results of the dexamethasone suppression test (DST) in children and adolescents with affective and other psychiatric disorders. The sensitivity of nonsuppression as a marker of major depressive disorder has varied enormously among studies of prepubertal children meeting DSM-III or RDC criteria. In two studies,[49, 87] less than 20 percent of children exhibited nonsuppression despite high frequencies of endogenous depression, while in an additional three[88-90] nonsuppression was documented in 56–87 percent of cases. Nonsuppression may be less specific to a diagnosis of major depressive disorder in prepubertal children than in adults. High rates of nonsuppression (60 to 83 percent) among youngsters with dysthymic disorder[88] and separation anxiety[91] may reflect a physiological as well as clinical association between these disorders and major depression, but nonsuppression has also been reported in a substantial percentage of children with schizophrenic spectrum disorders.[88] Only 10 percent of a sample of prepubertal children with conduct disorders exhibited nonsuppression.[92] In three studies[93-95] of adolescent populations employing DSM-III or RDC criteria, the DST was found to have a sensitivity for major depressive disorder of 40 to 64 percent and a specificity of 70 to 100 percent, values similar to those reported by Carroll et al.[96] and Meltzer et al.[97] in studies of adults. However, nonsuppression was also frequently observed in adolescents with eating disorders.[94] While the usefulness of the DST as a diagnostic tool remains controversial, the procedure has provided convincing evidence that similar abnormalities of pituitary-adrenal function are found in children, adolescents, and adults with major depressive disorder.[1, 49, 90] Hypersecretion of cortisol during a 24-hour assessment period has also been described in 20 percent of prepubertal children with endogenous depression[49] as well as in depressed adults.[98]

Puig-Antich and colleagues[99-102] have reported extensive studies of growth hormone secretion in prepubertal children fulfilling RDC criteria for major depressive disorder. Approximately two-thirds of children with endogenous depression exhibited significant hyposecretion of growth ho mone in response to insulin-induced hypoglycemia, versus one-third of children with nonendogenous depression and 10 percent of children with neurotic disorders but no history of depressed mood.[99] Individual and group results were not significantly different when depressed children were retested in a drug-free state following a sustained period of recovery of at least four months.[100] Furthermore, drug-free children with endogenous and nonendogenous subtypes of major depressive disorder secreted significantly more growth hormone during sleep before and after recovery than normal children and children with neurotic disorders.[101, 102] The authors concluded that the observed alterations in growth hormone secretion may be trait- rather than state-dependent markers of major depressive disorder, or markers of past illness. They further noted that similar patterns of growth hormone hyposecretion in response to insulin challenge had now been identified in children and adults[103-105] with endogenous depression, lending support to the hypothesis that major depressive disorder is a similar illness in prepuberty and adulthood.[99]

Studies of sleep architecture. Studies by Puig-Antich et al.[86] and Young et al.[106] have failed to identify differences in sleep architecture between children 13 years old and younger with major depressive disorder and their healthy peers. In contrast to populations of adults with major depression,[107-110] prepubertal children with endogenous and nonendogenous depression did not exhibit: decreased latency of onset of the first REM period; increased REM density; abnormalities in the temporal distribution of REM sleep; decreased slow-wave sleep; or decreased sleep efficiency.[86, 106] Puig-Antich[86] has hypothesized that the finding of altered sleep architecture in adults versus children with major depressive disorder is due to an interaction between depression and maturational processes, rather than to differences between age groups in pathophysiological mechanisms responsible for development of depression. In support of this theory, he has cited studies[110-112] documenting correlations between increasing age and decreased REM latency and sleep efficiency in both depressed and normal adults. Although the significance of the finding remains unclear, Puig-Antich and colleagues[113] have observed decreased REM latency in drug-free prepubertal children following a sustained period of recovery from an episode of major depression.

Genetic Models

Studies of potential genetic contributions to the etiology of affective disorders have been far less comprehensive in pediatric than in adult populations. To date, investigations of genetic factors operative in childhood affective disorders have been confined to family aggregation studies. Unfortunately, such studies do not adequately distinguish between genetic and environmental factors contributing to the onset of disorder. Several authors[114-117] have noted that parents suffering from affective disorders are often irritable or resentful of their children, and less capable of exercising adequate parenting skills. Klerman et al.[118] recently documented a progressive increase in the rate of major depressive disorder with decreasing age among first-degree relatives of probands with affective disorders, a trend which most likely results from an interaction between pervasive environmental or cultural factors and genetic factors. Adoption, twin, genetic linkage, and segregation studies are required to determine to what extent specific genetic vulnerability plays a role in the development of affective disorders during childhood and adolescence. Despite their limitations, family aggregation studies have suggested increased genetic loading for affective disorder in families of depressed prepubertal children and adolescents versus families of individuals with onset of depression in mid-life.[49, 119] Studies of affective disorders in children of depressed parents and in families of depressed children will be summarized.

Studies of children of depressed parents. Several studies have documented an increased rate of depression,[114, 120-123] as well as other psychiatric disorders including conduct disorder, attention deficit disorder, and separation anxiety disorder,[115, 120, 121, 124] in children of parents with affective disorders. Weissman and colleagues[114] found that 13 percent of 107 children ages 6 to 18 years of probands with major depressive disorder met DSM-III criteria for major depression and 2.8 percent criteria for dysthymic disorder, versus none of 87 children of parents with no history of psychiatric disturbance. Major depression was the most common psychiatric diagnosis among the children of the depressed probands. The risk of developing major depressive disorder was significantly higher in children from families in which both parents, rather than one parent, suffered from depression. In a study by Cytryn et al.,[122] 9 of 13 parents consecutively hospitalized at the National Institute of Mental Health for treatment of major affective disorders had offspring ages 5 to 15 years meeting DSM-III criteria for major depressive disorder or dysthymic disorder. In contrast, 3 of 13 healthy control parents matched for the number and ages of their children, as well as socioeconomic status, had offspring meeting criteria for depressive disorders.

Families of depressed children. A number of studies have suggested that onset of major depressive disorder before the third decade of life is associated with an increased prevalence of major depression among first-degree biological relatives.[2, 49, 119, 125, 126] Puig-Antich[49] reported a lifetime morbid risk for major depressive disorder of 0.42 among first-degree relatives (older than 16 years) of prepubertal probands meeting RDC criteria for major depression. Similarly, Strober and colleagues[125] described a morbid risk for affective disorder of 0.35 among first-degree relatives of adolescents hospitalized for treatment of depression. This figure was considerably higher than that for the risk of affective disorder among first-degree relatives of adolescents with other psychiatric disorders participating in the same study. In both of the above studies, the lifetime morbid risk for major depressive disorder in families of pediatric probands appeared to be higher than the risk determined for first-degree relatives of adult probands with major depression (0.18 to 0.30).[2] Moreover, Weissman et al.[119] found an inverse linear relationship between the age of onset of major depression in probands and the rate of major depressive disorder among first-degree relatives. Relatives of probands with early onset of depression were themselves more likely to have an early onset of disorder. These findings support the hypothesis that onset of major depressive disorder in prepuberty or adolescence is associated with greater genetic vulnerability.[49, 119]

Psychological Models

Despite differing conceptual frameworks, similar interpersonal and intrapsychic processes have been implicated in the evolution of depressive states in children by authors belonging to psychoanalytic, behavioral, and cognitive schools. Most formulations have stressed the importance of real or imagined loss of parental love and guidance in the genesis of depressed mood in children. Poor self-esteem, helplessness, social withdrawal, and aggression toward the self are prominent sequelae. A discrepancy in a child's perception of his true situation versus what he believes ought to be his lot has also been frequently cited as a factor in the development of depression. Physical abuse appears to be a common precipitant of depressive symptomatology in younger children.

Psychoanalytic models. Spitz,[52] Bowlby,[127] and Anna Freud[128] each reported profound reactions resembling grief and depression in infants indefinitely separated from their mothers between the ages of six months and three to four years. Bowlby[127] described a sequential three-phase response in young children removed from their mothers once attachment had taken place, characterized by protest, then despair manifest in grief and mourning, and finally detachment. He postulated that loss of the mother in early childhood results in a personality prone to depression and other psychiatric illnesses as a consequence of the predilection of children to invoke defense mechanisms commonly seen in pathological mourning in adults; these include repression of yearning for the lost object, denial of the reality of the loss, and displacement of reproach.[127, 129]

Rather than citing actual loss of the mother as the crucial determinant in the etiology of childhood depression, Sandler and Joffe[130] maintained that the "common factor" in depressive states in children is the child's perception of having lost or being unable to attain an ideal state of well-being embodied in a relationship to an important person. A "depressive reaction" occurs when the child responds to a discrepancy between his "actual state of self" and the ideal state with helpless resignation. The child experiences guilt when he cannot live up to ideals dictated by the superego, and may direct aggression toward a self perceived as unsatisfactory.

The onset of depressive states in preschool children has frequently been ascribed to disturbances in the parent-child relationship during the developmental phase of separation and individuation. Mahler[131] characterized the "rapprochement subphase" of the separation-individuation process, which extends from the latter half of the second year into the third year of life, as a period during which children are particularly vulnerable to develop depressed mood. Elation, associated with the preceding "practicing subphase," ceases to be the dominant affect as the child relinquishes fantasies of grandeur and omnipotence, and acquires a more realistic view of himself as small and relatively helpless. Drawing upon her extensive direct observations of young children and their mothers, Mahler described depressive symptomatology in several children whose mothers either failed to respond positively to their requests for admiration and approval or curtailed their efforts to exercise autonomy. Sandler and Joffe[130] noted that parents who undermine the individuation process interfere with the child's relinquishment of cathexes to infantile ideal states, rendering the child more vulnerable to subsequent disappointment and depression. Also focusing on the early parent-child relationship, Anna Freud[132] and Malmquist[133] observed that identification with a depressed parent can result in the development of a negative self-concept and a tendency toward depressed mood.

Behavioral and cognitive models. Behavioral models applied to the understanding of depressive states in children have focused on learned helplessness and the loss of positive reinforcement. Learned helplessness is a concept derived from studies by Seligman and Maier[134] of animals exposed to inescapable electroshock. Petti[25] observed that children were vulnerable to the development of depression when faced with a "no-win situation," which might result from parental rejection, neglect, or abuse, school failure, or unremitting poverty. He noted that media portrayal of exciting life-styles and free access to material possessions can promote unrealistic expectations which result in chronic frustration and demoralization. Expanding upon the work of Lewinsohn[135] in adults, Petti[25] described the importance of the loss of response-contingent positive reinforcement in the perpetuation of depressive states in children. Depressed children exhibit fewer social skills necessary to elicit positive reinforcement from others, and are less capable of responding positively when reinforcement is offered. Progressive isolation and loss of self-esteem is particularly likely when parents are unable to provide appropriate modeling for development of social skills.

Kovacs and Beck[136] have hypothesized that cognitive distortions associated with depression, including excessive self-castigation, exaggeration of problems, and hopelessness, have their origins in early childhood. While actual loss of a parent in childhood may facilitate the development of "depressogenic schemata," a child's relationship with a parent preoccupied with his or her own personal inadequacy, or with inflexible rules of conduct, is more frequently the decisive factor. The child not only models his self-concept after that of the parent, but fails to develop the capacity to revise negative perceptions in the face of achievement or positive reinforcement from other individuals.

Impact of abuse and neglect. Several authors have commented upon the virtually ubiquitous presence of depressive symptomatology in children who have been physically abused or neglected.[137-139] Rosenthal and Rosenthal[51] found that 81 percent of 16 preschool children with a history of serious suicidal behavior had been abused or neglected while only 38 percent of an equal number of age-matched, nonsuicidal children with behavioral problems had been mistreated. Kashani[7,40] noted that a history of abuse or neglect was frequently present in preschool children with depressive symptomatology.

ASSESSMENT OF DEPRESSIVE SYMPTOMATOLOGY

Traditionally, the assessment of psychopathology in children has relied heavily upon parental and school reports, and upon play interviews with the children themselves. Acknowledging that play sessions may be helpful in identifying worries and psychodynamic conflicts in depressed children, Puig-Antich[1,49,140] has stressed the necessity of directly questioning children about their feelings, concerns, and behavior during diagnostic assessment. Care must be taken to pose questions in language younger children can understand. Several expressions, including "very unhappy," "sad," "not ever feeling good," "blue," "down," "empty," and "low," should be used when inquiring about depressed mood.[140] Puig-Antich[140] has recently stated that a diagnosis of major depressive disorder should neither be made nor ruled out unless a semistructured interview derived from DSM-III or RDC criteria has been conducted with the child to define a symptom profile from the child's vantage point. Interview schedules appropriate for the assessment of depressive symptomatology include: the Interview Schedule for Children (ISC), developed by Kovacs;[141] the Schedule for Affective Disorders and Schizophrenia for School-Age Children (Kiddie-SADS), developed by Puig-Antich and Chambers;[142] and the Child Depression Rating Scale-Revised (CDRS-R), developed by Poznanski.[143]

Several studies have evaluated the correspondence of parents' versus children's reports of depressive symptomatology.[121,144-146] On the whole, findings suggest that parents tend to be better historians concerning observable behaviors and the chronological evolution of depressive symptoms in their children,[121,140,144] while children are best able to describe their moods and the presence of symptoms such as poor self-esteem, hopelessness, or guilt.[121,140,145] Both parents and children may minimize depressive symptoms,[1,144-146] while some depressed parents may exaggerate symptoms in their children through a process of projective indentification.[146] The final diagnostic impression must be based upon the clinician's evaluation of information obtained from both parents and children, as well as other appropriate sources.

TREATMENT

Pharmacology

Although a definitive study comparing the efficacy of antidepressant medication versus placebo in children or adolescents with major depressive disorder has yet to be published, several studies[2, 147-150] have suggested that tricyclic antidepressants are effective in the treatment of depression in prepubertal children. In a study of 30 school-age children treated with imipramine, Puig- Antich and colleagues[2] found that 100 percent of children with combined plasma levels of imipramine and desipramine greater than 155 ng/ml responded to treatment, while only 33 percent of children with lower plasma levels showed significant improvement. Although the response rate in a group of children treated with placebo was 60 percent,[2] 79 percent of these youngsters relapsed within one month after placebo was discontinued.[140] Using a double-blind crossover design, Kashani et al.[147] observed that six of nine prepubertal children responded to treatment with amitriptyline (1.5 mg/kg/day), while only two responded to placebo. Although emphasizing that rigorous studies are still required to firmly establish the efficacy of tricyclic antidepressants in the treatment of depressed prepubertal children, Cantwell[1] and Puig-Antich[2, 140] have stated that research demonstrating similar rates of response to pharmacological interventions in children and adults strengthens the argument that major depressive disorder is a similar entity in both age groups.

Little scientific evidence currently exists for the efficacy of antidepressant medications in the treatment of major depressive disorder in adolescents.[140] Kramer and Feiguine[151] reported that adolescents hospitalized for treatment of depression exhibited marked improvement when treated with amitriptyline (200 mg/day) or placebo, but current diagnostic criteria were not used, and drug levels were not obtained. In a study of 32 adolescents meeting RDC criteria for major depression, Puig-Antich and colleagues[140] found that only one-third responded to imipramine. No relationship was observed between plasma levels of drug and clinical response. Puig-Antich has hypothesized that high levels of sex hormones may interfere with the efficacy of imipramine during adolescence.[140] Geller and colleagues[152] recently reported that six of eight adolescents treated with nortriptyline (70-150 mg/day) had full responses, while two exhibited partial improvement. In his clinical experience, Puig-Antich[140] has observed that most adolescents ultimately experience full or partial remission of depressive symptomatology with pharmacological treatment, although two or three medication trials may be required. Some adolescents who fail to respond to tricyclic antidepressants may suffer from atypical depression[45, 140] and benefit from treatment with a monoamine oxidase inhibitor (MAOI).

Puig-Antich[140] has recommended administration of imipramine to prepubertal children in three equally divided doses resulting in a total dose of up to 6mg/kg/day. Beginning at 1.5 mg/kg/day, the dose should be increased incrementally by approximately 1 mg/kg/day every third or fourth day until combined plasma levels of imipramine and desipramine in excess of 155 ng/ml are achieved.[2, 140] Levels greater than 200 ng/ml may be required in some children before a response is noted.[45, 49] While Puig-Antich found a linear relationship between drug levels and clinical response to imipramine, Preskorn et al.[150] noted a curvilinear relationship. In the latter study, positive clinical response was associated with combined levels of imipramine and desipramine ranging from 125-225 ng/ml. Geller and colleagues[153] have used single dose kinetic studies to predict the dosage of nortriptyline required to establish steady-state plasma levels in the range associated with favorable clinical outcome in the authors' ongoing study of the efficacy of the drug in the treatment of depressed children and adolescents (60-100 and 75-150 ng/ml, respectively).

Pharmacological interventions must generally be modified for children and adolescents with psychotic depression. Puig-Antich and colleagues[45] have stated that an imipramine dose sufficient to produce combined plasma levels of 350 ng/ml is often required to adequately treat psychotically depressed prepubertal children with hallucinations. Addition of an antipsychotic agent may be necessary. Combined treatment is routinely required in cases where delusions are present. Geller et al.[152] have reported successful treatment of seven of eight delusionally depressed adolescents with a combination of chlorpromazine and nortriptyline. Well-controlled studies of the treatment of bipolar disorder in pediatric age groups have yet to be reported. Anecdotal evidence suggests that lithium is effective.[154]

Final assessment of the efficacy of pharmacological intervention should be made following five weeks of treatment.[140] Puig-Antich[140] has reported that antidepressant medication can be discontinued in prepubertal children three to four months after initial recovery unless the child has a history of rapid relapse. Adolescents typically require treatment for six months to one year.

The pattern of side effects in response to tricyclic antidepressants is somewhat different in prepubertal children than in adults. In children, anticholinergic side effects are generally minimal.[154] However, children appear to be more vulnerable than adults to cardiotoxic effects of tricyclic antidepressants, particularly first-degree heart block.[155-157] Elevation of diastolic blood pressure is often observed in children treated with imipramine.[155-158] Puig-Antich[140] has cautioned that an electrocardiogram (ECG) should be obtained and blood pressure measured supine and standing before commencing treatment with imipramine and before any increase in dosage is made. The dose should be decreased if: the PR interval is greater than 0.21 seconds; the QRS is prolonged over 130 percent of baseline; the resting heart rate is greater than 130 beats/min; the systolic blood pressure is greater than 145 mm Hg; or the diastolic blood pressure is greater than 95 mm Hg.[45] Children are also susceptible to withdrawal symptoms, including epigastric pain, vomiting, fatigue, tearfulness, apathy, headaches, and agitation, upon discontinuation of treatment with imipramine, even when the dose is decreased gradually.[159] Law and colleagues[159] have recommended that imipramine should be tapered over a period of at least two weeks.

Psychotherapy

Individual, group, or family psychotherapy is often indicated for children and adolescents with affective disorders. As previously discussed, children frequently continue to exhibit impaired relationships with family members and peers months following successful pharmacological treatment of the depressive episode. Depressed youngsters often have concomitant psychiatric disorders, some of which may not respond to antidepressant medication. Many children must contend with the chronic stress of residing with parents who also have psychiatric disturbances. The therapist may facilitate psychosocial development and reduce the impact of environmental stress by: providing a consistent and supportive relationship; assisting the child to label emotions, identify concerns, and resolve conflicts; helping the child to develop more effective coping strategies and age-appropriate social skills; counseling parents regarding child-rearing practices; intervening to reduce family discord; and, where required, serving as an advocate for the child with social agencies or school systems. A detailed discussion of specific psychotherapeutic modalities utilized in the treatment of children and adolescents with affective disorders is beyond the scope of this chapter.

While there is a consensus that psychotherapy is frequently an important factor in successful long-term management of children with affective disorders, controversy exists concerning the relative merits of psychotherapy versus medication in the treatment of depressive symptomatology per se. Many clinicians continue to favor psychotherapy as the initial treatment of choice for children who are mildly to moderately depressed; a trial of antidepressant medication may be considered for those who fail to respond. On the other hand, Puig-Antich[140] has reported that psychotherapy is rarely an effective treatment for youngsters who meet DSM-III criteria for major depressive disorder. He has suggested postponing a decision to proceed with formal psychotherapy with the child until the depressive episode has been successfully treated pharmacologically, and the degree of residual impairment has been assessed. In cases where medication is the primary treatment modality, it is important for the clinician to provide support to the child and family, as well as information about the disorder and treatment plan. Frequent contact with the child and parents is required during the phase of active depressive symptomatology to assess the risk of suicidal behavior and the response to medication.

Future research efforts should be directed toward establishing the relative efficacies of specific psychotherapeutic interventions, such as cognitive or exploratory psychotherapy, in the long-term management of depressed children and adolescents. Moreover, rigorous studies are required to firmly establish whether children with less severe forms of affective disorders are best served by specific psychotherapies, medication, or a combination of modalities.

SUMMARY

The preponderance of evidence supports the hypothesis that affective disorders presenting in childhood and adolescence are similar in both phenomenology and underlying pathophysiology to affective disorders with onset in later life. However, further research is required to assess effects of developmental and maturational processes upon symptom profile, physiological variables, and psychosocial functioning in children with affective disorders. Studies are also needed to delineate biological and environmental factors most important in the pathogenesis of affective disorders in pediatric age groups, and to establish the efficacy of pharmacological and psychotherapeutic approaches to treatment.

REFERENCES

1. Cantwell DP: Depressive disorders in children: Validation of clinical syndromes. *Psychiatr Clin North Am 1985; 8:* 779-792.
2. Puig-Antich J, Weston B: The diagnosis and treatment of major depressive disorder in childhood. *Ann Rev Med 1983; 34:* 231-245.
3. Kovacs M, Feinberg TL, Crouse-Novak MA, et al: Depressive disorders in childhood: I. A longitudinal prospective study of characteristics and recovery. *Arch Gen Psychiatry 1984; 41:* 229-237.
4. Kovacs M, Feinberg TL, Crouse-Novak M, et al: Depressive disorders in childhood: II. A longitudinal study of the risk for a subsequent major depression. *Arch Gen Psychiatry 1984; 41:* 643-649.
5. Strober M, Green J, Carlson G: Phenomenology and subtypes of major depressive disorder in adolescence. *J Affective Disord 1981; 3:* 281-290.

6. Freeman LN, Poznanski EO, Grossman JA, et al: Psychotic and depressed children: a new entity. *J Am Acad Child Psychiatry 1985; 24:* 95-102.
7. Kashani JH, Ray JS, Carlson GA: Depression and depressive-like states in preschool-age children in a child development unit. *Am J Psychiatry 1984; 141:* 1397-1402.
8. Chambers WJ, Puig-Antich J, Tabrizi MA, et al: Psychotic symptoms in prepubertal major depressive disorder. *Arch Gen Psychiatry 1982; 39:* 921-927.
9. Poznanski EO: The clinical phenomenology of childhood depression. *Am J Orthopsychiatry 1982; 52:* 308-313.
10. Carlson GA, Cantwell DP: A survery of depressive symptoms in a child and adolescent psychiatric population: Interview data. *J Am Acad Child Psychiatry 1979; 18:* 587-599.
11. Poznanski EO, Krahenbuhl V, Krull JP: Childhood depression: A longitudinal perspective. *J Am Acad Child Psychiatry 1976; 15:* 491-501.
12. Abraham K: Notes on the psychoanalytic investigation and treatment of manic depressive insanity and allied conditions, in *The Meaning of Despair: Psychoanalytic Contributions to the Understanding of Depression.* Edited by Gaylin W. New York, Science House 1968.
13. Freud S: *Mourning and Melancholia (Standard Ed), vol. XIV.* London, Hogarth Press 1957.
14. Bibring E: Affective disorders: the mechanism of depression, in *Affective Disorders: Psychoanalytic Contributions to their Study.* Edited by Greenacre P. New York, International Universities Press 1953.
15. Finch SM: *Fundamentals of Child Psychiatry.* New York, W.W. Norton & Co., 1960.
16. Rie HE: Depression in childhood: a survey of some pertinent contributions. *J Am Acad Child Psychiatry 1966; 5:* 653-685.
17. Toolan JM: Depression in children and adolescents. *Am J Orthopsychiatry 1962; 32:* 404-414.
18. Glaser K: Masked depression in children and adolescents. *Dev Med Child Neurol 1974; 16:* 340-349.
19. Cytryn L, McKnew DH: Proposed classification of childhood depression. *Am J Psychiatry 1972; 129:* 149-155.
20. Carlson GA, Cantwell DP: Unmasking masked depression in children and adolescents. *Am J Psychiatry 1980; 137:* 445-449.
21. Cytryn L, McKnew DH, Bunney WE: Diagnosis of depression in childhood: a reassessment. *Am J Psychiatry 1980; 137:* 22-25.
22. Kovacs M, Beck AT: An empirical-clinical approach toward a definition of childhood depression, in *Depression in Childhood.* Edited by Schulterbrandt, JG, Raskin, A, New York, Raven Press 1977.
23. Pearce JB: Childhood depression, in *Child Psychiatry.* Edited by Rutter M, Hersov L, London, Blackwell Press 1977.
24. Petti TA: Behavioral approaches in the treatment of depressed children, in *Affective Disorders in Childhood and Adolescence: An Update.* Edited by Cantwell DP, Carlson GA, New York, Spectrum Publications 1983.

25. Cantwell DP: Depression in childhood: clinical picture and diagnostic criteria, in *Affective Disorders in Childhood and Adolescence: An Update*. Edited by Cantwell DP, Carlson GA, New York, Spectrum Publications 1983.

26. Waters BGH, Storm V: Depression in pre-pubertal children. Australian New Zealand *J Psychiatry 1985; 19:* 6-17.

27. Puig-Antich J: The use of RDC criteria for major depressive disorder in children and adolescents. *J Am Acad Child Psychiatry 1982; 21:* 291-293.

28. Robbins DR, Alessi NE, Cook SC, et al: The use of the Research Diagnostic Criteria (RDC) for depression in adolescent psychiatric inpatients. *J Am Acad Child Psychiatry 1982; 21:* 251-255.

29. Strober M: Clinical and biological perspectives on depressive disorders in adolescence, in *Affective Disorders in Childhood and Adolescence: An Update*. Edited by Cantwell DP, Carlson GA, New York, Spectrum Publications, 1983.

30. *Diagnostic and Statistical Manual of Mental Disorders*, third edition. Washington, D.C., American Psychiatric Association 1980.

31. Spitzer RL, Endicott J, Robins E: Research diagnostic criteria. *Arch Gen Psychiatry 1978; 35:* 773-782.

32. Carlson GA, Cantwell DP: Diagnosis of childhood depression: A comparison of Weinberg and DSM-III criteria. *J Am Acad Child Psychiatry, 1982; 21:* 247-250,

33. Strober M, Carlson G: Bipolar illness in adolescents with major depression: Clinical, genetic, and psychopharmacologic predictors in a three- to four-year prospective follow-up investigation. *Arch Gen Psychiatry 1982; 39:* 549-555.

34. Ling W, Oftedal G, Weinberg W: Depressive illness in childhood presenting as severe headache. *Am J Dis Child 1970; 120:* 122-124.

35. Weinberg WA, Rutman J, Sullivan L, et al: Depression in children referred to an educational diagnostic center. *J Pediatr 1973; 83:* 1065-1072.

36. Malmquist CP: Depression in childhood and adolescence, 1. *N Engl J Med, 1971; 284:* 887-893.

37. Petti TA: Depression in hospitalized child psychiatry patients: approaches to measuring depression. *J Am Acad Child Psychiatry 1978; 17:* 49-59.

38. Poznanski E, Cook S, Carroll B: A depressive rating scale for children. *Pediatrics 1979; 64:* 442-450.

39. Feighner JP, Robins E, Guze SB, et al: Diagnostic criteria for use in psychiatric research. *Arch Gen Psychiatry 1972; 26:* 57-63.

40. Kashani JH, Carlson GA: Major depressive disorder in a preschooler. *J Am Acad Child Psychiatry 1985; 24:* 490-494.

41. Carlson GA, Strober M: Affective disorders in adolescence, in *Affective Disorders in Childhood and Adolescence: An Update*. Edited by Cantwell DP, Carlson GA, New York, Spectrum Publications 1983.

42. Kashani JH, Cantwell DP, Shekin WO, et al: Major depressive disorder in children admitted to an inpatient community mental health center. *Am J Psychiatry 1982; 139:* 671-672.

43. Puig-Antich J, Blau S, Marx N, et al: Prepubertal major depressive disorder: a pilot study. *J Am Acad Child Psychiatry 1978; 17:* 695-707.

44. Liebowitz MR, Klein DF: Hysteroid dysphoria. *Psychiatr Clin North Am 1979; 2:* 555-575.

45. Ambrosini PJ, Puig-Antich J: Major depression in children and adolescents, in *The Clinical Guide to Child Psychiatry.* Edited by Shaffer D, Ehrhardt AA, Greenhill LL, New York, Free Press 1985.

46. Annell AL: Manic-depressive illness in children and effect of treatment with lithium carbonate. *Acta Paedopsychiatrica 1969; 36:* 292-301.

47. Brumback RA, Weinberg WA: Mania in childhood. *Am J Dis Child, 1977; 131:* 1122-1126.

48. Carlson GA, Strober M: Manic depressive illness in early adolescence. *J Am Acad Child Psychiatry 1978; 17:* 138-153.

49. Puig-Antich J: Affective disorders in childhood. *Psychiatr Clin North Am 1980; 3:* 403-424.

50. Toolan JM: Suicide and suicidal attempts in children and adolescents. *Am J Psychiatry 1962; 118:* 719-724.

51. Rosenthal PA, Rosenthal S: Suicidal behavior by preschool children. *Am J Psychiatry 1984; 141:* 520-525.

52. Spitz RA: Anaclitic depression. *Psychoanal Study Child 1946; 2:* 313-342.

53. Eastgate J, Gilmour L: Long-term outcome of depressed children: A follow-up study. *Dev Med Child Neurol 1984; 26:* 68-72.

54. Chess S, Thomas A, Hassibi M: Depression in childhood and adolescence: a prospective study of six cases. *J Nerv Ment Dis, 1983; 171:* 411-420.

55. Puig-Antich J, Lukens E, Davies M, et al: Psychosocial functioning in prepubertal major depressive disorders: II. Interpersonal relationships after sustained recovery from affective episode. *Arch Gen Psychiatry 1985; 42:* 511-517.

56. Puig-Antich J: Major depression and conduct disorder in prepuberty. *J Am Acad Child Psychiatry 1982; 21:* 118-128.

57. Geller B, Chestnut EC, Miller MD, et al: Preliminary data on DSM-III associated features of major depressive disorder in children and adolescents. *Am J Psychiatry 1985; 142:* 643-644.

58. Hershberg SG, Carlson GA, Cantwell DP, et al: Anxiety and depressive disorders in psychiatrically disturbed children. *J Clin Psychiatry 1982; 43:* 358-361.

59. Kolvin I, Berney TP, Bhate SR: Classification and diagnosis of depression in school phobia. *Br J Psychiatry 1984; 145:* 347-357.

60. Bernstein GA, Garfinkel BD: School phobia: The overlap of affective and anxiety disorders. *J Am Acad Child Psychiatry 1986; 25:* 235-241.

61. Puig-Antich JA, Lukens E, Davies M et al: Psychosocial functioning in prepubertal major depressive disorders: I. Interpersonal relationships during the depressive episode. *Arch Gen Psychiatry 1985; 42:* 500-507.

62. Cantwell DP, Sturzenberger S, Burroughs J et al: Anorexia nervosa: An affective disorder? *Arch Gen Psychiatry 1977; 34:* 1087-1093.

63. Halmi KA, Goldberg SC, Eckert E, et al: Pretreatment evaluation in anorexia nervosa, in *Anorexia Nervosa.* Edited by Vigersky RA New York, Raven Press 1978.

64. Hendren RL: Depression in anorexia nervosa. *J Am Acad Child Psychiatry 1983; 22:* 59-62.

65. Kashani JH, Lababidi Z, Jones RS: Depression in children and adolescents with cardiovascular symptomatology: The significance of chest pain. *J Am Acad Child Psychiatry 1982; 21:* 187-189.

66. Kashani JH, Barbero GJ, Bolander FD: Depression in hospitalized pediatric patients. *J Am Acad Child Psychiatry 1981; 20:* 123-124.

67. Rutter M, Grahame P, Chadwick OFD, et al: Adolescent turmoil: fact or fiction. *J Child Psychol Psych 1976; 17:* 35-65.

68. Kandel DB, Davies M: Epidemiology of depressive mood in adolescents: an empirical study. *Arch Gen Psychiatry 1982; 39:* 1205-1212.

69. Offer D: *The Psychological World of the Teen-Ager.* New York, Basic Books 1969.

70. Carlson GA, Cantwell DP: Suicidal behavior and depression in children and adolescents. *J Am Acad Child Psychiatry 1982; 21:* 361-368.

71. Pfeffer CR, Plutchik R, Mizruchi R: Suicidal and assaultive behavior in children: Classification, measurement, and interrelations. *Am J Psychiatry 1983; 140:* 154-157.

72. Waller DA, Rush AJ: Differentiating primary affective disease, organic affective syndromes, and situational depression on a pediatric service. *J Am Acad Child Psychiatry 1983; 22:* 52-58.

73. Kashani J, Simonds JF: The incidence of depression in children. *Am J Psychiatry 1979; 136:* 1203-1205.

74. Kashani JH, McGee RO, Clarkson SE, et al: Depression in a sample of 9-year-old children. *Arch Gen Psychiatry 1983; 40:* 1217-1223.

75. Earls F: The epidemiology of depression in children and adolescents. *Pediatr Ann 1984; 13:* 23-31.

76. Albert N, Beck AT: Incidence of depression in early adolescence: A preliminary study. *J Youth Adolesc 1975; 4:* 301-307.

77. Kaplan SL, Hong GK, Weinhold C: Epidemiology of depressive symptomatology in adolescents. *J Am Acad Child Psychiatry 1984; 23:* 91-98.

78. Weissman MM, Myers J: Affective disorders in a US urban community: The use of research diagnostic criteria in an epidemiological survery. *Arch Gen Psychiatry 1978; 35:* 1304-1311.

79. Boyd JH, Weissman MM: Epidemiology of affective disorders. *Arch Gen Psychiatry 1981; 38:* 1039-1047.

80. Akiskal HS, McKinney WT: Overview of recent research in depression: Integration of ten conceptual models into a comprehensive clinical frame. *Arch Gen Psychiatry 1975; 32:* 285-305.

81. Cantwell DP: Overview of etiologic factors, in *Affective Disorders in Childhood and Adolescence: An Update.* Edited by Cantwell DP, Carlson GA, New York, Spectrum Publications 1983.

82. Kashani JH, Cantwell DP: Etiology and treatment of childhood depression: a biopsychological perspective. *Compr Psychiatry 1983; 24:* 476-486.

83. Lewis M, Lewis DO: Depression in childhood: a biopsychosocial perspective. *Am J Psychother 1981; 35:* 323-329.

84. Mandell AJ: Neurobiological mechanisms of adaptation in relation to models of psychobiological development, in *Psychopathology and Child Development*. Edited by Schopler E, Reichler RJ, New York, Plenum Press, 1967.

85. Barchas PR, Barchas JD: Social behavior and adrenal medullary function in relation to psychiatric disorder, in *Neuroregulators and Psychiatric Disorders*. Edited by Usdin U, Hamburg DA, Barchas JD, New York, Oxford University Press 1977.

86. Puig-Antich J, Goetz R, Hanlon C, et al: Sleep architecture and REM sleep measures in prepubertal children with major depression: A controlled study. *Arch Gen Psychiatry 1982; 39:* 932-939.

87. Geller B, Rogol AD, Knitter EF: Preliminary data on the dexamethasone suppression test in children with major depressive disorder. *Am J Psychiatry 1983; 140:* 620-622.

88. Petty LK, Asarnow JR, Carlson GA, et al: The dexamethasone suppression test in depressed, dysthymic, and nondepressed children. *Am J Psychiatry 1985; 142:* 631-633.

89. Weller EB, Weller RA, Fristad MA, et al: The dexamethasone suppression test in hospitalized prepubertal depressed children. *Am J Psychiatry 1984; 141:* 290-291.

90. Poznanski EO, Carroll BJ, Banegas MC, et al: The dexamethasone suppression test in prepubertal depressed children. *Am J Psychiatry 1982; 139:* 321-324.

91. Livingston R, Reis CJ, Ringdahl IC: Abnormal dexamethasone suppression test results in depressed and nondepressed children. *Am J Psychiatry 1984; 141:* 106-108.

92. Targum SD, Chastek CT, Sullivan AC: Dexamethasone suppression test in prepubertal conduct disorder. *Psychiatry Res 1981; 5:* 107-108.

93. Klee SH, Garfinkel BD: Indentification of depression in children and adolescents: The role of the dexamethasone suppression test. *J Am Acad Child Psychiatry 1984; 23:* 410-415.

94. Hsu LSK, Molcan K, Cashman MA, et al: The dexamethasone suppression test in adolescent depression. *J Am Acad Child Psychiatry 1983; 22:* 470-473.

95. Robbins CR, Alessi NE, Yanchyshyn GW: Preliminary report on the dexamethasone suppression test in adolescents. *Am J Psychiatry 1982; 139:* 942-943.

96. Carroll BJ, Feinberg M, Greden JF, et al: A specific laboratory test for the diagnosis of melancholia. *Arch Gen Psychiatry 1981; 38:* 15-22.

97. Meltzer HY, Fang VS: Cortisol determination and the dexamethasone suppression test. *Arch Gen Psychiatry 1983; 40:* 501-505.

98. Sachar EJ, Hellman L, Roffwarg HP, et al: Disrupted 24 hour pattern of cortisol secretion in psychotic depression. *Arch Gen Psychiatry 1973; 28:* 19-25.

99. Puig-Antich J, Novacenko H, Davies M, et al: Growth hormone secretion in prepubertal children with major depression: I. Final report on response to insulin-induced hypoglycemia during a depressive episode. *Arch Gen Psychiatry 1984; 41:* 455-460.

100. Puig-Antich J, Novacenko H, Davies M et al: Growth hormone secretion in prepubertal children with major depression: III. Response to insulin-induced hypoglycemia after recovery from a depressive episode and in a drug-free state. *Arch Gen Psychiatry 1984; 41:* 471-475.

101. Puig-Antich J, Goetz R, Davies M, et al: Growth hormone secretion in prepubertal children with major depression: II. Sleep-related plasma concentrations during a depressive episode. *Arch Gen Psychiatry 1984; 41:* 463-466.

102. Puig-Antich J, Goetz R, Davies M, et al: Growth hormone secretion in prepubertal children with major depression: IV. Sleep-related plasma concentrations in a drug-free, fully recovered clinical state. *Arch Gen Psychiatry 1984; 41:* 479-483.

103. Sachar EJ, Frantz A, Altman N et al: Growth hormone and prolactin in unipolar and bipolar depressed patients: responses to hypoglycemia and L-dopa. *Am J Psychiatry 1973; 130:* 1362-1367.

104. Mueller PS, Heninger GR, MacDonald RK: Studies on glucose utilization and insulin sensitivity in affective disorders, in *Recent Advances in Psychobiology of Depressive Illnesses.* Edited by William TA, Katz MM, Shield JA US Dept. Health Education Welfare 1972.

105. Gruen PH, Sachar EJ, Altman N, et al: Growth hormone responses to hypoglycemia in postmenopausal depressed women. *Arch Gen Psychiatry 1975; 32:* 31-33.

106. Young W, Knowles JB, MacLean AW, et al: The sleep of childhood depressives: Comparison with age-matched controls. *Biol Psychiatry 1982; 17:* 1163-1168.

107. Gillin JC, Duncan W, Pettigrew KD, et al: Successful separation of depressed, normal, and insomniac subjects by EEG sleep data. *Arch Gen Psychiatry 1979; 36:* 85-90.

108. Vogel GW, Vogel F, McAbee RS, et al: Improvement of depression by REM sleep deprivation: new findings and a theory. *Arch Gen Psychiatry 1980; 37:* 247-253.

109. Kupfer D, Foster FG: EEG sleep and depression, in *Sleep Disorders: Diagnosis and Treatment.* Edited by Williams RL, Karacan I, New York, John Wiley & Sons 1979.

110. Coble P, Kupfer DJ, Spiker DG, et al: EEG sleep and clinical characteristics in young primary depressives. *Sleep Res 1980; 9:* 165.

111. Ulrich R, Shaw DH, Kupfer DJ: The effects of aging on sleep. *Sleep 1980; 3:* 31-40.

112. Gillin JC, Duncan WC, Murphy DL, et al: Age related changes in sleep in depressed and normal subjects. *Psychiatry Res 1981; 4:* 73-78.

113. Puig-Antich J, Goetz R, Hanlon C, et al: Sleep architecture and REM measures in drug-free recovered prepubertal major depressives. *Arch Gen Psychiatry 1983; 40:* 187-192.

114. Weissman MM, Prusoff BA, Gammon GD, et al: Psychopathology in the children (ages 6-18) of depressed and normal parents. *J Am Acad Child Psychiatry 1984; 23:* 78-84.

115. Beardslee WR, Bemporad J, Keller MB, et al: Children of parents with major affective disorder: a review. *Am J Psychiatry 1983; 140:* 825-832.

116. Orvaschel H, Weissman MM, Kidd KK: Children and depression; the children of depressed parents; the childhood of depressed patients; depression in children. *J Affective Disord 1980; 2:* 1-16.

117. Puig-Antich J, Perel JM, Lupatkin W, et al: Plasma levels of imipramine (IMI) and desmethylimipramine (DMI) and clinical response in prepubertal major depressive disorder: a preliminary report. *J Am Acad Child Psychiatry 1979; 18:* 616-627.

118. Klerman GL, Lavori PW, Rice J et al: Birth-cohort trends in rates of major depressive disorder among relatives of patients with affective disorder. *Arch Gen Psychiatry 1985; 42:* 689-693.

119. Weissman MM, Wickramaratne P, Merikangas KR, et al: Onset of major depression in early adulthood. *Arch Gen Psychiatry 1984; 41:* 1136-1143.

120. McKnew DH, Cytryn L, Effron AM, et al: Offspring of patients with affective disorders. *Br J Psychiatry 1979; 134:* 148-152.

121. Orvaschel H, Weissman MM, Padian N, et al: Assessing psychopathology in children of psychiatrically disturbed parents. *J Am Acad Child Psychiatry 1981; 20:* 112-122.

122. Cytryn L, McKnew DH, Bartko JJ, et al: Offspring of patients with affective disorders: II. *J Am Acad Child Psychiatry 1982; 21:* 389-391.

123. Welner Z, Welner A, McCrary MD, et al: Psychopathology in children of inpatients with depression: a controlled study. *J Nerv Ment Dis 1977; 164:* 408-413.

124. O'Connell RA, Mays JA, O'Brien JD, et al: Children of bipolar manic-depressives, in *Genetic Aspects of Affective Illness*, Edited by Mendlewicz J, Shopsin B, New York, Spectrum Publications 1979.

125. Strober M, Burroughs J, Salkin B et al: Ancestral secondary cases of psychiatric illness in adolescents with mania, depression, schizophrenia, and conduct disorders. *Biol Psychiatry*, in press.

126. Brumback RA, Dietz-Schmidt S, Weinberg WA: Depression in children admitted to an educational diagnostic center: Diagnosis and treatment and analysis of criteria and literature review. *Dis Nerv Sys 1977; 38:* 529-535.

127. Bowlby J: Grief and mourning in infancy and early childhood. *Psychoanal Study Child 1960; 15:* 9-52.

128. Freud A, Burlingham D: *Infants Withhout Families; The Case for and Against Residential Nurseries.* New York, International Universities Press, 1944.

129. Bowlby J: Pathological mourning and childhood mourning. *J Am Psychoanal Assoc 1963; 11:* 500-541.

130. Sandler J, Joffe WG: Notes on childhood depression. *Int J Psychoanal 1965; 46:* 88-96.

131. Mahler MS, Pine F, Bergman A: *The Psychological Birth of the Human Infant: Symbiosis and Individuation.* New York, Basic Books 1975.

132. Freud A: *Normality and Pathology in Childhood*, New York, International Universities Press 1965.

133. Malmquist CP: The theoretical status of depression in childhood, in *Three Clinical Faces of Childhood*. Edited by Anthony EJ, Gilpin DC, New York, Spectrum Publications 1976.

134. Seligman M, Maier S: Failure to escape traumatic shock. *J Exp Psychol 1967; 74:* 1-9.

135. Lewinsohn PM: Behavioral study and treatment in depression, in *Progress in Behavior Modification*. Edited by Hersen M, Eisler R, Miller P, New York, Academic Press 1974.

136. Kovacs M, Beck AT: Maladaptive cognitive structures in depression. *Am J Psychiatry 1978; 135:* 525-533.

137. Green A: Child abuse and neglect, in the *Clinical Guide to Child Psychiatry*. Edited by Shaffer D, Ehrhardt AA, Greenhill LL, New York, The Free Press 1985.

138. Blumberg ML: Depression in abused and neglected children. *Am J Psychother 1981; 35:* 342-355.

139. Martin HP, Beezely P: Personality of abused children, in *The Abused Child*. Edited by Martin HP, Cambridge, Mass., Ballinger Publishing Co. 1976.

140. Puig-Antich J: Clinical and treatment aspects of depression in childhood and adolescence. *Pediatr Ann 1984; 13:* 37-41, 44-45.

141. Kovacs M: *Interview schedule for children (ISC)*. Pittsburgh, University of Pittsburgh School of Medicine 1978.

142. Puig-Antich J, Chambers W: *The schedule for affective disorders and schizophrenia for school-age children* (Kiddie-SADS). New York, New York State Psychiatric Institute 1978.

143. Poznanski EO, Grossman JA, Buchsbaum Y, et al: Preliminary studies of the reliability of the children's depression rating scale. *J Am Acad Child Psychiatry 1984; 23:* 191-197.

144. Orvaschel H, Puig-Antich J, Chambers WJ, et al: Retrospective assessment of child psychopathology with the Kiddie-SADS-E. *J Am Acad Child Psychiatry 1982; 21:* 392-397.

145. Moretti M, Fine S, Haley G et al: Childhood and adolescent depression: Child report versus parent report information. *J Am Acad Child Psychiatry 1985; 24:* 298-302.

146. Kazdin AE, French NH, Unis AS, et al: Assessment of childhood depression: Correspondence of child and parent ratings. *J Am Acad Child Psychiatry 1983; 22:* 157-164.

147. Kashani JH, Shekim WO, Reid JC: Amitriptyline in children with major depressive disorder: A double-blind crossover pilot study. *J Am Acad Child Psychiatry 1984; 23:* 348-351.

148. Petti TA, Law W: Imipramine treatment of depressed children: A double-blind pilot study. *J Clin Psychopharmacol 1982; 2:* 107-110.

149. Petti TA, Conners CK: Changes in behavioral ratings of depressed children treated with imipramine. *J Am Acad Child Psychiatry 1983; 22:* 355-360.

150. Preskorn SH, Weller EB, Weller RA: Depression in children: Relationship between plasma imipramine levels and response. *J Clin Psychiatry 1982; 43:* 450-453.
151. Kramer AD, Feiguine BA: Clinical effects of amitriptyline in adolescent depression: A pilot study. *J Am Acad Child Psychiatry 1981; 20:* 636-644.
152. Geller B, Cooper TB, Farooki ZQ, et al: Dose and plasma levels of nortriptyline and chlorpromazine in delusionally depressed adolescents and of nortriptyline in nondelusionally depressed adolescents. *Am J Psychiatry 1985; 142:* 336-338.
153. Geller B, Cooper TB, Chestnut EC, et al: Child and adolescent nortriptyline single dose kinetics predict steady state plasma levels and suggested dose: preliminary data. *J Clin Psychopharmacol 1985; 5:* 154-158.
154. Wiener JM: Psychopharmacology in childhood disorders. *Psychiatr Clin North Am 1984; 7:* 831-843.
155. Preskorn SH, Weller EB, Weller RA, et al: Plasma levels of imipramine and adverse effects in children. *Am J Psychiatry 1983; 140:* 1332-1335.
156. Winsberg B, Goldstein S, Yepes L, et al: Imipramine and electrocardiographic abnormalities in hyperactive children. *Am J Psychiatry 1975; 132:* 542-545.
157. Hayes TA, Pavitch ML, Baker E: Imipramine dosage in children: a comment on "Imipramine and electrocardiographic abnormalities in hyperactive children." *Am J Psychiatry 1975; 132:* 546-547.
158. Saraf KR, Klein DF, Gittelman-Klein R: Imipramine side effects in children. *Psychopharmacologia 1974; 37:* 265-274.
159. Law W, Petti TA, Kazdin AE: Withdrawl symptoms after graduated cessation of imipramine in children. *Am J Psychiatry 1981; 138:* 647-650.

Chapter 10

GERIATRIC DEPRESSIVE DISORDERS*

George S. Alexopoulos, M.D.
Robert C. Young, M.D.
Jonathan H. Holt, M.D.

Depression is the most frequent psychiatric disorder of old age. Surveys of elderly people who live in the community show that approximately 15 percent have at least mild depression.[1] To some extent the incidence of depression depends on the method of assessment. When self-reports are used, mild depression seems to be more frequent in populations older than 65 years.[2] However, some investigators who based their findings on psychiatric diagnoses report higher incidence of depression in younger adults.[2-4] More severe depressive syndromes occur for the first time between 45 and 65 years, but their frequency may start to decrease after the age of 65.[5] Some studies suggest that in recent decades the onset of the first depressive episode has occurred at an increasingly younger age.[6] This chapter discusses clinical aspects of geriatric depression and similarities and differences between geriatric depression and depression in younger adults.

CLINICAL PICTURE

Aging seems to influence the course of depression. Older women are more prone to develop chronic syndromes when they become depressed,[2] while men probably have more frequent depressive episodes as they grow older.[7]

---

*This work has been supported by funds of the Xerox, Link and Greenwall Foundations.

In general, the symptomatology of geriatric depression is similar to that of young adults. It includes: depressed and anxious mood, preoccupation with guilt, hopelessness, helplessness, worthlessness, appetite and weight loss, inability to fall or stay asleep, early morning awakening, lack of energy, physical symptoms, diurnal variation of mood, and in some cases, delusions. There is some evidence that patients with onset of first depressive episode late in life have more delusions,[8] agitation, hypochondriacal preoccupations and insomnia.[9] There is also some indication that late onset depression has more frequent relapses than early onset depression.[7] Late onset depressives have fewer first degree relatives with affective disorders than patients with early onset depression.[10] Finally, more brain atrophy[11, 12] and higher platelet monoamine oxidase activity[13] have been reported in late compared to early onset depressed patients. While further research is needed, these differences suggest that late onset depression may be a distinct nosological entity.

Cognitive dysfunction often occurs in the context of depression. Deficits in attention, memory, and conceptualization are frequently part of the depression syndrome in any age.[14-21] In elderly patients cognitive dysfunction occurring in the context of depression may be severe enough to meet criteria for dementia.[22-24] This cognitive dysfunction often subsides when the affective symptoms improve.[16, 24-27] A reversible dementia syndrome can also develop in the context of various psychiatric disorders and is therefore not specific to depression.[26-28] In the elderly, however, depression is the psychiatric condition most frequently associated with reversible dementia.[23, 15]

Many authors have emphasized the clinical importance of distinguishing this reversible dementia syndrome, often called pseudodementia, from irreversible dementia.[26, 27, 15, 24] Wells described eleven cases of reversible dementia associated with psychiatric disorders and pointed to clinical characteristics that distinguished such patients from irreversibly demented patients. These features included: presence of psychiatric history, recent onset of symptoms that could be dated with some precision, relatively rapid progression, complaints of severe cognitive loss that are disproportionate to the observed disability, and marked dependency on others.

The cognitive disturbances of depressed patients with reversible dementia are as a rule mild, and do not reflect any particular pattern of deficit. Marked inconsistency in cognitive test performance is probably characteristic of reversible dementia.[27] Ron et al.[29] (1979) noted that patients with reversible dementia did not have a significant difference in Wechsler verbal vs. performance IQ, whereas irreversibly demented patients showed a discrepancy between the two. In a series of eleven patients, Caine[15] (1981) observed that they all had a memory disturbance and most showed inattention, slowed mental processing, and a paucity of verbal elaboration. The picture resembled subcortical dementia of early stages. In three of these patients, neuropsychological findings were observed that were consistent with focal dysfunction.

While cognitive dysfunction can develop in depressed patients, it has also been observed that some patients with irreversible dementia initially have depression.[30] Depressive symptoms may be so prominent that they obscure the diagnosis of dementia. Approximately 20 percent of demented psychiatric outpatients have been reported to meet criteria for major depression,[28] while up to 50 percent of demented individuals living in the community or in nursing care facilities have various degrees of depression.[31, 32] Depression has been observed in histopathologically confirmed cases of Alzheimer's disease,[33, 34] and multi-infarct dementia.[33] It has been suggested that approximately 15 percent of Alzheimer's patients have depression.[35] Some authors believe that depression occurs in the early stages of the disease.[36] However, a recent investigation failed to identify significant depressive symptoms in patients with early Alzheimer's disease.[37] In another study, a cluster of depressive symptoms—retardation, agitation, lack of reactivity, severely depressed mood, depressive delusions, self-reproach or guilt, loss of interest—correlated with the severity of dementia.[38] This finding suggests that more affective symptoms develop in the severely demented and presumably less aware group of Alzheimer's patients.

Minimal information exists on the outcome of patients who develop a dementia syndrome when they become depressed. Rabins et al.[24] (1984) followed 18 psychiatrically hospitalized patients who met DSM-III criteria for major depression and dementia. On discharge from hospital, three of these patients (17 percent) remained demented even after improvement of their mood. Two of these patients remained demented two years later and one died. A much higher percentage of development of dementia (52 percent) has been reported recently in a three year follow-up study of depressed patients (N = 28).[39] These subjects were not initially demented, but complained about memory problems and sought evaluation in a dementia research center. In neither of these studies was the criteria of dementia quantified adequately. It seems more appropriate to consider that both a reversible and an irreversible component of cognitive dysfunction exists in a large number of patients who originally present depression and dementia.

A considerable proportion of geriatric depression develops in the context of medical or neurological disease.[40] Recent myocardial infarction, thyroid or adrenal disease, malignancy, B12 deficiency, Parkinsonism, and stroke are the most frequent disorders associated with depression.[41] There is evidence that left-sided strokes lead to depression more often than strokes of the right hemisphere.[42]

Another major cause of depression in the elderly is the use of addictive or nonaddictive drugs. Sedatives are the most frequently abused drugs in the elderly and can lead to chronic confusion with motor agitation or retardation, labile depressed mood and ideation, and suicidal thoughts or attempts.[43] Prescribed drugs, such as reserpine, beta-blockers or steroids may also precipitate depression of various intensity.

PSYCHOSOCIAL FACTORS

Psychosocial factors contribute to the development of geriatric depression and are relevant for its treatment. The life structures of the geriatric population have distinct though not homogeneous characteristics. Life structure denotes the pattern of key relationships in a person's life at a given time and over time.[44] In later adulthood the relationships to self (self-concept), to family (spouse, children, and others) and to vocation and avocation are particularly fraught with peril that predispose to bereavement, depression, and anomie. Anomie describes a state of hopelessness and meaninglessness.[45] Even individuals fortunate in health and socioeconomic circumstances fall under the spectrum of the society's expectations for old age. These involve loss of occupational position, of prowess, of significant others, of prospects for future achievement, and finally of life itself.

The social structure of the elderly population has in common certain general patterns. Occupational activities as a rule undergo more change than extraoccupational activities. Most have reduced work loads if not total retirement from work and the organization or structures connected with work. Certain extra-occupational connections continue (religion, community, recreation). In some areas these are specifically organized for this age group. The degree of involvement for the elderly varies from case to case.

The construct of life structure can be extended to include the relationship of a person to his body. Within the periods of late adulthood the body provides a different habitat for the person. Presence of chronic illness is the rule in contrast to previous periods. This provides a psychological background to all other life events, and may help explain the hypochondriacal preoccupation of some geriatric depressed patients.

These issues are not unique to geriatric patients but particularly characterize this phase of life. Erikson was among the first to conceptualize the later adult years.[46] His theory focused on personality and was organized around the concept of key tasks or conflicts for a given age. The conflict identified for the elderly population was that of "integrity vs. despair." Old age forces one to consider one's life as nearly complete. One either accepts this and thus achieves integrity, or despairs about one's life or of its approaching end. This challenge may predispose towards affective chopathology. Erikson's theory is not easily put to statistical validation. Some clinicians argue that the integrity vs. despair conflict is not a prominent feature within the geriatric psychotherapy practice.[47, 48] However, we have found it to be a helpful concept in the treatment of geriatric patients with problems related to self-acceptance.

The family structure undergoes drastic changes within the geriatric years. Themes of loss and change pervade this stage of life. Patients in the early years of later adulthood still have or are in the process of losing parents or relatives of the previous and their own generation. The recent increase of more advanced elderly results in greater heterogeneity in the family structure of the geriatric population. Again, the overall trend is loss and bereavement, at least of contemporaries. There are, of course, additions at the other generational end of the family. Loss of independence is a recurrent theme in the geriatric group, particularly for the advanced elderly. This mandates the involvement of family members in the treatment of the depressed patient. Family participation, often optional with other age groups, becomes crucial with the depressed elderly. The overall emotional tone of the family's relationship to the patient has been found to affect the clinical course in depression and schizophrenia.[49] The expressed emotion (EE) construct has been developed to investigate this effect.[49] EE denotes the negative and positive communications and attitudes between family members and the identified patient. Increased EE has been associated with high relapse rate in schizophrenic and in depressed patients.[49] Although the EE research is based on mixed-age populations, the relevance to geriatric patients is clear. Studies specific to geriatric depressed patients are under way.

TREATMENT

When the clinician is presented with a depressed geriatric patient, the first task is to ascertain whether the depression is due to a drug or a physical illness. Treatment of addiction or of physical illness causing depression may lead to remission of depression.[41, 40] If, however, the depression persists, antidepressant treatment should be considered. The efficacy of antidepressants in depressed medical patients is not well studied, but the available literature is encouraging. Use of nortriptyline led to significant improvement in depressed patients after stroke.[50] Both monoamine inhibitors[51] and electroconvulsive therapy[52] have been used successfully in depression of medically ill patients. Antidepressant treatment is particularly important in patients with both depression and dementia, since the dementia syndrome may remit with improvement of depression. In fact, a trial of adequate antidepressant treatment may be the only way to confirm the diagnosis of depression with reversible dementia in the elderly.

A comprehensive approach including psychotherapy, family counseling, and somatic therapies has been effective in the treatment of geriatric depression. Counseling or psychotherapy is often sufficient in mild depression while somatic therapies are essential in the treatment of more severe cases.

NONBIOLOGICAL THERAPIES

The nonbiological therapies used in the treatment of depression are heterogeneous. They include individual psychotherapy, group therapy, family therapy, and activity therapies. In inpatient treatment of depression, most or all are used concurrently.

The efficacy of psychotherapy in geriatric patients has been undervalued since the days of Freud who believed that it was not worthwhile, defenses presumably having "ossified" after age 50.[48] Contrary opinion came in fairly early. Figures from within the psychoanalytic movement, particularly Karl Abraham,[53] (1927) and other personality theorists, e.g., Jung and Adler, used psychotherapy for depression of the elderly.[48] Nevertheless the notion of unsuitabillity continued and perhaps has even gained strength over the past 25–30 years as effective physical treatments have developed.

The use of psychotherapy in elderly patients with psychiatric disorders has not been studied adequately.[54] Most recently, an analysis of data from studies on the efficacy of psychotherapy in geriatric patients suggests that this treatment is not only beneficial but also cost-effective.[55] In fact, higher cost-effectiveness was observed in geriatric populations compared to younger adults.[55]

To date there has been little effort to adapt psychodynamic psychotherapy techniques to the elderly. Early psychoanalytic authors recommended that therapists of geriatric patients should be active and provide structure in therapy.[53, 56] Lazarus et al.[57] (1984) observed that therapists treating geriatric patients with psychodynamic psychotherapy tended to use more supportive techniques. Most psychotherapists of geriatric patients individualize their work, and use a problem-oriented approach while offering both structure and support.

Cognitive therapy and interpersonal psychotherapy have been found to be as effective as imipramine in the treatment of mixed-age depressives.[58] These are relatively short-term therapies that have been standardized and can be used reliably by trained therapists. Although the use of cognitive or interpersonal therapy has not been studied systematically in elderly depressives, we expect that these treatments will be effective when adapted to the needs of geriatric populations.

Group therapy is extensively used as part of both the inpatient and outpatient treatment or geriatric depressed patients. Groups with homogeneous membership facilitate identification of group members with each other, thus leading to group cohesion. This process permits sharing of oppressive feelings of guilt and anger while it reinforces self-acceptance and acceptance of illness. In the psychiatric ward, groups are often task or activity-oriented. Groups of geriatric outpatients generally focus on life problems such as loneliness, abandonment by children, practical everyday difficulties, etc. These approaches provide a focus and reduce resistances originating from poor cultural acceptance of psychotherapeutic methods often found in geriatric populations.[59]

The patient's family plays a critical role in the care of the geriatric patient. A major predictor of institutionalization of ill or disabled geriatric patients is the degree of stress and burdening that their caretakers experience.[60-62] Four emotional experiences have been described in families with an older person who has an acute or chronic illness[60]: 1) a painful conflict is experienced when a decision for a major life change has to be made against the wishes of the older family members; 2) grief develops when irreversible physical or emotional changes take place in a parent or a spouse; 3) resurfacing of old family conflicts occur in the face of crisis; 4) emotional depletion and exhaustion follows overwhelming responsibilities.

In working with these predictable family stresses, a first step is to educate family members about the nature, the treatment and the outcome of depression. This is particularly important because of the social stigma and the broad misconceptions associated with this disorder. The family should be helped in finding and using community services that can be therapeutic for the patient. In chronic cases of depression or where some degree of irreversible dementia coexist, various other steps need to be taken. Adult children should be helped to assume a managerial role and negotiate a relationship with the aged parents that includes reciprocal sharing of obligations and decisions. Clarification of roles and expectations among the rest of the family members usually minimizes conflicts. Finally, family members should be advised that caring for their own personal needs is important, so that they can continue to function without guilt.

Use of therapeutic activities is an essential part of the treatment of depression. As a rule, geriatric patients have well developed skills. When depressed, however, these persons develop lack of initiatives, self-preoccupation to the exclusion of other interests, disturbances in psychomotor activity, and lack of self-confidence. These symptoms impair psychosocial skills necessary for independent function in the areas of self-care, leisure, or work. Their disability may be further compounded by the loss of significant people, i.e., death of spouse or relocation of children, who performed certain functions important for them. The patients' difficulties in everyday functioning confirm and reinforce feelings of worthlessness that develop initially as part of the depression syndrome. Assessment of functional disability, acceptance of changes in function, reorientation to realistic activities, and guidance in learning some new skills are all crucial for the rehabilita tion of elderly depressed patients. For these reasons therapeutic activity programs have been incorporated in geriatric psychiatric units, while many geriatric depressed outpatients can benefit from a referral to an activity therapy specialist.

SOMATIC THERAPIES

Somatic antidepressant therapies include treatment with tricyclic antidepressants, monoamine oxidase inhibitors, ECT or one of the newer antidepressants. In major depression the treatment of first choice is usually a trial of a tricyclic antidepressant. Tricyclics may be not used if there is a history of poor responsiveness to adequate treatment with these drugs, or the patient has a contraindication to tricyclics. Cardiac conduction abnormalities, recent myocardial infarction, active angina pectoris, severe orthostatic hypotension, and severe prostatic enlargement are probably the most frequent contraindications to tricyclic antidepressants in this population.[63] Nortriptyline is the best studied tricyclic antidepressant drug in geriatric populations.[64, 65] Nortriptyline has mild anticholinergic activity compared to amitriptyline and imipramine and therapeutic blood level range has been established. At therapeutic dosages, nortriptyline may have less of a conduction-slowing effect.[64-66] A therapeutic trial of nortriptyline is considered adequate if the patient develops blood levels of 50-150 mg/ml and is exposed to the drug for longer than two weeks. Desipramine is another tricyclic antidepressant with an even milder anticholinergic effect than nortriptyline, and there is increasing information about its pharmacokinetics in the elderly.[66]

If tricyclic antidepressants are ineffective or not tolerated, a monoamine oxidase inhibitor (MAOI) or electroconvulsive therapy (ECT) should be considered. MAOIs are effective in atypical depressions with anxiety, phobias, and possibly a reverse vegetative syndrome which includes somnolence, increased appetite and weight gain.[67] There is, however, evidence that some geriatric patients with major endogenous depression respond to MAOIs.[68] The limitations of MAOIs are that they require a low tyramine diet, and interact adversely with drugs such as sympathomimetrics, L-dopa, meperidine, tricyclic antidepressants, barbiturates, and anticholinergic drugs, which are frequently used in the elderly. Another limitation is that they cause orthostatic hypotension in a considerable percentage of patients.[66] This side effect develops usually after 2–3 weeks of treatment with MAOIs and is poorly tolerated by geriatric patients.

ECT is effective in approximately 75 percent of patients with major depression.[69] ECT is often the treatment of choice in depression with delusions.[69] Delusional depression as a rule does not improve with tricyclics alone,[70, 71] but may respond well to ECT. ECT probably is the safest somatic treatment. The only absolute contraindications to ECT are recent myocardial infarction and space-occupying lesion with elevated intracranial pressure.[69] The poor cultural acceptance of ECT is a considerable limitation of this treatment. Patients with recurrent depression need to be maintained on tricyclic antidepressants or lithium carbonate. Prevention of future depressive episodes is most effective when these patients receive a drug to which they have responded. When ECT is used, however, this information is not available.

The use of newer antidepressants in the elderly has not been adequately studied. Trazodone is probably the most useful drug among the recently developed antidepressants because it probably does not prolong cardiac conduction substantially and may be considered in elderly patients with conduction defects.[72, 73] There is, however, evidence that trazodone may cause arrhythmias.[74] Another major problem is that the dosage of trazodone is not established and, although its blood concentration can be assayed, the therapeutic range is not known. Given the limited clinical and research experience with trazodone, this drug should be prescribed only in cases for which other somatic therapies are either contraindicated or have been ineffective.

In summary, despite their fragile physical health and the easy development of side effects, most elderly patients respond favorably to modern antidepressant treatment. Systematic use of somatic therapies combined with a comprehensive psychological approach of the patient and his family are the major recent advances of the field and have improved the prognosis of geriatric depression significantly.

REFERENCES

1. Blazer D, Williams CD: Epidemiology of dysphoria and depression in an elderly population. *Am J Psychiatry 1980; 137:* 439-444.
2. Gurland B: The comparative frequency of depression in various age groups. *J Gerontol 1976; 31:* 283-292.
3. Post F: The factors of aging in affective illness. In Recent Developments in Affective Disorders. Edited by Coppen A, Wulk A. *Brit J Psychiatry.* Special Publication No. 2, 1968.
4. Post F: Diagnosis of depression in geriatric patients and treatment modalities appropriate for the population. In *Depression,* Edited by Gallant DM, Simpson GD, New York, Spectrum Publications Inc., 1974.
5. Post F: Affective disorders in old age. In *Handbook of Affective Disorders.* Edited by Paykel ES, New York, Guilford Press, 1982, pp. 393-402.
6. Klerman GL, Lavori PW, Rice J, Reich T, Endicott J, Andreasen NL, Keller MB, Hirschfeld RMA: Birth-cohort trends in rates of major depressive disorder among relatives of patients with affective disorders. *Arch Gen Psychiatry 1985; 42:* 689-693.
7. Zis AP, Goodwin FK: Major affective disorder as a recurrent illness: a critical review. *Arch Gen Psychiatry 1979; 36:* 835-839.
8. Meyers BS, Kalayam B, Mei-Tal V: Late-onset delusional depression: a distinct clinical entity? *J Clin Psychiatry 1984; 45:* 345-349.
9. Brown RP, Sweeney J, Loutsch E, Kocsis J, Frances A: Involutional melancholia revisited. *Am J Psychiatry 1984; 141:* 24-28.

10. Winokur G, Behar D, Schlesser M: Clinical and biological aspects of depression in the elderly. In *Psychopathology in the Aged*. Edited by Cole JO, Barrett JE New York, Raven Press, 1980.

11. Jacoby RJ, Levy R: Computed tomography in the elderly. 3. Affective disorder. *Brit J Psychiatry 1980; 136:* 270-275.

12. Jacoby RJ, Levy R, Bird JM: Computed tomography and the outcome of affective disorder: a follow-up study of elderly patients. *Brit J Psychiatry 1981; 139:* 286-292.

13. Alexopoulos GS, Lieberman KW, Young RC, Shamoian CA: Platelet MAO activity and age at onset of depression in elderly depressed women. *Am J Psychiatry 1984; 141:* 1276-1278.

14. Friedman A: Minimal effects of severe depression on cognitive functioning. *J Abnorm Social Psychol 1964; 69:* 237-243.

15. Caine ED: Pseudodementia. *Arch Gen Psychiatry 1981; 38:* 1359-1964.

16. Sternberg DF, Jarvik ME: Memory function in depression. *Arch Gen Psychiatry 1976; 33:* 219-224.

17. McAlister TW: Cognitive functioning in the affective disorders. *Compr Psychiatry 1981; 22:* 572-586.

18. Stromberg LS: The influence of depression on memory. *Acta Psychiatr Scand 1977; 56:* 109-128.

19. Albert M: Assessment of cognitive functions in the elderly. *Psychosomatics 1984; 25:* 310-317.

20. Weingartner H, Silverman E: Models of cognitive impairment: cognitive changes in depression. *Psychopharmacol Bull 1982; 18:* 27-41.

21. Plotkin DA, Mintz J, Jarvik LF: Subjective memory complaints in geriatric depression. *Am J Psychiatry 1985; 142:* 1103-1105.

22. Folstein MF, McHugh PR: Dementia syndrome of depression. In *Alzheimer's Disease, Senile Dementia and Related Disorders*, Edited by Katzman R, Terry RD, Bick KL. New York, Raven Press, 1978.

23. Post F: Dementia, depression and pseudodementia. In *Psychiatric Aspects of Neurologic Disease*. Edited by Benson DF, Blumer D, New York, Grune and Stratton, 1975.

24. Rabins PV, Merchant A, Nestadt G: Criteria for diagnosing reversible dementia caused by depression: validation by 2-year follow-up. *Brit J Psychiatry 1984; 144:* 488-492.

25. Nott PN, Fleminger JJ: Presenile dementia: the difficulties of early diagnosis. *Acta Psychiatr Scand 1975; 51:* 210-217.

26. Kiloh LG: Pseudodementia. *Acta Psychiatr Scand 1961; 37:* 336-351.

27. Wells CE: Pseudodementia. *Am J Psychiatry 1979; 136:* 895-900.

28. Reifler BV, Larson E, Hanley R: Coexistence of cognitive impairment and depression in geriatric outpatients. *Am J Psychiatry 1982; 139:* 623-626.

29. Ron MA, Tooye BK, Gerraloa ME et al.: Diagnostic accuracy in presenile dementia. *Brit J Psychiatry 1979; 134:* 161-168.

30. Liston EF: Occult presenile dementia. *J Nerv Ment Dis 1977; 164:* 263-267.

31. Miller NE: The measurement of mood in senile brain disease: examiner ratings and self-reports. In *Psychopathology in the Aged*. Edited by Cole JO, Barrett JE New York, Raven Press, 1980.

32. Ernst P, Badash D, Beran B, Kosovsky R, Kleinhaus M: Incidence of mental illness in the aged: unmasking the effects of diagnosis of chronic brain syndrome. *J Am Ger Soc 1977; 8:* 371-375.

33. Rosen WG, Terry RD, Fuld PA, Katzman R, Peck A: Pathological verification of ischemic score in differentiation of dementias. *Ann Neurol 1980; 7:* 486-488.

34. Coblentz JM, Mattis S, Zingesser LH, Kasoff SS, Wisniewski HM, Katzman R: Presenile dementia. *Arch Neurol 1973; 29:* 299-308.

35. Kral VA: The relationship between senile dementia (Alzheimer's type) and depression. *Can J Psychiatry 1983; 28:* 304-306.

36. Roth M: Diagnosis of senile and related forms of dementia. In *Alzheimer's Disease: Senile Dementia and Related Disorders*. Edited by Katzman R, Terry RD, Bick KL, New York, Raven Press, pp. 205-232, 1978.

37. Knesevich JW, Martin RL, Berg L, Dunziger W: Preliminary report on affective symptoms in the early stages of senile dementia of the Alzheimer's type. *Am J Psychiatry 1983; 140:* 233-235.

38. Greenwald BS, Mathe AA, Mohs RC, Levy MI, Johns CA, Davis KL: Cortisol and Alzheimer's disease, II: Dexamethasone suppression, dementia severity, and affective symptoms. *Am J Psychiatry 1986; 143:* 442-446.

39. Reding M, Haycox J, Blass J: Depression in patients referred to a dementia clinic. A three-year prospective study. *Arch Neurol 1985; 42:* 894-896.

40. Rodin G, Voshart: Depression in the medically ill: An overview. *Am J Psychiatry 1986; 143:* 696-705.

41. Salzman C: Depression and physical disease. In *Physician's Guide to the Diagnosis and Treatment of Depression in the Elderly*. Edited by Crook P, Cohen GD, New Canaan, Connecticut, Mark Powley Associates, 1983, pp. 9-17.

42. Robinson RG, Szetela B: Mood change following left hemisphere brain injury. *Ann Neurol 1980; 9:* 447-453.

43. Salzman C, Shader RI: Depression in the elderly II. Possible drug etiologies; differential diagnostic criteria. *J Am Geriatr Soc 1978; 36:* 303-308.

44. Levinson D, et al.: *The Seasons of a Man's Life*, New York, Ballantine, 1978.

45. Durkheim E: *Le Suicide*, 1897, Republished in translation, *Suicide*, New York, Macmillan, 1951.

46. Erikson E: *Childhood and Society*, New York, W.W., Norton & Co., 1st ed. 1950; 2nd ed. 1963.

47. Butler RN: Life review. In *New Thoughts on Old Age*. Edited by Kastenbaum RJ, New York, Springer, 1964.

48. Brink TL: *Geriatric Psychotherapy*, New York, Human Sciences Press, 1979.

49. Leff J, Vaughn C: *Expressed Emotion in Families*. New York, Guilford Press, 1985.

50. Lipsey RJ, Robinson RG, Pearlson GD, et al.: Nortriptyline treatment of poststroke depression: a double-blind study. *Lancet 1984; 1:* 297-300.

51. Lehman H: Affective disorders in the aged. *Psychiatr Clin North Am 1982; 5:* 27-44.

52. Bidder TG: Electroconvulsive therapy in the medically ill patient. *Psychiatr Clin North Am 1981; 4:* 391-405.
53. Abraham K: *Seleccted Papers of Karl Abraham*. New York, Basic Books, 1927.
54. Lazarus L: *Clinical Approaches to Psychotherapy with the Elderly*. Washington, D.C., American Psychiatric Press Inc., 1984.
55. Mumford E, Schlesinger H, Glass G, et al.: A new look at evidence of reduced cost of medical utilization following mental health treatment. *Am J Psychiatry, 141:* 10: 1143-1158.
56. Wayne G: Psychotherapy in senescence. *Annals of Western Medicine & Surgery 1952; 6:* 88-91.
57. Lazarus L, et al.: Brief psychotherapy with the elderly: a review and preliminary study of process and outcome. In *Clinical Approaches to Psychotherapy with the Elderly*. Washington, D.C., American Psychiatric Press Inc., 1984.
58. Elkin I, Shea T, Watkins JT, Collins JF, Docherty JT, Shaw BF: *Outcome Findings and Therapist Performance*. Presented at the American Psychiatric Association Annual Meeting, Washington, D.C., May, 1986.
59. Thurston F: *Issues in family therapy with the elderly*. Presented at the American Psychiatric Association Annual Meeting, Dallas, May, 1985.
60. Brody EM: Parent care as a normative family stress. *Gerontologist 1985; 25:* 19-29.
61. Cobe GM: Family of the aged: issues in treatment. *Psychiat Annuals 1985; 15:* 343-347.
62. Mace NL, Rabins PV: *The Thirty-six Hour Day*. Baltimore: Johns Hopkins University Press, 1981.
63. Glassman AH, Bigger T: Cardiovascular effects of therapeutic doses of tricyclic antidepressants: a review. *Arch Gen Psychiatry 1981; 38:* 815-820.
64. Reed L, Smith RC, Schoolar JC et al.: Cardiovascular effects of nortriptyline in geriatric patients. *Am J Psychiatry 1980; 137:* 986-989.
65. Ziegler VE, Co BT, Bigger JT: Plasma nortriptyline levels and ECG findings. *Am J Psychiatry 1977; 134:* 441-443.
66. Goldman LS, Alexander RC, Luchins DJ: Monoamine oxidase inhibitors and tricyclic antidepressants: comparison of their cardiovascular effects. *J Clin Psychiatry 1986; 47:* 225-229.
67. Ravaris CL, Robinson DS, Ives JD, et al.: Phenelzine and amitriptyline in the treatment of depression: a comparison of present and past studies. *Arch Gen Psychiatry 1980; 37:* 1075-1080.
68. Georgotas A, Friedman E, McCarthy M, et al.: Resistant geriatric depressions and therapeutic response to monoamine oxidase inhibitors. *Biol Psychiatry 1983; 18:* 195-203.
69. Weiner RD: The psychiatric use of electrically induced seizures. *Am J Psychiatry 1979; 136:* 1507-1517.
70. Nelson JC, Bowers MB: Delusional unipolar depression—description and drug response. *Arch Gen Psychiatry 1978; 35:* 1321-1328.
71. Glassman AH, Kantor SJ, Shustake M: Depression, delusions, and drug response. *Am J Psychiatry 1979; 132:* 716-719.

72. Robinson DS, Corsella J, Feigner JP, et al.: A comparison of trazodone, amoxapine and maprotilene in the treatment of endogenous depression: results of a multicenter study. *Curr Ther Res 1984; 35:* 549-560.

73. Gerner R, Estabrook W, Stener J et al.: Treatment of geriatric depression with trazodone, imipramine, and placebo. *J Clin Psychiatry 1980; 41:* 216-220.

74. Janowsky D, Curtis G, Zisook S, et al.: Ventricular arrhythmias possibly aggravated by trazodone. *Am J Psychiatry 1983; 140:* 796-797.

RECOMMENDED READING

Blazer II DG: *Depression in Late Life.* St. Louis, CV Mosby Co, 1982.

Murphy E: The prognosis of depression in old age. *Brit J Psychiatry 1983; 142:* 111-119.

Post F: Affective disorders in the old age. *In Handbook of Affective Disorders.* Edited by Paykel S. New York, Guilford Press, 1982, pp. 393-402.

Chapter 11

DEPRESSION AND PHYSICAL ILLNESS*

David F. Cella, Ph.D.
Samuel W. Perry, M.D.

> In order to cure the human body it is necessary to have a knowledge of the whole of things.
>
> Hippocrates

The relationship between depression and physical illness has held a long-standing fascination for clinicians. However, like many relationships that hold a sustained interest, this one, too, is replete with subtleties and complexities. At first glance, the relationship would appear to be a simple one: people get depressed because they are sick ("No wonder he's depressed; he's got cancer") and conversely, people get sick because they are depressed ("After her husband was gone, she died of a broken heart").

Looking at these two statements more closely, one finds that simple answers are replaced with difficult questions: Is it normal to be depressed when physically ill? If so, why don't most people get depressed when they have a severe illness with a bad prognosis? Does the physical illness cause the depression in some biological manner or is the depression a purely psychological reaction? What about all the drugs and procedures given to the physically ill; can they cause depression or do they make it better? If people really are more vulnerable to physical illness because they are depressed, what exactly happens in the body that makes the person more vulnerable? And what about all those people who have physical complaints but no apparent illness; are they depressed and just don't know it?

*Supported in part by NIH Grant #P50GM26145.

Because many of these questions have not yet been adequately answered and because physical illness and its medical treatment introduce so many confounding variables, psychiatric investigators often choose to exclude physically ill patients from their research protocols; but the clinician does not have this option. This chapter, therefore, provides a conceptual framework for the clinician who is confronted with a physically ill patient who is depressed (or a depressed patient who is physically ill). We begin by briefly summarizing the difficulties in establishing the prevalence of depression in the physically ill. Next, we describe now the DSM-III-R helps conceptualize some diagnostic issues in this area, yet leaves other issues unclear. Based on this review, we conclude with suggestions for the clinician when evaluating and diagnosing a depressed, physically ill patient.

PREVALENCE

Depression is the most prevalent major psychological problem in the physically ill. This is partly because the lifetime prevalence of major depression and dysthymia in the general population is 10 to 15 percent.[1,2] However, the occurrence of depression in medical patients exceeds this figure. The reasons for this include: the physiological effects of disease and treatments on the central nervous system (CNS), the psychological impact of illness as a precipitating stressor, and the secondary maladaptive behaviors of preexisting depressive disorders which make it more likely that a depressed individual will become ill and remain ill.

Depression is often missed by clinicians trained to treat physical illness; and physical illness is often missed by those trained to treat psychiatric disorders. The rate of recognition of depression by primary care physicians is reportedly as low as 10 to 33 percent.[6,7] This certainly points out the need for more vigilance on the part of those providing treatment for physical illnesses.

The warning applies equally to mental health professionals when presented with depressed patients. In a review of the literature, LaBruzza[11] concluded that 1 out of every 20 patients that seek psychiatric consultation is actually suffering from an underlying medical condition. Koranyi[12] demonstrated that of 902 psychiatric patients with concurrent major medical illnesses, the psychological symptoms of 18 percent were caused by the medical problem. In 51 percent of those same patients, the psychological symptoms were exacerbated by physical illness. In nearly half of the 902 cases, physical illness was undiagnosed prior to Koranyi's study.

Studies indicate that the percentage of physically ill individuals who suffer from a depression severe enough to warrant intervention is 15 to 42 percent.[3-9] This range is wide because different studies have used different diagnostic criteria (pre- and post-DSM-III), different assessment strategies (e.g., self-report, interview, standardized instruments, chart review), and different types of patients (e.g., inpatients, outpatients, the acutely ill with good prognoses, and the chronically ill with poor prognoses). Furthermore, many studies have not distinguished: 1) affective disorders from either normal grief reactions or adjustment disorders with depression; 2) patients with preexisting depression from those whose depression is precipitated by (or at least temporarily associated with) the physical illness; and 3) depressions primarily caused by systemic disease or its treatment from those depressions that are more clearly psychological. By now discussing these distinctions, we hope to help clarify these diagnostic difficulties.

DIFFERENTIAL DIAGNOSIS

Organic Affective Syndrome

When considering the differential diagnosis of any patient who presents with a depression (regardless of whether the patient has experienced previous depressions and regardless of whether the patient is physically ill), the clinician must first ask: "Does this depression have any possible organic basis?" The answer to this question is never a simple yes or a no. We know, for instance, that all depressions at some level must affect the brain biologically and are therefore "organic." However, this use of the term organic is not the traditional one. By "organic" we usually mean associated with some structural damage or at least driven primarily by some biological or biochemical process. We also know that individuals vary in their susceptibility to acquire a depression when physiologically stressed. For example, many patients with hypoglycemia, endocrinopathies, or brain tumors do *not* become depressed; therefore, one cannot presume that the presence of even a severe organic illness is necessarily the cause of a depression.

Dealing with problems of correlation and causality.   We must recognize the difference between correlation and cause. For example, both myocardial infarction and pancreatic carcinoma have been associated with depression. In the absence of an established mechanism, it would be an error to assume that the depressive syndrome is biologically driven. Nevertheless, although the distinction between organic and nonorganic is not always as well demarcated as we would like, and given that the modern biopsychosocial model precludes a Cartesian division between body and mind,[10] clinically it remains useful to follow DSM-III-R guidelines is differentiating organic from nonorganic affective syndromes. The identification of possible predisposing biological factors can be helpful in early intervention or even prevention of depressive disorders.

The high prevalence of occult physical illnesses in presumed psychiatric patients is a significant clinical problem worthy of selective medical screening based upon aspects of symptomatology, onset, or demography which are atypical. For example, Hall and Beresford[13] have recommended including carcinoma of the pancreas in the differential diagnosis with "individuals in their fifties who present with moderately depressive feelings of worthlessness or psychomotor retardation and who have a previous negative history of depression" (p. 13). This type of informed, comprehensive approach can help identify depression secondary to physical illness without subjecting patients to an unnecessary and expensive barrage of tests.

When to look for organic affective syndrome. As defined by the DSM-III-R, organic affective syndromes can be caused by systemic illness, by direct CNS disease, and by treatment of either a physical or psychological disorder. Using these guidelines, the diagnosis would be considered in the presence of any medical condition strongly associated with depression. These conditions have been summarized elsewhere[11-15] and include: hypothyroidism, slow-onset hyperthyroidism, hypoparathyroidism, hyperparathyroidism, hyperadrenalism (Cushing's disease), Addison's disease, pernicious anemia, hyperglycemia, hypoglycemia, diabetes, chronic pain syndromes, spinal cord injury, hypopituitarism, brain trauma, intracranial tumor, CNS brain metastases, pancreatic carcinoma, lymphoma, systemic lupus erythematosis, viral infections, and chronic obstructive pulmonary disease.

Many pharmacological treatments are also associated with organic affective syndromes.[15-19] In fact, there are few medications that have not been linked to depression.[19] Of these, the more commonly prescribed drugs include: reserpine, methyldopa, propanolol and most other antihypertensives, corticosteroids and adrenocorticotrophic hormone (ACTH), fenfluramine, cimetidine, digitalis, narcotic analgesics, antipsychotics, sedative hypnotics, and antianxiety medications. Less frequent depressive reactions have been reported with: L-dopa, carbamazepine, oral contraceptives, disulfiram, amantadine, and some anticancer agents (e.g., vincristine, vinblastine, l-asparaginase, and procarbazine).

A point that must be emphasized, however perplexing for the clinician, is that in the presence of either a medical condition or a drug associated with depression, the *presumptive* diagnosis is an organic affective disorder, even though: 1) not all patients with these illnesses or administered these medications develop a depression; 2) the development of a depression depends in part on psychological factors such as the meaning of the illness or drug and the patient's particular psychodynamics, situation, age, or past psychiatric history (e.g., patients who are elderly or have a prior psychiatric history are more prone to develop organically induced depressions); 3) a given individual may become depressed on one occasion and not another (e.g., after a bout of systemic lupus erythematosis or after administration of steroids); and 4) the biological mechanism of the induced depression may be only hypothetical (e.g., the reduction of catecholamines following the administration of many antihypertensives, or the competitive binding of serotonin receptor sites secondary to immunological alterations in cancer patients).[20]

The question of trauma-induced depression. There is no doubt that many patients become depressed following intensive surgery,[21] radiation[22] and head injury, but are these depressions "organic"? Geshwind,[23] for example, has called depression an understandable *psychological* reaction to the cognitive impairment following brain trauma. Gainotti[24] has challenged this view by citing evidence that patients with right hemisphere lesions tend to be apathetic whereas those with left hemisphere lesions tend to have catastrophic, depressive reactions. This argument is supported by Robinson and colleagues who have empirically demonstrated this apparent lateralization of a depressive response in left anterior brain injury.[25, 26] These studies are cited to illustrate that advances in the neurosciences continually modify our previous notions of what is "functional" and what is "organic."

Major Depression

If an organic affective syndrome is ruled out because neither the medical condition nor its treatment are believed to have induced the depression, the next diagnosis to consider is major depression. This diagnosis is complicated in the presence of physical illness.[27, 28]

Limitations of DSM-III-R. A DSM-III-R diagnosis of major depressive episode requires the presence of a dysphoric mood and at least four of eight associated symptoms. Five of these eight symptoms are commonly produced by physical illness itself: 1) anorexia or significant weight loss; 2) insomnia or hypersomnia; 3) motor slowing or agitation; 4) loss of energy or fatigue; and 5) diminished ability to think or concentrate.

Because these diagnostic criteria occur so commonly with physical illness and because at least some dysphoria is usually present in these patients, a rigid application of the DSM-III-R would undoubtedly result in the overdiagnosis of a major depression. This problem of overdiagnosis cannot be solved by relying on a dexamethasone suppression test, for it is commonly abnormal in the absence of a depressive disorder in patients who are physically ill.[29, 30] Similarly, standardized scales such as the Beck Depression Inventory[31] or the Hamilton Depression Rating Scale,[32] also emphasize somatic aspects of the diagnosis.[9, 33, 34]

Toward resolving the limitations of DSM-III-R. As suggested by others,[8, 9, 33-35] a possible way to circumvent this problem of overdiagnosis is to rely more heavily upon the three remaining DSM-III-R associated symptoms that are more psychological in nature: 1) loss of interest or pleasure; 2) feelings of worthlessness, self-reproach or guilt; and 3) thoughts of death or suicide. Somatic symptoms of depression can be used as supportive data when they are severe and clearly out of proportion to the extent of illness, or when they fluctuate in conjunction with the more affective, psychological symptoms.

An approach which emphasizes the nonsomatic aspects of depression still has some limitations, because even in the absence of depression, physical illness itself *normally* alters a patient's behavior and self-view. Parsons,[36] for example, has described "the sick role," in which physical complaints, dependency, and relinquishment of responsibility are expected, sanctioned and encouraged. Similarly, "illness behavior" as described by Mechanic[37] and Mumford[38] indicates that physically ill patients normally experience a psychological state that overlaps with the DSM-III-R diagnostic criteria for major depression. Furthermore, as Fabrega[39] has pointed out, the diagnosis of depression in general relies heavily upon culturally and socially determined notions of "acceptable" behavior and view of oneself. Since we know that the response to physical illness is strongly influenced by one's culture and social status, "deviance" from the norm may be especially prominent during the throes of physical illness, again leading to an overdiagnosis of depression.

Resolution of these sociocultural biases inherent in diagnosing depression can be approached by using patients as their own controls. In other words, input from close family members and friends becomes extremely valuable in determining if patients are reacting within the normal spectrum of their response repertoire, or if their withdrawal or sadness is pathologial.

The question of secondary depression. Some[27] have argued that all depressions following either medical illness or psychiatric disorder should be labeled secondary, thereby homogenizing a group of primary depressives for research investigation. Andreasen and Winokur,[28] however, have pointed out that labeling all depressions after any physical illness as "secondary" would produce a diagnostic concept so broad it would lose any meaning (and might also reduce the pool of so-called primary depressives for research).

There are two other potential dangers in labeling depressions in the physically ill as "secondary." First, the label implies that the depression is related to the physical illness. To the contrary, it is estimated that the two conditions are truly independent at least one-third of the time.[12, 13] As with many "primary" depressions, a precipitating stressor (e.g., the physical illness) can be found retrospectively to appear to explain the psychological condition.

A second potential danger of the label "secondary depression" is that the psychopathological condition will be erroneously viewed as normal: "People who are sick have every reason to be depressed." Actually, most people who are physically ill do not develop a major depression by DSM-III-R criteria,[5, 34, 40-42] and although the prevalence of a severe depression is highest among those who suffer major physical impairment,[3, 4, 9, 42] the clinician must remember that the majority of patients who face even a dreadful prognosis do not become severely depressed. They cope remarkably well.

Because somatic, psychological, and "reactive" clinical features are not always reliable in establishing the diagnosis of a major depression in the physically ill, what criteria can the clinician use? Departing from rigid adherence to the DSM-III-R, we would recommend that the clinician rely primarily on the *severity* of the dysphoria and its interference with adaptive or self-helping behavior.

Dysthymic Disorder

This less severe depressive disorder is both more prevalent and easier to diagnose than major depression in the physically ill. By using quantitative rather than qualitative diagnostic criteria, the clinician would make the diagnosis of a dysthymic disorder when the physically ill patient has suffered a mild or moderate depression for at least two years with some associated symptoms, such as social withdrawal, hopelessness, and a diminished productivity that is disproportionate to the constraints posed by the physical illness. The most difficult differential is between dysthymia and realistic pessimism and resignation about one's capacities. An example would be a man with a below-knee amputation who develops a persistent negative attitude towards his family, work and physical rehabilitation.

Adjustment Disorder with Depressed Mood

Although this diagnosis is the most prevalent of the DSM-III-R disorders involving depression in the physically ill,[5] exactly how and when this diagnosis should be made is also confusing. On the surface, the diagnostic criteria would appear to be simple enough. An adjustment disorder is diagnosed if the patient: 1) has a maladaptive response to a precipitating stress (i.e. physical illness); 2) does not have a personality pattern of overreaction or another depressive disorder (organic affective syndrome, major depression, dysthymia); and 3) presumably would be psychologically normal were it not for the precipitating stressor, or is suffering impairment in social or occupational functioning. A closer look at these three criteria discloses some difficulties when applied to the physically ill.

Challenges to clinical judgment. Reactions to physical illness are enormously varied and determined by one's intelligence, culture, socio-economic status, life situation, character style, phase in the life cycle, and the conscious and unconscious meanings of the illness. Given this wide range of responses, it is not always clear what adjustments should be regarded as maladaptive. The DSM-III-R leaves this decision to clinical judgment, but we know that the looser the diagnostic criteria, the greater risk of bias: a response different from what the clinician desires or expects might arbitrarily be considered maladaptive. For example, when a woman becomes dissatisfied and sad over the result of her plastic surgery and seeks a second or third opinion for additional procedures, under what conditions—in the patient and in the clinician—would her behavior be labeled an adjustment disorder with depressed mood? Or when a man becomes discouraged and withdrawn after a rather minor sprained ankle, would the diagnosis of an adjustment disorder be different if the patient were a professional athlete versus a sedentary corporate executive?

To limit bias towards either over- or underdiagnosis of a *maladaptive* response to physical illness, it is helpful to have for comparison some general guidelines about what an *adaptive* response entails. In this regard, the adaptive functions developed by Hamburg and Adams[43] are quite useful. They are: keeping distress within normal limits; maintaining a sense of personal worth; restoring relations with significant others; enhancing prospects for recovery; and increasing the likelihood of working out the most desirable situation for oneself, given one's physical illness.

Problems in ruling out other depressive disorders. As we have already described, there are several reasons that an organic affective syndrome, a major depression and dysthymia may be underdiagnosed or overdiagnosed in the physically ill. Logically, therefore, ruling them in or out is not always so easy. For example, if a patient becomes depressed following the recurrence of lung cancer, how does the clinician determine if the diagnosis is an adjustment disorder or if the affective disturbance is secondary to a hormone-secreting tumor warranting the diagnosis of an organic affective syndrome? Would an elevation in the urinary steroids be sufficient to consider the depression "organic" in its etiology? And if a patient becomes profoundly depressed four months after a burn injury but has no neurovegetative symptoms, is an adjustment disorder a reasonable diagnosis even though it is not within three months of the burn or would a diagnosis of a major depression be more appropriate? And if a patient with chronic arthritis remains depressed for over two years while her physical problems persist, would she be diagnosed as having an adjustment disorder or would she now meet the diagnostic criteria for dysthymia?

These questions are presented to raise the possibility that the high prevalence of an adjustment disorder with depressed mood in the physically ill may not always be based on careful reasoning, but may be due to a tendency among clinicians to use this diagnosis whenever a patient becomes depressed in the context of a physical illness. In some situations the diagnosis of an organic affective syndrome, a major depression, or dysthymia would be more appropriate.

The presumption of normality. A final point of confusion about the diagnosis of an adjustment disorder in the physically ill concerns the presumption that the patient would be psychologically normal if the stressor were not present. There are two inherent problems with this presumption. First, in some individuals who are chronically ill or physically impaired, their depression no longer appears to be reactive but rather appears to have become characterologically ingrained or to have "a life of its own." In these situations, it is not always clear at what point the depressive disorder should no longer be regarded as a maladaptive response to the illness.

A second problem with the presumption of normality in the absence of the physical illness is the implication, however subtle, that the patient is not currently psychologically disturbed, that he or she is merely "under stress." But an adjustment disorder in a *disorder*, a maladaptive behavioral and emotional response. Moreover, the depression accompanying this disorder can be quite severe, even to the point of suicidal ideation or acts. The diagnosis is not intended to denote that the depression is mild, but the presumption that the patient "would be normal" sometimes inadvertently leads the clinician to take the depressed mood less seriously.

Normal Sadness

As elaborated elsewhere in this book, it is often difficult to distinguish normal grief from pathological depression. For several reasons, this distinction is especially difficult in the physically ill and, once again, can lead to both the underdiagnosis and overdiagnosis of depression.

Common misconceptions about grief and depression. One common misconception is that normal grief and pathological depression can be distinguished by their severity; that is, that grief is relatively mild and depression more intense. On the contrary, a grief response can be quite profound whereas depressed feelings may be mild. Therefore, when a patient becomes overwhelmed by the loss of a limb or breast or cardiac function, the diagnosis of depression should not be based simply on the severity of the feelings, especially if the loss holds a particular dynamic meaning to that patient.

A second common misconception is that depression and grief can be distinguished by their duration; that is, that grief is short-lived and depression lingers. On the contrary, many grief responses are prolonged, and may intermittently recur throughout one's life, whereas many depressions, even untreated major depressions, resolve after several months. Therefore, if a patient with ulcerative colitis continues to grieve from time to time over the loss of a more normal life, the duration of these sad feelings would not in itself warrant the diagnosis of "depression" any more than the diagnosis would be given to a bereaved widow who feels sad on those holidays or anniversaries when she is reminded of her lost loved one.

Differentiating grief from depression.   Since neither severity nor duration are sufficient to distinguish grief from depression, the clinician must use other criteria. Of these, the most important is determining whether or not a diminished self-esteem is associated with the loss.[44] Because one's sense of self is so intermeshed with one's sense of body, this determination in the physically ill is difficult, but not impossible. Following a myocardial infarction or disfiguring surgery, patients may feel understandably sad about the loss of their physical being, yet not feel in any way less "lovable." Despite their limitations, they still feel like basically worthy human beings. A depressive response, on the other hand, would lead the patient to make such statements as "I'm no good" or "I'm worthless" or "I'm being punished."

Along with diminished self-esteem, feelings of hopelessness and helplessness are also helpful in distinguishing depression from normal sadness; but here, too, the presence of physical illness makes this distinction difficult. For example, a patient crippled with a metastatic terminal cancer may have a sense of being helpless and having a hopeless prognosis; yet even if she were understandably sad about this realization, we would not label her "depressed" if she felt confident about her capacity to handle whatever lay ahead.

This difference between grief and depression is more than semantic, for each requires a different clinical response. Whereas a communication of empathic understanding is a sufficient response to a patient with normal grief, depression requires more active psychotherapeutic or psychopharmacological interventions. If a patient is appropriately mourning the occurrence of a physical illness and working through that loss, it would be an error for the clinician to consider the normal intense sadness as "depression" and convey to the patient that the emotional responses are pathological. Similarly, if a patient feels totally worthless as a human being and overwhelmed by the prospects of dealing with the future, it would be an error for the clinician to consider these responses as "normal" and thereby fail to treat the psychopathology.

Suicide.   Long associated with depression, suicide has also been linked to physical illness.[45, 46] In a study by Dorpat and colleagues,[46] 70 percent of people who committed suicide had one or more active illnesses, and in one-half of the cases the illness was considered to be contributory.

The highest numbers of suicides were found in rheumatoid arthritis, peptic ulcer, and hypertension patients. Cancer patients had the highest suicide-to-illness prevalence ratio within the study sample, however.

Holland[47] has concluded that the link between cancer and suicide has been inflated in the past, and that most suicides occur in patients during the terminal period, or in patients with limited social supports. Brown et al.[48] have pointed out that the suicidality of cancer patients in their study was only present in the context of some major psychiatric diagnosis. Nevertheless, at the very least, the higher rate of emotional and mental disturbance in people with cancer and other serious medical conditions places them at higher risk for suicide.

Somatoform Disorders

In the 1960s, as tricyclic antidepressants started to be used more widely, clinicians began prescribing these drugs for groups of patients who traditionally had responded poorly to other psychotherapeutic interventions. Among these were patients with various somatic symptoms: hypochondriacal complaints, persistent unexplained fatigue, vaguely described headaches, and chronic pain without clear pathophysiological causes. Because many of these patients responded to tricyclic antidepressants, the term "masked depression" was used to categorize these patients.[49]

We have since learned that tricyclic antidepressants are useful for many psychiatric problems other than depression (e.g., vascular headaches, panic disorders, chronic organically-induced pain, some sleep disorders). Therefore, unless patients have either signs or symptoms of a depression, they probably should not be labeled as "depressed," masked or otherwise. A clinical response to antidepressant medication is not so specific that it can be used diagnostically.

Chronic pain. Chronic pain syndromes address the relationship between somatoform disorders and depression. It is true that chronic pain is associated with many signs and symptoms that are similar to depression (hopelessness, helplessness, and losses of self-esteem, libido, weight, appetite, energy, or concentration). It is also true that some patients with chronic pain syndromes respond favorably to antidepressant medication. However, the clinician should not conclude on this basis that all patients with chronic pain are depressed and that is the primary source of their complaints. This is an error for three reasons: 1) many chronic pain patients have an analgesic response to psychotropic drugs other than antidepressants (e.g., anxiolytics, neuroleptics); 2) the chronic pain rather than the depression may have produced the psychological and neurovegetative signs and symptoms, possibly by depletion of serotonin; and 3) if the clinician presumes that depression is the primary source of the pain complaints, an organic cause may not be searched for vigorously, and the clinician may inadvertently convey that the pain is being taken less seriously.

Psychological Factors Affecting Physical Condition

This diagnostic category is similar to somatoform disorders in that both relate in part to physical complaints that develop as a result of psychological factors (as opposed to depression and other psychological problems that develop as a result of physical illness); however, in somatoform disorders the physical complaints are considered "functional," whereas with "psychological factors affecting physical condition" the physical complaints are considered to have an "organic" basis.

The conceptual understanding of the relationship between "psyche" and "soma" has been greatly modified in recent years. During the early days of "psychosomatic medicine," psychoanalysts believed that specific conflicts or even specific personality types were associated with specific "psychosomatic disorders."[50] This early view has been modified in three ways.

First, the "specificity" theory has been replaced with the biopsychosocial model,[10] which maintains a system view of the organism in which psychological and physiological factors inevitably interact in *all* diseases. The extent of this interaction will depend upon individual psychological factors (e.g., personality, coping style, neurotic conflicts, perceived stress) as well as upon individual pathophysiological factors (e.g., genetic predisposition, severity, and duration of pathological condition). In this more modern view, both psychological and physical illnesses are seen as heterogeneous; therefore, depression would be regarded as a major contributing factor in the initiation or perpetuation of a particular disease in some individuals but would not be seen as significantly contributory in others.

Another shift in what was termed "psychosomatic medicine" has been a far more systematic epidemiological approach towards documenting the widely-held belief that psychological distress, including depression, makes one more vulnerable to physical illness.[51-53] Stress, life change, and resulting sequelae have been linked to increased morbidity from myocardial infarction,[54, 55] bronchial asthma,[56] diabetes,[57] and depression.[58]

Researchers are now conducting studies that are prospective, controlled and focused. For example, some early studies[59-61] provided provocative evidence for depression being a significant factor in the onset of malignancy. In a 17-year prospective study of over 2,000 men, a high depression score of the MMPI was associated with a twofold increase in the odds of dying from cancer over that period.[62] However, in an equally well designed study,[63] no causal relationship between depression and the development of cancer was found in 191 unipolar and bipolar depressives. A thorough review of this area[64] concluded that psychological factors (including depression) do not have a major impact on the development or progression of cancer. The point here is not that clinicians doubt that there is a relationship between psychological distress and physical illness, but that well-controlled studies to document this presumed causal relationship continue to be necessary.

A third shift in "psychosomatic medicine" has been towards looking for a pathophysiological rather than a psychodynamic mechanism to explain the relationship between psychological distress and physical disease. An early indication of this shift was various psychoendocrinologic studies that showed how stress and loss can alter the sympathetic adrenomedullary system.[65] A more recent indication has been the rapidly advancing field of psychoneuroimmunology.[66-68] For example, in two separate studies of individuals who were bereaved (but not necessarily pathologically depressed), alterations were found in lymphocyte response to mitogen stimulation,[69, 70] suggesting that one's affective state may make one more vulnerable to disease. More recently, lymphocyte function was found to be decreased in psychiatric inpatients with severe depression when compared to psychiatric outpatients with mild depression, schizophrenia, and healthy controls;[71] and individuals subjected to sleep deprivation were found to have a decrease in lymphocyte stimulation and phagocytosis by neutrophils,[72] suggesting a possible relationship between the sleep disorders of depression, immune compromise, and vulnerability to illness.

Although we are getting closer to a scientific understanding of how depression may make one more susceptible to physical illness, at the present time the diagnosis of "psychological factors affecting physical condition" should be used cautiously by the clinician who speculates that the patient's physical illness may have been *caused* by a depression; however, this DSM-III-R diagnostic category can be used more generously when categorizing the patient whose depression has no doubt led to a progression or perpetuation of the physical illness because of poor compliance either with treatment or participation in prescribed rehabilitation programs. Depressive withdrawal and treatment noncompliance can lead to premature deterioration or even death.[35] For example, the depressed diabetic who won't take insulin, the depressed renal patient who refuses dialysis, or the depressed cancer patient who doesn't take prescribed chemotherapy would all meet the criteria for this diagnosis.

CONCLUSIONS

In this chapter we have discussed the interesting but complex relationship between depression and physical illness. We have pointed out why clinicians must be cautious before speculating that depression has contributed to either "functional" somatic complaints or to "organic" physical disease. Our main emphasis throughout has been how conceptual problems can lead to either the overdiagnosis or underdiagnosis of depression in the physically ill.

Organic affective syndromes. These syndromes are often underdiagnosed because many patients do not have marked cognitive impairment or because iatrogenic causes are not considered. They are often overdiagnosed because clinicians presume that the presence of a physical illness in itself warrants the diagnosis even if the pathophysiological mechanisms affecting the CNS is unknown.

Major depression. This is often overdiagnosed because physical illness itself causes neurovegetative changes, and because the expected sick role is confused with depressive behavior. It is often underdiagnosed because clinicians erroneously view depressive reactions to illness as normal and expected rather than pathological and relatively infrequent (i.e. most physically-ill patients are *not* depressed).

Adjustment disorder with depressed mood. This is often overdiagnosed because the possibility of an independent major depression or dysthymia is not considered and because bias leads to labelling certain illness behaviors as maladaptive when they deviate from the clinician's personal or sociocultural standards. It is often underdiagnosed because of a confusion between depression and normal grief in which self-esteem and confidence in one's coping is maintained.

The need for conceptual and diagnostic clarity has clinical relevance. The risks of overdiagnosis are unnecessarily burdensome treatments and perhaps an injudicious prescription of antidepressant medication. The risk of underdiagnosis of depression in the physically ill is a failure to recognize and treat a disorder that not only causes psychological distress but also may increase the likelihood of suicide, and impede compliance with medical treatment and ultimate recovery from the illness. Our hope is that this chapter will help meet this need of understanding the most prevalent major psychological disorder in the physically ill.

REFERENCES

1. Weissman MM, Klerman GL: Epidemiology of mental disorders. *Arch Gen Psychiatry 1978; 35:* 705-712.
2. Teuting P, Koslow SH, Hirschfield RMA: *Special Report on Depression.* Bethesda, M.D., National Institute of Mental Health, 1981.
3. Stewart MA, Drake F, Winokur G: Depression among medically ill patients. *Dis Nerv Syst 1965; 26:* 479-485.
4. Moffic HS, Paykel ES: Depression in medial inpatients. *Br J Psychiatry 1975; 126:* 346-353.

5. Derogatis IR, Morrow G, Fetting J, Perman D, Piasetsky S, Schmale AM, Hendrichs M, Carnicke CL: The prevalence of psychiatric disorders among cancer patients. *JAMA 1983; 249:* 751-757.

6. Kline NS: Incidence, prevalence and recognition of depressive illness. *Dis Nerv Syst 1976; 37:* 10-14.

7. Nielsen AC III, Williams TA: Depression in ambulatory medical patients: Prevalence by self-report questionnaire and recognition by non-psychiatric physicians. *Arch Gen Psychiatry 1980; 37:* 999-1004.

8. Rodin G, Voshart K: Depression in the medically ill: An overview. *Am J Psychiatry 1986; 143:* 696-705.

9. Bukberg J, Perman D, Holland JC: Depression in hospitalized cancer patients. *Psychosom Med 1984; 46,* 3: 199-212.

10. Engel G: The need for a new medical model: A challenge for biomedicine. *Science 1977; 196:* 129-136.

11. LaBruzza AL: Physical illness presenting as psychiatric disorder: Guidelines for differential diagnosis. *Journal of Operational Psychiatry 1981; 12:* 24-31.

12. Koranyi EK: Morbidity and rate of undiagnosed physical illness in a psychiatric clinic population. *Arch Gen Psychiatry 1979; 36:* 414-419.

13. Hall RCW, Beresford TP: Psychiatric manifestations of physical illness. In Michels R, Cavenar JO (Eds): *Psychiatry* (Vol. 2) Philadelphia; J.B. Lippincott Co., 1985, (ch. 88).

14. Loewenstein RJ, Black HR: Recognition, evaluation and differential diagnosis of psychiatric and somatic conditions. In Leigh H (Ed.): *Psychiatry in the practice of medicine.* Menlo Park, CA, Addison-Wesley, 1983, 57-81.

15. Hall RCW (Ed.): *Psychiatric Presentations of Medical Illness: Somatopsychic Disorders.* New York, Spectrum Publications, 1980.

16. Shader RJ (Ed.): *Psychiatric Complications of Medical Drugs.* New York, Raven Press, 1972.

17. Lipowski ZJ: Intoxication with medical drugs. In Kugelmass IN (Ed.): *Delirium.* Springfield, IL, Charles C. Thomas, 1980, 255-316.

18. Johnson DAW: Drug-induced psychiatric disorders. *Drugs 1981; 22:* 57-69.

19. Perry S: Substance-induced organic mental disorder. In Hales RE, Yudofsky SC (Eds.): *American Psychiatric Press Textbook of Neuropsychiatry.* Washington, D.C.: American Psychiatric Press, Inc. 1987, 157-176.

20. Brown JH, Paraskevas F: Cancer and depression: Cancer presenting with depressive illness. *Br J Psychiatry 1982; 141:* 227-232.

21. Chapman CR, Cox GB, Anxiety, pain and depression surrounding elective surgery: A multivariate comparison of abdominal surgery patients with kidney donors and recipients. *J Psychosom Research 1977; 21:* 7-15.

22. Forester BM, Kornfeld DS, Fleiss J: Psychiatric aspects of radiotherapy. *Am J Psychiatry 1978; 135,* 8: 960-963.

23. Geschwind N: The organization of language and the brain. *Science 1970; 170:* 940-944.

24. Gainotti G: Emotional behavior and hemispheric side of the brain. *Cortex 1972; 8:* 41-55.

25. Robinson RG, Szetela B: Mood change following left hemispheric brain injury. *Annals of Neurology 1981; 9:* 447-453.

26. Lipsey JR, Robinson RG, Pearlson GS, Rao K, Price TR: Mood change following bilateral hemispheric brain injury. *Br J Psychiatry 1983; 143:* 266-273.

27. Gold MS, Pottash ALC, Extein I, Sweeney DR: Diagnosis of depression in the 1980's. *JAMA 1981; 245,* 15: 1562-1564.

28. Andreasen NC, Winokur G: Secondary depression: Familial, clinical, and research perspectives. *Am J Psychiatry 1979; 136,* 1: 62-66.

29. Risch SC, Janowsky DS: Limbic-hypothalamic-pituitary-adrenal axis dysregulation in melancholia. In Michels M, Cavenar JO (Eds.): *Psychiatry* Vol. 3. Philadelphia, J.B. Lippincott Company, 1985 (Ch. 54).

30. Carroll BJ, Feinberg M, Greden JF et al.: A specific laboratory test for the diagnosis of melancholia: Standardization, validation and clinical utility. *Arch Gen Psychiatry 1981; 38:* 15-22.

31. Beck AT, Ward CH, Mendelsohn M, Mock J, Erbaugh J: An inventory for measuring depression. *Arch Gen Psychiatry 1961; 4:* 561-571.

32. Hamilton M: A rating scale for depression. *J. Neurol Neurosurg Psychiatry 1960; 23:* 56-62.

33. Endicott J: Measurement of depression in patients with cancer. *Cancer 1984; 53* (Suppl.): 2243-2248.

34. Stoudemire A: Depression in the medically ill. In Michels R, Cavenar JO (Eds.): *Psychiatry* (Vol. 2). Philadelphia: J.B. Lippincott Co., 1985 (Ch. 99).

35. Leigh H: Evaluation and management of depression and affective disorders. In Leigh H (Ed.): *Psychiatry in the Practice of Medicine.* Menlo Park, CA, Addison-Wesley, 1983, 123-137.

36. Parsons T: *Social Structure and Personality.* Glencoe Il, Free Press, 1965.

37. Mechanic D: *Medical Sociology: A Selective View.* New York, Free Press, 1968.

38. Mumford E: On being a patient. In Simons RC, Pardes H: *Understanding Human Behavior in Health and Illness,* 2nd ed., Baltimore, Williams and Wilkins, 1981, 31-35.

39. Fabrega H: Problems implicit in the cultural and social study of depression. *Psychosom Med 1974; 36,* 5: 377-398.

40. Streltzer J: Diagnostic and treatment considerations in depressed dialysis patients. *Clin Exper Dialysis and Apheresis 1983; 7* (4): 257-274.

41. Plumb M, Holland J: Comparative studies of psychological function in patients with advanced cancer II. Interviewer-rated current and past psychological symptoms. *Psychosom Med 1981; 43:* 243-253.

42. Hong BA, Smith MD: Depressive symptomatology in kidney failure. *Proceedings of the American Psychiatric Association Annual Meeting,* Washington, D.C., May, 1986 (No. 82B), p. 153.

43. Hamburg DA, Adams JE: A perspective on coping behavior: Seeking and utilizing information in major transitions. *Arch Gen Psychiatry 1967; 17:* 277-284.

44. Viederman M, Perry SW: Use of a psychodynamic life narrative in the treatment of depression in the physically ill. *Gen Hosp Psychiatry 1980; 3:* 177-185.

45. Fawcett J: Suicidal depression and physical illness. *JAMA 1972; 219,* 10: 1303-1306.
46. Dorpat TL, Anderson WF, Ripley HS: The relationship of physical illness to suicide. In Reskick HLP (Ed.): *Suicidal Behaviors.* Boston, Little Brown & Co., 1968.
47. Holland JC: Psychologic aspects of cancer. In Holland JF, Frei E: *Cancer Medicine.* Philadelphia, Lea & Febiger, 1982, 1175-2331.
48. Brown JH, Henteleff P, Barakat S, Rowe CJ: Is it normal for terminally ill patients to desire death? *Am J Psychiatry 1986; 143:* 2, 208-211.
49. Lopez-Ibor JJ: Masked depressions. *Br J Psychiatry 1972; 120:* 245-258.
50. Alexander F: *Psychosomatic Medicine: Its Principles and Applications.* New York, W.W. Norton, 1950.
51. Kagan A: Epidemiology, disease and emotion. In Levi L (Ed.): *Emotions: Their Parameters and Measurement.* New York, Raven Press, 1975, 531-540.
52. Rabkin JG, Streuning EL: Life events, stress and illness. *Science 1976; 194:* 1013-1029.
53. Kraus A, Lilienfield A: Some epidemiological aspects of the high mortality rate in the young widowed group. *J Chron Dis 1959; 10:* 207-217.
54. Theorell T: Life events before and after onset of a premature myocardial infarction. In Dohrenwend BS, Dohrenwend BP (Eds.): *Stressful Life Events: Their Nature and Effects.* New York, John Wiley & Sons, 1973, 101-118.
55. Lundberg U, Theorell T, Lind E: Life change and myocardial infarction: Individual differences in life change scaling. *J Psychosom Res 1975; 19:* 27-32.
56. Groen JJ: The psychosomatic theory of bronchial asthma. *Psychother Psychosom 1979; 31:* 38-48.
57. Grant I, Kyle GC, Teichman A, et al.: Recent life events and diabetes in adults. *Psychosom Med 1974; 36:* 121-128.
58. Schlesser MA, Winokur G, Sherman BM: Hypothalamic-pituitary-adrenal axis activity in depressive illness. *Arch Gen Psychiatry 1980; 37:* 737-743.
59. Watts CAH: *Depressive Disorders in the Community.* Bristol, John Wright, 1966.
60. Ken TA, Schapiro K, Roth M: The relationship between premature death and affective disorders. *Br J Psychiatry 1969; 115:* 1277-1282.
61. LeShan L, Worthington RE: Some recurrent life history patterns observed in patients with malignant disease. *J New Ment Dis 1956; 124:* 460-465.
62. Shekelle RB, Raynor WJ, Ostfeld AM, Garron DC, Bieliauskas LA, Liu SC, Maliga C, Paul O: Psychological depression and 17-year risk of death from cancer. *Psychosom Med 1981; 43:* 117-125.
63. Niemi T, Jaaskelainen J: Cancer morbidity in depressive persons. *J Psychosom Res 1978; 22:* 117-120.
64. Fox BH: Current theory of psychogenic effects on cancer incidence and prognosis. *J Psychosocial Oncology 1983; 1:* 17-31.
65. Levi L (Ed.): Stress and distress in response to psychosocial stimuli. *Acta Med Scand Suppl 1972; 528:* 1-166.
66. Ader R, (Ed.): *Psychoneuroimmunology.* New York, Academic Press, 1981.
67. Schiavi R, Stein M: Disorders of immune mechanism. In Arieti S (Ed.): *American Handbook of Psychiatry—IV.* New York, Basic Books, 1975, 709-725.

68. Locke SE: Stress, adaptation and immunity: Studies in humans. *Gen Hosp Psychiatry 1982; 4:* 49-58.
69. Bartrop RW, Lazarus L, Luckhurst E, Kiloh LG, Penny R: Depressed lymphocyte function after bereavement. *Lancet 1977; 1:* 834-836.
70. Schleifer SJ, Keller SE, Camerino M, Thornton JC, Stein M: Suppression of lymphocyte stimulation following bereavement. *JAMA 1983; 250:* 374-377.
71. Schleifer SJ, Keller SE, Siris SG, Davis KL, Stein M: Depression and immunity: Lymphocyte function in ambulatory depressed patients, hospitalized schizophenic patients, and patients hospitalized for hernorrhapshy. *Arch Gen Psychiatry 1985; 42:* 129-133.
72. Palmblad J: Stress and immunologic competence: Studies in man. In Ader R (Ed.): *Psychoneurroimmunology.* New York, Academic Press, 1981, 229-257.

RECOMMENDED READING

Fawcett J: Suicidal depression and physical illness. *JAMA 1972; 219:* 10: 1303-1306.

Hall RCW (Ed.): *Psychiatric Presentations of Medical Illness: Somatopsychic Disorders.* New York, Spectrum Publications, 1980.

Koranyi EK: Morbidity and rate of undiagnosed physical illness in a psychiatric clinic population. *Arch Gen Psychiatry 1979; 36:* 414-419.

Viederman M, Perry SW: Use of a psychodynamic life narrative in the treatment of depression in the physically ill. *Gen Hosp Psychiatry 1980; 3:* 177-185

Chapter 12

PATHOLOGICAL GRIEF RESPONSES

Milton Viederman, M.D.

Mourning in response to loss is one of the most powerful and universal human experiences. Though generally ascribed to the loss of an important person, mourning responses can be evoked by other losses such as loss of a body part, loss of bodily function, loss of an ideal or a symbolic loss, etc. Indeed one may view the whole fabric of experience through the life cycle from the vantage point of gain and loss with the latter reflecting progressive relinquishment of roles and associated gratifications such as the relinquishment of the freedom from responsibility as a child grows older, the loss of the dependency relationship with the parents in the second separation-individuation phase at the end of adolescence, the loss of children as they leave the home, the loss of childbearing capacity, etc. It is the intent in this chapter, however, to focus on responses to loss of important people through death or separation.

An introductory comment about definitions may be useful. Although the recent publication by the National Academy of Science[1] defines a group of terms frequently utilized in discussing mourning and grief, this usage is not general and often confusion results. The authors state that bereavement should be considered the fact of loss through death, and bereavement reactions, any psychologic, physiologic, or behavioral response to bereavement. They relegate grief to the feeling states and behavior accompanying these states such as crying, agitation, etc. The grieving process refers to the change of affective state over time. Mourning is used to mean a social expression of grief in the social science sense (pp. 9–10). Bowlby's terminology is simpler and will be utilized in the presentation below. For

Bowlby,[2] mourning is used to describe the psychological processes accompanying loss, and grief or is used to connote the subjective states that accompany mourning.

THE LITERATURE

The literature on bereavement is rich and diverse and reflects different perspectives ranging from phenomenologic to psychodynamic and psychoanalytic. Many of the points of view have implicit or explicit theoretical models that relate to the view of mourning as the adaptive response to loss.

Freud,[3] in his classic paper, "Mourning and Melancholia," distinguished normal mourning from melancholia which he viewed as a pathological response to loss. Freud emphasized that these two states shared certain characteristics, in particular: painful dejection, loss of interest in the outside world, the inability to love and cathect objects, and the inhibition of activity. This psychological experience reflects the gradual process of "decathexis" of the lost object during which each memory and expectation is reevoked, reexperienced, and decathected, all with considerable pain. In the process energy is released for the recathexis of new objects in the outside world. Melancholia, or pathological grief, is characterized by painful and guilty self-reproaches and occurs in the context of the loss of an object with whom the individual had had a previously highly ambivalent relationship based upon a narcissistic object choice. It is the repressed hostile component of the ambivalent relationship which leads to intense guilt. Freud views the self-recriminations of the melancholic as an attack upon the "object now residing in the ego." Abraham[4] presented a theoretical model that was in some ways similar to Freud's but he theorized that introjection occurred in normal bereavement to mute the pain of separation until the individual could adjust to an altered reality. Deutsch[5] focused on delayed grief in individuals who had lost important figures many years before. Lindemann[6] systematically studied grief responses in the survivors of a nightclub fire in Boston. He described the symptomatology of normal grief and included: 1) somatic distress; 2) preoccupation with the image of the deceased; 3) guilt; 4) hostile reactions; and, 5) the loss of normal patterns of conduct. There is some question as to whether all of these features are characteristic of normal grief. Important was Lindemann's characterization of morbid grief reactions as including a delay or postponement of reaction (in his experience, the most common manifestation of pathological grief), and a group of distorted reactions, the main features of which included overactivity without a sense of loss; the acquisition of symptoms belonging to the last illness of the deceased; intense hostility against specific individuals; medical disease; and severe alterations in patterns of social intereaction with family, at work, etc. He also included the picture of a classical agitated depression as an aberrant form of grief.

Bowlby[2] has examined mourning in the context of his broader study of attachment behaviors. He disputes Freud's view of mourning as primarily a process devoted to instinctual decathexis of a love object and disagrees with Melanie Klein[7] who states that the anlage of mourning responses relate to the development experience of the loss of the breast through the weaning experience of infancy. Bowlby's view is that mourning represents a disruption of attachment bonds that have their antecedents in separation from the maternal object. He views pathological mourning as involving two primary symptom complexes, one of chronic grieving and the other of a prolonged absence of grieving. The former is characterized by extremely painful emotional states with persistent anger, ruminating self-reproach, a sense of worthlessness and the welcoming of death. Particularly striking is an intense, persistent and unremitting yearning for the lost object, a phenomenon present to a lesser degree in normal mourning and reflective of his view that mourning represents the psychological wish of the mourner to regain the lost object. The prolonged absence of grieving on the other hand is characterized rather by numbing, forced cheerfulness, control, an unwillingness to share the feelings of loss. The maladaptive nature of such behavior is reflected in the persistent difficulty such individuals have in establishing affective social bonds. Moreover they are vulnerable to depressive reactions on anniversaries of the loss, in the context of another even minor loss, or when a child, for example, reaches the age of a lost parent. An important feature of such pathological mourning responses may be compulsive caretaking of others or what Bowlby calls "mummification," the maintenance of material aspects of a shared life together in an undisturbed state such as to preserve the illusion of the presence of the lost person. Bowlby agrees with Freud[3] and Parkes and Weiss[8] that antecedent, highly ambivalent relationships often lead to pathological grief. He also notes that markedly dependent relationships reflective of early loss or conflictual relationships with parents lay the groundwork for pathological grief responses. His work remains a conceptual landmark in the understanding of the mourning process.

Raphael and Maddison[9] delineated specific items which they felt important in the development of pathological mourning responses and designed interventions to effect these elements. Their study population improved significantly as compared with controls. Important were: 1) perceived nonsupport or the presence of a support system that discouraged expression of grief; 2) a pathological relationship with the deceased characterized by ambivalence or dependence; 3) suddenness and nature of the death such as suicide or youthful death[10]; and 4) a terminal course which led to a deterioration of the relationship with the dying person. Raphael and Maddison[10] emphasized that early loss of the spouse before the age of forty was a poor prognostic sign. The interventions

utilized involved abreaction or supporting the expression of grief; the interpretation of defense (in particular denial) as well as the interpretation of
hostile ambivalence and the gratification of regressive needs activated
during the mourning process.

Parkes and Weiss,[8] strongly influenced by Bowlby's conceptual framework, did an extensive long-term study of the grieving process. Parkes's
early work[11] studied the impact of pathological mourning in psychiatrically
ill patients and confirmed Anderson's[12] conclusion that a large percentage
of psychiatric patients were suffering from chronic pathological grief with
restlessness and self-reproach. In this group of patients unremitting
painful grieving was more frequent than delayed grief, though the fact that
the study was done on psychiatric patients may have influenced this
finding. Parkes and Weiss[8] studied bereaved individuals longitudinally, in
the early phases of bereavement, 3 and 8 weeks after loss, 13 months after
the loss, and 2–4 years later. They defined three syndromes of pathological
grief: 1) unexpected grief; 2) conflicted grief; and 3) chronic grief.
Unexpected, sudden loss of a spouse was a major factor in poor long-term
adjustment. These individuals were extremely distressed early in the
bereavement process and at 2–4 years after the loss, they appeared to have
poorly accepted the loss. They were moderately to severely anxious and
depressed and expressed the feeling that there was little reason to go on.
Self-reproach and loneliness were common and there was poor social
recovery in the form of difficulty in establishing relationships and poor
work performance. The second category, conflicted grief, was found in
individuals who had had particularly ambivalent previous relationships.
Paradoxically, this group appeared to be doing reasonably well in the early
phase of bereavement, at which time they established social contacts and
seemed to experience little pain of loss. There was a tendency toward idealization of even highly conflicted previous relationships. Two to four years
later they were frequently depressed, highly anxious, guilty and yearning
for the return of the deceased spouse. Their physical health was worse and
they were dissatisfied in their social relationships. Chronic grief, the third
category, seemed to occur more frequently in individuals who had had
excessively dependent relationships with their spouses. Relentless and
overwhelming yearning dominated their experience and they maintained
the fantasy of a continued relationship with the dead partner in order to
sustain an illusion of security. They were insecure, fearful, and lacked confidence in their capacity to effectively engage in the world. Normal and
pathological grief are not to be viewed as categorically different but on a
spectrum and the research strategy of Parkes and Weiss was to compare
extremes of normal and pathological bereavement.

Horowitz, et al.[13] used a dynamic-regressive model in differentiating
between normal grief and pathological grief. Normal grief involves the
painful separation and relinquishment of an attachment to an adult object
that has been lost. Pathological grief involved the regressive reevocation of

early self-object constellations that are conflicted. The existence of these conflicts has been muted by the presence of an adult object relationship until the loss occurs.

> The essential point is that recent internalization of ambivalent attitudes toward attributes of the lost person is not the major reason for states of pathological grief. Although these new identifications and attitude formations are important processes, a major cause of pathological grief appears to be the reemergence of earlier self-images and role relationship models. These were established before the loss, but were held in check by a more positive relationship... (with the adult object). (p. 1159)

Horowitz and his coauthors emphasize that the relationship with the lost person tends to mute underlying regressive anxiety about neediness, lovability, worthiness, etc. Hence, before the death and by virtue of the relationship with the other person, the individual can feel strong, worthy, lovable in the context of the sustenance generated by the relationship. With loss, however, there is a regressive reactivation of the unconscious conflicted infantile relationship.

Cognitive and behavioral theorists have also addressed the issue of pathological grief. Extrapolating from Beck et al.'s cognitive model[14] of depression, they speculate that individuals with a premorbid tendency to see themselves and the world in a negative light may instigate "a chain of negative thoughts that could intensify or prolong grief" when the death "might be interpreted as a deliberate rejection based upon their inherent defectiveness" (p. 63). The authors cite Gauthier and Marshall's[15] paper that suggests that social reinforcement may prolong grieving behavior and in situations where expression of grief is discouraged may lead to delayed grief. Some individuals will avoid painful memories, thereby impeding the grief process. Ramsey[16] has commented on individuals who avoid situations that would evoke painful memories of grief and in this context develop an increasingly constricted and phobic attitude about the world.

Clayton[17] views grief itself as fundamentally a depressive syndrome of varying length and approaches it phenomenologically. Using descriptive criteria, she has determined that from 25 to 42 percent of individuals at 1 month and from 16 to 70 percent at 13 months have the descriptive criteria of depression using Feighner's criteria.[18-20] She notes a decrease in vegetative signs at 13 months in many individuals but the persistence of symptoms of disturbed sleep, restlessness and low mood in over 40 percent of individuals. This is consistent with the study by Blanchard et al.[21] She agrees with Lindemann[6] and Parkes[22-23] that the depression is always of the agitated and never of the retarded sort. Her studies fail to measure the intensity and persistence of the symptoms and the degree to which they pervasively affect the life experience. Hence, the presence or absence of

symptoms may not be an adequate indication of the presence of pathological grief. Characteristic of the mourning process are marked fluctuations in
mood alternating between extreme dysphoria and periodic positive interaction with the environment. These considerations are not adequately
addressed in symptom surveys.

The need to more closely examine the total life experience of the
bereaved person becomes evident when we consider the fact that individuals become more aware of distress, painful feelings, and obsessive worri-
some ruminations when inactive, alone, and especially in
middle-of-the-night awakenings. Moreover, activity may be a defense
against underlying depression. However, if a bereaved person finds relief
in a job or social engagement, are we to interpret the residue of painful preoccupations with loss as a reflection of unresolved grief and to ignore the
activity as a beginning engagement in life? Moreover, the continued preoccupation with a dead person in memory and fantasy may go on for many
years or until death and does not in itself necessarily reflect a pathological
grief response.[24] We live in a world of internal representations. Internal
representations of objects long dead persist. Of critical importance is the
determination as to whether these representations act as benign or malevolent influences. It becomes apparent that the entire adaptive status of an
individual must be examined and weighed in order to determine the
degree of resolution of bereavement or success in coping with loss.

Ultimately, our view of response to loss must reflect our normative
expectations of object relations and one of the failures in object relations
theory may be reflected in the minimal emphasis placed on functioning
without the object. In this regard there is a considerable difference of
opinion as to whether pathological grief can be characterized simply by
intensity and duration of grief.[25] Variations in response to loss may relate to
the intensity of attachment and the degree of exclusiveness of the relationship. Intensely exclusive and close relationships seen as pathologically
dependent relationships have been described as antecedent to chronic
grief.[8] Yet such "babes-in-the-woods relationships" sustained over many
years and gratifying to both parties may be judged as pathological only by
virtue of the intensity of the disruption which is imposed by the loss of one
partner. It may be quite unreasonable to call the persistence of such a disruption pathological grief in the situation of couples that have lived most of
their lives together and when loss occurs at a late age. Clearly value judgments are involved in such a decision. Healthy and intimate relationships
must include the capacity to tolerate aloneness, if not loneliness, and individuals develop and grow in the absence of the other. Furthermore,
normal and pathological do not exist in pure culture and represent the
extremes of a bell-shaped curve. The diagnosis of a pathological response
can only be made by a total assessment of the individual's interpsychic,
interpersonal, and behavioral adaptation.

NORMAL GRIEF RESPONSES

With the above reservations in mind the "normal process of grief" will be elaborated. Bowlby's[2] description is the richest and the most generally agreed upon description of the normal process of bereavement.*

Initial Response to Loss: Numbing/Denial

The initial response to the fact of a loss (even after a period of prolonged anticipatory grieving) involves the requirement that one adapt to a changed reality. As is the case of any major overwhelming stressful event, the first psychological protection against the threat of a dramatic shift in one's experience of reality involves some distancing from the change in reality. This has been called numbing, denial, distancing, etc. This behavior, designed to defend against the initial impact of a threatening change in reality, permits the organism to gradually integrate the change and to effect an adaptation over time. In the case of a sudden unanticipated loss, the numbing or denial phase may last for a few weeks but in general this phase is brief and rapidly gives way to the next phase of mourning.

A moving description of this stage is described in a recent book on Monet.[26]

> At the time of Camille's death an incident took place that has become a part of the Monet legend. He painted a study of her on her deathbed. This was not in itself extraordinary. What is extraordinary was his later comment on it, which Georges Clemenceau quoted in his book on his friend's work. Monet used the episode to dramatize his bondage to painting. Rather than describing his act as a last devotion to his dead wife, he exclaimed at the unnaturalness of what he had done. For he had been aware even at her bedside of the detachment with which his painter's eye had accessed the fall of light across her face, had identified the sequence of values, had translated her ravaged and irreplaceable features into a painting problem. It was perverse and he had compared

---

*The process outlined will apply to the normal course of grief after loss of a spouse. Clearly there are variations in the bereavement process depending upon the nature of the relationship that is disrupted. Therefore, it is to be assumed that an adult's loss of a parent or an adult's loss of a child will be somewhat different from the adult's loss of a spouse. In the circumstance of the adult's loss of the parent, much will depend upon the configuration of the relationship, i.e., whether the adult child remains dependent or whether the dependency relationship has been reversed as the parent ages. Similarly in the adult's loss of a child, an examination of the dynamics of the couple will strongly influence the outcome. For the sake of brevity, the loss of the spouse will be described in detail with the presumption that other losses will represent variations on a theme. It is generally assumed, however, that the adult loss of a young child is one of the most painful experiences and one which leaves considerable residuum.

himself to a beast of burden harnessed to a millstone—the millstone of his metier, which cut him off from ordinary human experience. (pp. 55–56)

This behavior reflects a defense against the immediate trauma of loss and death. In this situation the painter transforms a painful and intolerable reality into something that is familiar and a normal and central part of his life. He detached himself by changing the experience into a problem in the execution of a painting. In recognizing his detachment he unjustly recriminates himself for heartlessness, this in spite of his profound attachment to Camille. Subsequently, he underwent an intense normal grief response with ultimate recovery and remarriage. It is not uncommon for individuals to recriminate themselves for this early defensive behavior and to improperly attribute it to a lack of feeling and callousness. It is often useful to reassure the bereaved that this is a normal response during this phase of the grief response.

The Phase of Yearning and Searching for the Lost Figure—Distress and the Work of Mourning

This second phase is a prolonged one that involves much pain. Bowlby[2] divided it into two subphases; the first, dominated by intense yearning for the lost object with attempts to re-find it; and the second by increasing discouragement and despair as the individual progressively integrates the reality and permanence of the loss. These phases are likely to prevail for many months during the grieving process though in normal grief they tend to be completed by the end of one year. This phase is characterized by pangs of intense yearning for the lost object with periodic sobbing often accompanied by restlessness, insomnia, powerful feelings of sadness, and anxiety. This painful dysphoric state may alternate with states of relative detachment and more relaxed engagement in life which may include pleasure and humor. Characteristic is an episodic and wavelike quality, though initially longer periods of profound despair may dominate. This relief that comes from what Bowlby called "distancing" represents a defense by which the individual is able to protect himself from an overpowering sense of loss. This alternates with an intrusive and painful preoccupation with the lost person and experiences with the lost person often stimulated by encounters with people, situations and material things that remind the mourner of the loss. Memories, previously forgotten, of the lost person and experiences with the lost person emerge each time with painful distress as if the loss is being discovered anew. Freud described this as the working through of the loss and the gradual decathexis of the lost person. Representations of the lost person may reemerge in dreams, illusions, or even brief hallucinations which in themselves are not abnormal. Parkes[23] characterizes this behavior in the following way. There is "restless moving about and scanning of the environment; thinking intensely about the lost person; developing a perceptual set for the person, namely a disposition to perceive and to pay attention to any stimuli that suggests the presence of the person and to ignore all those who are not relevant to the same; directing attention to those parts of the environment in which the person is likely to be found; and calling for the lost person." The strong perceptual set toward seeing the lost person leads to frequent visual and auditory misperceptions. Bowlby[2] describes anger as a normal component of this phase of grief, viewing it as a characteristic biological and adaptive response to separation stemming from childhood when anger in the child has an adaptive function in leading to a reunion with mother and making her more reluctant to leave on future occasions. Anger may not be a central feature of grief and, especially when intense, may be more characteristic of pathological responses to loss. This phase is accompanied frequently by the vegetative signs of depression, though many individuals are capable of distinguishing the mood disturbance which they describe as intense sadness from depression which is experienced as a dictinctly different feeling state. Not everyone is capable of making this distinction. Unlike pathological grievers, those undergoing normal responses experience either no guilt about the loss or guilt of omission rather than commission. They ruminate about what they might have done to prevent the death, but do not have guilt about having caused it. Self-esteem is maintained and these individuals do not experience shame. Though the feeling of hopelessness about the future may dominate them, they have a cognitive awareness of their experience as a response to loss and are aware of the fact that there will be a resolution of the painful state. The wavelike quality of their sadness is also unlike a depressive response to loss. Suicidal ideation is very rare. Important to note is that neither the intensity of the dysphoria nor the vegetative signs of depression are discriminating elements between normal and pathological grief.

This process of relinquishment of the lost object requires an internal "redefinition of self and situation... which... is no mere release of affect but a cognitive act on which all else turns. It is a process of realization," of reshaping internal representational models so as to align them with the changes that have occurred in the bereaved's life situation (Bowlby[2]).

Reorganization and Recovery

The third phase of the bereavement process begins imperceptibly as the individual progressively comes to terms with the loss and is more free to attend to the outside world which is now recognized as altered in ways that go beyond the loss of the loved person. The survivor may find himself in many situations in which he has to assume roles previously accomplished by the lost person. In traditional households the widower may find himself responsible for housekeeping duties he had not previously performed and the widow required to cope with finances and house repairs. The absence of a mate with whom to share responsibility for the upbringing of young children may pose difficulty and the responses to loss of the children themselves must be taken into account. Often a child's rage generated toward the dead parent will be repressed and displaced to the surviving one, a source of considerable pain. Gradually a new engagement in an altered world must occur.

Successful mourning does not imply the relinquishment of a relationship with the internal representations of the lost object. Often evocations of memories of the dead act as a comforting presence to individuals who have coped well.[27-28] Minor identifications with the dead person and the continuation of activities characteristic of the relationship with the dead person do not reflect pathological outcome and may imply a strengthening of resources.

ABNORMAL GRIEF RESPONSES

It has already been emphasized that abnormal grief responses must be viewed from a point of view of the total constellation rather than as a summation of symptoms. Ultimately success or failure in response to loss resides in the quality and completeness of the individual's capacity to reengage in life. Considerations of age of the bereaved and social possibilities for reintegration must be taken into account. It is also to be emphasized that normal and pathological grief do not exist in pure culture but represent extremes on a bell-shaped curve.

The following is a suggested scheme for considering varying responses to loss such that the clinician may be alerted to potential long-range difficulties. Though the elements will be presented as components of potential pathological grief responses, it is to be understood that the whole is greater than the sum of its parts. Pathological grief is to be considered a global syndrome rather than a disorder and it must be recognized that it is a syndrome embedded in a dynamic life experience that is being influenced by many other demands of living.

ANTECEDENTS TO PATHOLOGICAL GRIEF

There is good evidence to suggest that antecedent conflictual relations will influence the response to loss.[8] Highly ambivalent relationships with repressed hostility are likely to lead to severe guilt and chronic grief. Similarly, highly dependent relationships may well leave the mourner full of rage and without the sense that he has appropriate resources to cope independently. There is considerable difference of opinion in the literature about the role of anticipation of death and the potential values and liabilities of anticipated grief. Parkes and Weiss[8] argue that sudden and unanticipated death is a high risk factor for poor outcome. Clayton[17] states that this is not a generally held point of view. The actual experience of caring for a dying person may have positive or negative implications. In some situations antecedent conflict may be reevoked by the anticipated death with a possibility of resolution in the context of a transaction with the dying person.[29] Raphael and Maddison[9] have described increased difficulty in mourning in the following situations: death by suicide; self-inflicted death; untimely death, deaths in youth; deaths in which there is excessive involvement of the bereaved in the terminal care of a deteriorating patient; deaths that involve extreme guilt or those in which the relationship sours when the dying person resents the dependency needs evoked by the illness and attacks the survivor.

EARLY PHASES OF PATHOLOGICAL GRIEF

In evaluating a response to loss, one must always consider the intensity of attachment. There are relationships that seem nominally close but on closer examination do not reveal a high degree of attachment and therefore do not lead to intense grief. Some losses are experienced as a relief. However, assuming reasonably intense attachment, there are two broad categories of abnormal response.[6] These appear in the early months after loss and persist. The first involves the absence of an expected response and the second, the persistence of a severe dysphoric response. The first category may involve a delay of response[8] as in conflicted grief where an overactive, euphoric or hypomanic response covers depression and leads by the end of a year to a failure of social reintegration and reestablishment of object relations. Depression and intense yearning assert themselves at that time.
Identification with the symptoms of the lost person may occur and lead to a mistaken diagnosis of physical disease.[30]

The second category involves a highly dysphoric response occurring in the early months after the loss. This may involve a combination of any of the following elements. Here the important question is the pervasiveness of these elements and the degree to which they interfere with relatedness and social adaptation.

1. Intense and persistent anger toward the lost object is an indication of pathological grief though minor and inconsistent fantasies do not have the same implication. The anger may be manifested overtly in the form of recurrent hostile images and memories of the lost person or it may be displaced upon others in the surround, the doctors, other family members, etc. This may be accompanied by a predominance of intrusive negative and critical representations of the lost person to be contrasted with the emer-

gence of positive representations and memories of the interaction with the lost person that are evocative of pain by virtue of the awareness of loss of pleasurable interaction with the beloved. Anger may be repressed and take the form of extreme guilt with self-reproach and feelings of unworthiness and unlovability.

2. The loss may generate a powerful sense of incompetence and help-lessness with the conviction that one is unable to manage alone. This may be accompanied by feelings of worthlessness, low self-esteem and intense and persistent yearning which goes beyond the periodic yearning described above in normal grief responses. Anxiety generated by the loss of a dependency adaptation associated with the belief that the bereaved needs another person to permit adequate functioning and survival may lead to agoraphobic responses and a general avoidance of life. Phobic avoidance reflective of a fear of incompetence may be coupled with avoid-ance of situations which painfully remind the mourner of the lost person. This may extend to an inability to talk about the loss with others and lead to increasing isolation and perceived nonsupport.

3. A severe depressive constellation may be a primary manifestation of pathological grief. In this situation depression as a mood state is to be dis-tinguished from sadness. Characteristically, such individuals do not have the fluctuations of positive and negative mood states and are incapable of the distancing which characterizes the normal grief response. Suicidal ide-ation may be present in such a situation and retarded depression, unchar-acteristic of normal grief, may ensue. This response has the characteristics of what Freud[3] described as melancholia and what is now termed a major depressive disorder. The feeling of hopelessness is pervasive both on an emotional level and on a cognitive level, and these individuals have no sense that they will ultimately experience relief.

4. An extension of the persistence of the attachment and of its mainte-nance in the form that existed before the death may occur in what Bowlby has called mummification.[31] In this situation the individual maintains intact an essential and central part of a previous life experience connected with the lost person, thereby attempting to avoid disrupting the fantasy of a continuing presence of the lost person. This may be concretized by the maintenance of a room of the beloved as it was before the loss, as Mrs. Haversham maintained her wedding room from the day the bridegroom abandoned her.[32] Identification with the lost person by acquiring his habits, his feelings or even the symptoms of his illness may consolidate the uncon-scious fantasy of his continued presence.[33]

5. Compulsive caretaking may be a manifestation of pathological grief.[2] In this situation the person cares for others as he would be cared for and fantasizes that he was cared for in the previous relationship. The mechanism involves a vicarious identification with the person being cared for. Characteristically these individuals are unable to enter relationships that have other configurations.

6. Individuals who are unable to utilize available support systems in families and friends and thereby have inadequate perceived support are likely to experience later difficulty. The issue here is complex and may relate to previous personality structure as well as a need to avoid memories of a lost person in the context of supportive relationships with others.

In summary, one must note that a grief response after the loss of an individual to whom one was attached is a painful experience and takes time to resolve. In general, in the early months after loss, there are indications that predict a pathological outcome. These indications include extremely dysphoric responses of various sorts outlined above that are unremitting and may persist for years. In some situations the absence of an appropriate response may pressage future difficulties.

RESOLUTION AND FAILURE OF RESOLUTION OF GRIEF

Most studies[17] reveal that about 15 percent of individuals who have suffered a significant loss are depressed at 13 months (13 months generally chosen so as not to confound outcome with anniversary reactions). It is to be emphasized however, that there is no necessary reason why one year should be a magical cutoff point for the experience of some of the painful aspects of even normal grief responses. There is evidence[33] that some normal responses last longer than this. However, one must distinguish the persistence of grief as a syndrome from the reemergence of occasional distressing memories of the lost person or even brief anniversary reactions in the context of loss. Under special circumstances, tearful episodes may surprise individuals many years after loss even when they have quite successfully adapted to it. The vast majority of individuals who will resolve their grief probably have done so by about one year. The best criterion for such an evaluation is the degree to which the individual has reestablished the broad pattern of his previous homeostasis, with the additional element of reorganization of roles and activities demanded by the loss. Parkes and Weiss's[8] Assessment Score is a useful and broad framework for considering the success of the mourning process. They include the following items:

1. Level of functioning in comparison with pre-bereavement level
2. Movement towards resolution of outstanding problems
3. Acceptance of the loss
   a) Absence of distortion; no expectation of lost person's return or disbelief that death has occurred; no undue idealization or denigration of the deceased.

   b) Access of the grief to dissipation through interchange/
       increasing comfort in talking about the death and dead
       person.

   c) Integration of the event into the respondent's
       worldview/acceptance of rational explanation for the
       death.

4. Socializing: reentry into social life

5. Attitude toward the future; positive, including realistic
    plans

6. Health; no evidence of disturbance, including symptoms
    such as insomnia, anorexia, etc.

7. Anxiety or depression at normal pre-bereavement level

8. Guilt or anger at normal pre-bereavement level

9. Evaluation of self; pre-bereavement level of self-esteem

10. Resilience, respondent's capacity to cope with future loss
    (pp. 32–33, slightly modified by author)

The extensive literature devoted to the examination of the effect of
bereavement on health will not be examined in detail. In a most recent
review of the data Klerman & Clayton,[34] arrive at the following
conclusions.

> Following bereavement, there is a statistically significant increase in
> mortality for men under the age of 75. Although especially pronounced
> in the first year, the mortality rate continues to be elevated for perhaps
> as long as six years for men who do not remarry. There is no higher
> mortality in women in the first year; whether there is an increase in the
> second year is unclear.
>   There is an increase in suicide in the first year of bereavement, par-
> ticularly by older widowers and single men who lose their mothers...
> Among widowers there is an increase in the relative risk of death from
> accidents, cardiovascular disease and some infectious diseases. (p. 39)

The authors go on to indicate that all studies document an increase in
alcohol consumption and smoking and greater use of tranquilizers and
hypnotics. Although there are associations between bereavement and specific diseases, particularly cardiovascular disease and certain infectious diseases as well as depression, the data establishing strong links is sparse.
There is a difference of opinion about whether self-reported physical
symptoms and perceived deterioration in health status increase, although
poor previous physical and mental health and alcoholism and substance
abuse as well as the perceived lack of social supports are high risk factors

for poor outcome. The authors underline that perceived adequacy of social support in remarriage protect the bereaved from adverse outcome.

MANAGEMENT OF PATHOLOGICAL GRIEF RESPONSES

Multiple forms of intervention have been utilized in the bereaved population. Considerable usefulness has been attributed to mutual support groups (of widows, for example) and to the establishment of outreach programs and programs related to hospices that are designed not only to offer support in the early intensely distressing period of bereavement but also to effect outcome by facilitating more effective long-range adaptation. The goals are to decrease psychological symptoms, prevent the development of alcohol and drug dependence, and affect physical health status favorably.

In the presence of pathological grief, some consideration must be given to the use of psychotherapeutic and psychopharmacological approaches. The diverse psychotherapeutic approaches to pathological grief are guided by the theoretical underpinning of each approach. Insight-oriented psychotherapy is based upon an evaluation of intrapsychic conflict. The work of Raphael and Maddison[9] and Horowitz et al.[35] and Horowitz[36] exemplify this approach. Each suggest time-limited therapy addressed to specific issues, such as repressed ambivalence with unconscious rage and guilt; modification of the negative self-perceptions exposed by the loss of the partner; helplessness generated by the disruption of a highly dependent relationship; the role and influence of previous loss, etc. These therapeutic approaches encourage the patient to face the distressing reminders of the loss with a gradual working through and increased toleration of the loss. All of these approaches are based upon the idea that the patient must experience the distress generated by the loss. Behavioral approaches use this as a central focus as they attempt to desensitize the patient to the painful memories. Indeed, the fear of reminders of loss evoked by everyday experience and contact may lead the bereaved person to an increasing phobic construction in his life-style. Cognitive approaches though conceptualized slightly differently also encourage revision of the image of the lost person and in particular, involve a reorganization of the view of the relationship which has some resemblance to working through with cognitive reframing.

The use of psychotropic drugs in pathological grief has not been carefully studied. Minor tranquilizers are most commonly used during the initial phase of the grief response and although they clearly diminish distress, the danger of tolerance and dependence is a real one and must be carefully monitored by the treating physician. It is generally recommended that they be used for limited periods of time and with caution especially in elderly patients who may experience cognitive disruption with the minor tranquilizers. Similar precautions should apply to the use of hypnotic agents through careful and well controlled use of such drugs by the physician during the early intensely distressing phases of bereavement may be indicated.

The use of antidepressants is more controversial. The prevailing view is that a painful experience of grief is part of the normal grieving process and that antidepressants are not indicated in normal grief. The issue is less clear in the depressive form of a pathological grief response. Since the vegetative signs of depression are often present in intense normal grief, it is not always easy to use the diagnostic criteria of depression as an indication for antidepressant treatment. In general, it would seem reasonable to use antidepressants in the presence of severe and persistent depressive responses to loss. A psychotherapeutic approach should be used in conjunction with medication.

REFERENCES

1. Osterweis M, Solomon F, Green M (Eds.): *Bereavement, Consequences and Care*, Washington, D.C., National Academy Press, 1984.
2. Bowlby J: *Loss, Sadness and Depression—Attachment and Loss.* Vol. III. New York, Basic Books, 1980.
3. Freud S (1917): *Mourning and Melancholia.* Standard Edition 14:237-258, 1957.
4. Abraham K: A short history of development of the libido. *Selected Papers on Psychoanalysis.* New York, Basic Books, 1953.
5. Deutsch H: Absence of grief. *Psychoanalytic Quarterly 1937; 6:* 12-22.
6. Lindemann E: Symptomatology and management of acute grief. *Am J Psychiatry 1944; 101:* 141-149.
7. Klein M: Mourning and its relationship to manic depressive states, in: *Love, Guilt and Reparation and Other Papers 1921-1946.* London, Hogarth, 1940.
8. Parkes CM, Weiss RS: *Recovery from Bereavement.* New York, Basic Books, 1983.
9. Raphael B, Maddison DC: The care of bereaved adults. In *Modern Trends in Psychosomatic Medicine.* Edited by O.W. Hill. London, Butterworth, 1976.
10. Maddison D, Walker WL: Factors affecting the outcome of conjugal bereavement. *Brit J Psychiatry 1967; 113:* 1057-67.
11. Parkes CM: Bereavement and mental illness. *Brit J Medical Psychology 1965; 38:* 1-26.
12. Anderson C: Aspects of pathological grief and mourning. *Int J Psychoanalysis 1949; 30:* 48-55.
13. Horowitz M, Wilner N, et al.: Pathological grief and the activation of latent self-images. *Am J Psychiatry 1980; 137:* 1157-1162.
14. Beck A, Rush J, et al.: *Cognitive Therapy of Depression.* New York, Guilford Press, 1979.
15. Gauthier Y, Marshall W: Grief: A cognitive behavioral analysis. *Cognitive Therapy and Research 1977; 1:* 39-44.

16. Ramsey RW: Bereavement: A behavioral treatment of pathological grief. In *Trends in Behavioral Therapy*. Edited by Sioden PO, Bates S, Darkens III WS. New York, Academic Press, 1979.

17. Clayton PJ: Bereavement, in Paykel ES, Ed. *Handbook of Affective Disorders*. New York, Guilford Press, 1982, pp. 403-415.

18. Clayton PJ, Halikas JA, Maurice WL: The depression of widowhood. *Brit J Psychiatry 1972; 120:* 71-78.

19. Clayton PJ, Herjanic M et al.: Mourning and depression: Their similarities and differences. *Can Psychiatric Assoc J 1974; 19:* 309-312.

20. Bornstein PE, Clayton PJ, Halikas JA et al.: The depression of widowhood after thirteen months. *Brit J Psychiatry 1973; 122:* 561-566.

21. Blanchard GG, Blanchard EG, Becker JV: The young widow: depressive symptomatology through the grief process. *Psychiatry 1976; 39:* 394-399.

22. Parkes CM: The first year of bereavement: a longitudinal study of the reaction of London widows to the death of their husbands. *Psychiatry 1970; 33:* 444-467.

23. Parkes CM: "Seeking" and "Finding" a lost object: Evidence from recent studies of reaction to bereavement. *Soc Sci & Med 1970; 4:* 187-201.

24. Goin MK, Burgoyne RW, Toin JM: Timeless attachment to a dead relative. *Am J Psychiatry 1979; 136:* 988-989.

25. Wahl C: The differential diagnosis of normal and neurotic grief. *Psychosomatics 1970; 11:* 104-106.

26. Gordon R, Forge A: *Monet*. New York, Abrams, 1985.

27. Glick, I.O., Weiss, R.G. & Parkes, C.M.: *The First Year of Bereavement*. New York, John Wiley, 1974.

28. Rees, W.D.: The hallucinations of widowhood. *Brit Medical Journal, 4:* 37-41, 1971.

29. Viederman, M.: *Personality change through life experience III: Response to object loss.* (submitted for publication)

30. Zisook, S., Devand, R.A. and Click, M.A.: Measuring symptoms of grief and bereavement. *Amer. J. Psychiatry, 139:* 1590-1593, 1982.

31. Gardner, A., Prichard, M.: Mourning and mummification and living with the dead. *Brit J Psychiatry, 130:* 23-28, 1977.

32. Dickens C: *Great Expectations*. London, Oxford University Press, 1861.

33. Zisook S, Schucter S, Schuckit M: Factors in the persistence of unresolved grief among psychiatric outpatients. *Psychosomatics 1985; 26:* 497.

34. Klerman G, Clayton P: in *Bereavement, Reactions, Consequences and Care*. Edited by Osterweis M, Solomon F, Green M, Washington D.C., National Academy Press, 1983.

35. Horowitz MJ, Marmar C, Weiss D, DeWitt K, Rosenbaum R: Brief psychotherapy of bereavement reactions: the relationship of process to outcome. *Arch Gen Psychiatry 1984; Dec.*

36. Horowitz MJ, Weiss DS, Kaltreider N, Krupnick J, Wilner N, Marmar C, DeWitt K: Response to death of a parent: a follow-up study. *J Nerv Ment Dis 1984;* (in press).

RECOMMENDED READING

Raphail B: *The Anatomy of Bereavement*. New York, Basic Books, 1983.

Bowlby J: Loss: Sadness and Depression. Volume III of *Attachment and Loss*. New York, Basic Books, 1980.

Bereavement: Reactions, Consequences and Care. Washington DC, National Academy Press, 1984.

Parkes CM, Weiss RS: *Recovery from Bereavement*. Basic Books, New York, 1983.

AFTERWORD

From Burton's Anatomy of Melancholy:

> "I will no light nor company,
> I find it now my misery
> The scene is turn'd my joys are gone,
> Fear, discontent, and sorrows come."

Depressive illnesses are among the most treatment-responsive conditions in medicine, yet less than half the affected population in the United States and probably a smaller proportion in most other countries receive treatment.

Kraepelin observed: "Notwithstanding manifold external differences certain common fundamental features recur in all the morbid states mentioned."

Recognizing depression creates the possibility of its treatment and places research into these syndromes on a meaningful foundation.

J. John Mann, M.D.
New York, 1986

INDEX